The
Stormy
Voyage
of
FATHER'S
DAY

ALSO
BY

HUGO VIHLEN

APRIL FOOL

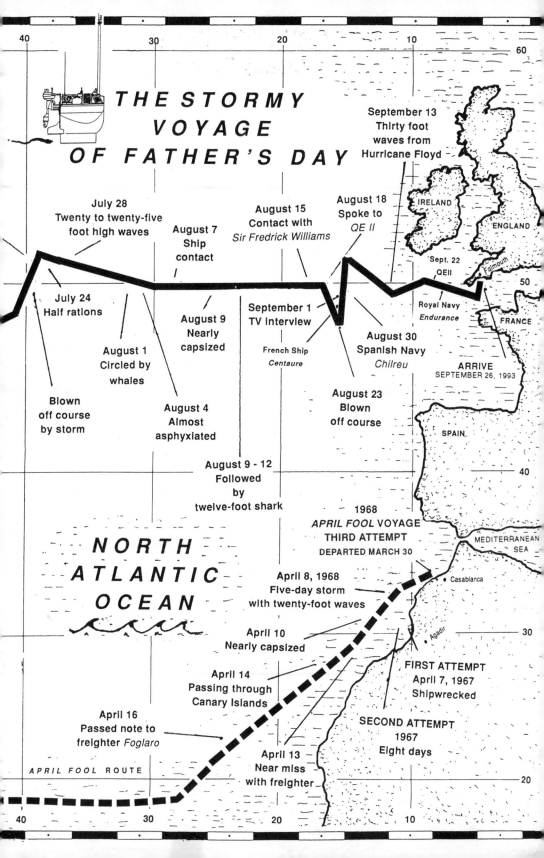

The
Stormy
Voyage
of
FATHER'S DAY

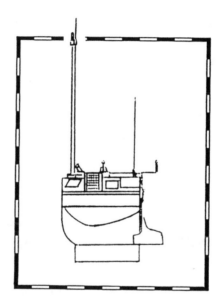

Hugo Vihlen
with
Joanne Kimberlin

Marlor Press, Inc.
Saint Paul, Minnesota

THE STORMY VOYAGE
OF *FATHER'S DAY*

A Marlin Bree Book

Copyright 1997 © Hugo Vihlen with Joanne Kimberlin

Mary Strasma, Assistant Editor
Cover Design by Maclean & Tuminelly
Drawings of Father's Day by Michael Edwards

Distributed in the U.S.A. to the book trade
by Contemporary Books, Inc., Chicago, Illinois

ISBN 0-943400-91-0
Manufactured in the United States of America
First edition

Library of Congress Cataloging-in-Publication Data

Vihlen, Hugo, 1931-
    The stormy voyage of Father's Day : solo across the North Atlantic in the smallest
sailboat ever / Hugo Vihlen, with Joanne Kimberlin.
    -- 1st ed.
    p. c.m.
    ISBN 0-943400-91-0 (pbk.)
    1. Vihlen, Hugo, 1931 - --Journeys. 2. Father's Day (Sailboat) 3. North Atlantic
    Ocean.   I. Kimberlin, Joanne, 1957- .
    II. Title.
    G470.V65 1997   96-47272
    910'.91631--dc21   CIP

MARLOR PRESS, INC.
4304 Brigadoon Drive
Saint Paul, Minnesota 55126

CONTENTS

**This book is dedicated
to those who went to sea
dreaming of world records
— and never returned again.**

William Albert Andrews

Andrews' 1892 world record trans-Atlantic crossing, set in the fourteen-foot, six-inch *Sapolio*, stood for three-quarters of a century. Andrews disappeared at sea, along with his new bride, on their 1901 honeymoon cruise aboard the ill-fated *Flying Dutchman*.

Josiah Lawlor

Lawlor and his fifteen-foot *Sea Serpent* held the record for one year, before Andrews swept it away in a race across the Atlantic that cost Lawlor his life. Andrews made it to Spain. Lawlor didn't.

Bas Jan Ader

Bas Jan Ader left Falmouth, England in June of 1975. His twelve-foot boat was found ten months later, floating empty one hundred and fifty miles west of Ireland.

John Riding

Thirty-three year old John Riding, after crossing the Atlantic bound for Australia, was lost in the Pacific Ocean in the summer of 1973. His twelve-foot *Sea Egg* is believed to have foundered in a hurricane.

William Willis

Willis was seventy-seven years old when he went to sea for the final time in 1968. He was heading from New York to England, but his twelve-foot *Little One* was found adrift by a freighter, 400 miles off the coast of Ireland. He was not on board.

William Dunlap

Dunlap held the Atlantic west to east record in the nine-foot, one-inch *Winds Will* for six months in 1982. He was lost in the Pacific on a subsequent voyage.

**And to those who dream
of following after me.**

FATHER'S DAY

Equipment & design details
for a five-foot, four-inch
North Atlantic passagemaker

Drawings by
MICHAEL EDWARDS

SIDE VIEW

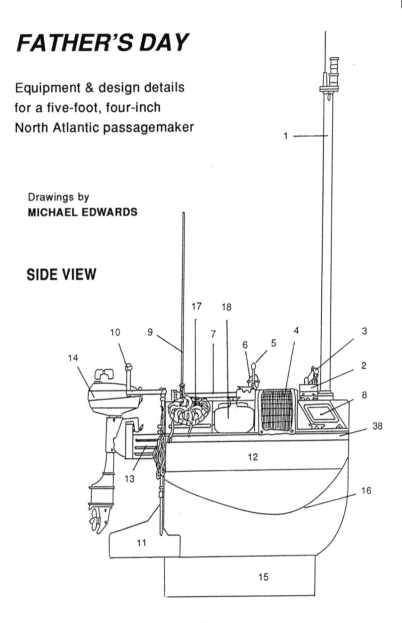

1. Mast (2.5 inch diameter).
   Spins on base to allow
   furling of sails.
2. Boom box or birdhouse. Used
   as snorkel, with booms
   mounted on top.
3. Booms (1.25 inch diameter).
   Stainless steel.
4. Solar panels (2).
5. Boom gallows. Prevents injury
   from swinging booms.
6. Compass.
7. Main hatch track. Made of
   high density plastic.
8. Window, made of Lexan. Side
   windows measure 10 inches by
   5 inches.

FRONT VIEW

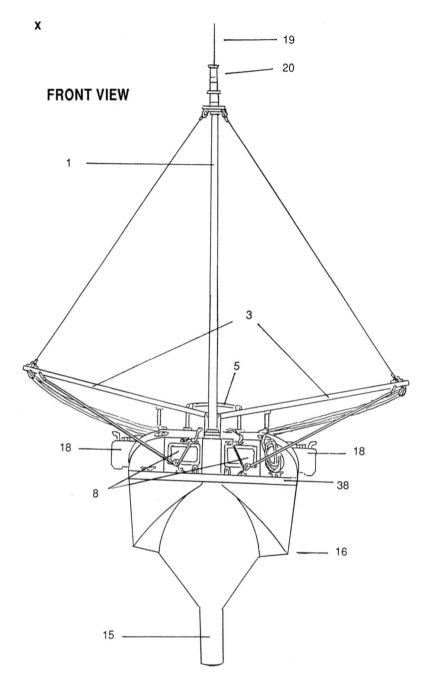

9. Outbacker single side band antenna.
10. Tiller bar.
11. Stainless steel rudders.
12. Water line. Bottom is painted with high-speed Teflon paint.
13. Stainless steel engine mount.
14. Four horsepower Evinrude engine with snorkel.
15. Keel.
16. Sponson.
17. Eighteen-inch sea anchor draped over two-speed winch.
18. Six gallon gasoline tank.

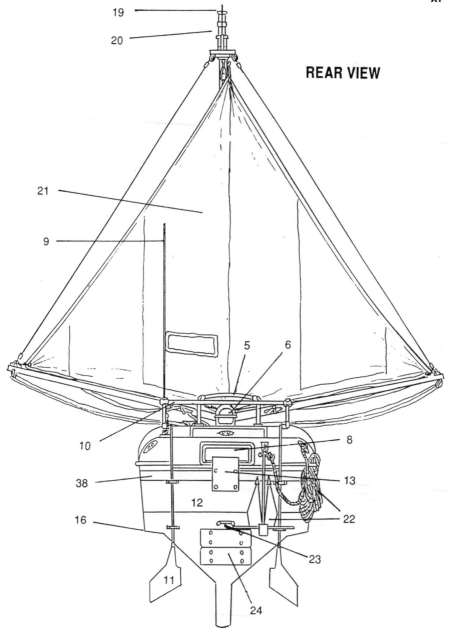

REAR VIEW

19. Marine VHF radio antenna.
20. Tri-color masthead light with emergency strobe.
21. One-piece sail with alternating panels of orange radar-reflecting material.
22. Danforth anchor with line.
23. Hand or foot hold for reboarding.
24. Two sintered bronze grounding plates for SSB radio.
25. Inside hatch handle.
26. Padded hatch opening (15.5 x 15.5 inches opening).

INSIDE VIEW
(Aft looking forward)

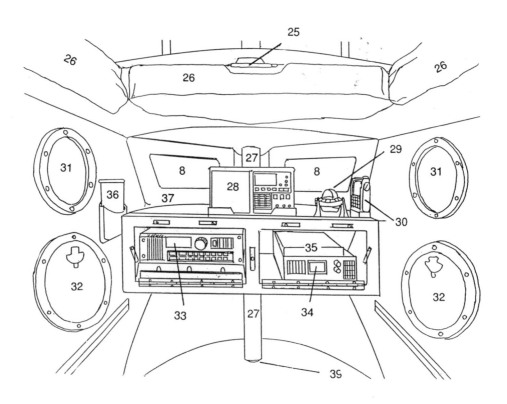

27. Keel-mounted mast post.
28. World-wide band radio receiver.
29. Backup compass (with severe deviation because of radios).
30. Garmin GPS.
31. Six-inch access plate to Top Forward compartment.
32. Eight-inch access plate to Bottom Forward Compartment.
33. ICOM M-600 single side band radio.
34. ICOM M-120 marine VHF radio.
35. King Aircraft KY 96A VHF radio

36. Drinking cup in holder.
37. Amp hour gauge (not shown.)
38. Retroflective tape.
39. 1968 penny placed under mast step for "good luck."

For a full inventory of items carried on board the record-breaking 105-day voyage of *Father's Day* across the North Atlantic Ocean, please see Appendices.

FOREWORD

I FEEL HONORED to be writing this foreword, because long before I ever met Hugo Vihlen, he'd already become something of a personal guru. People had crossed oceans in small boats long before we made our modest contribution, and they will again. But Hugo has the special distinction of being the first "micro" yachtsman. The smaller the boat, the bigger the sea, and his crossing from Casablanca to Florida in the six-foot *April Fool* set the yachting world on its ear in 1968.

His record stood unchallenged for a quarter of a century.

I, too, had world-record dreams in 1968. I was set to make a crossing of my own in a ten-foot boat. But Hugo's achievement took the wind out of my sails.

Twenty-five years and a few ocean crossings later, I came face to face with the man who unknowingly scuttled my earlier ambitions. It didn't surprise me the least that Hugo was an ordinary, unassuming, mild-mannered man. In this line of work people often expect you to be built like an American footballer and twice as thick. We were both poised to take his old record. With a sporting gesture rare between competing athletes today, Hugo insisted on sharing some of his provisions with me. I was impressed. Friendship grows from respect, and we had so much in common it was inevitable.

Month after month of total isolation at sea, against some of nature's most awesome forces, tests the body and soul to the very limits of self-sufficiency. If there's a defect in your character, the sea will find it. It's an unforgiving place. One silly mistake is likely to be your last. Nerves are stretched like piano wire, wondering what terror lurks around the next corner. Until it finally dawns on you that the real struggle is taking place within yourself, and the ocean, for all its inherent dangers, is only the arena in which the battle takes place.

Voluntarily confronting the fear is the challenge, and it's quite a deliberate strategy. Stupidity is the absence of fear; bravery is the mastery of it. The coward and the hero both experience the same terrors. They just react differently. In a world where everything is moving fast and getting faster, it takes a lot of audacity, great psychological strength, a fair bit of humility and a pinch of luck to tackle an ocean at a snail's pace in a boat the size of a coffee table.

If men like Hugo Vihlen are driven, it's possibly by the ultimate challenge: the need to confront themselves. We all measure our lives differently, some with empires, others with coffee spoons. But there are other yardsticks, and there can be few who don't applaud, if only from the comfort of their armchairs, or aren't uplifted by the courageous feats of people like Hugo Vihlen.

So why do men like Hugo risk their lives stubbornly, flying in the face of adversity? In our ancestral past some reckless troglodyte must have risked the condescending tuts of the elders when he left his warm cave to see what lay beyond the hill. Times may have changed a little, but there are still a few hills around, and we can hope that there will always be a few unreasonable men like Hugo prepared to go beyond them.

Don't let them steal your dreams.

Tom McNally

Atlantic Ocean Record Holder
From East to West

The
Stormy Voyage
of
Father's Day

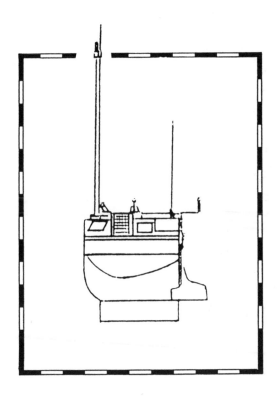

PREFACE

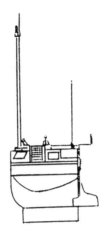

July 1, 1993
Day 18
398 miles out of St. John's, Newfoundland

A STORM WAS STALKING the North Atlantic.

I could taste it in the electrified air. All around, the ocean heaved, cold and compassionless, agonized by the mounting gale.

My homemade boat rode the swelling sea just as she'd been designed to do, like a cork, bobbing along from crest to crest. Except suddenly the crests were getting taller. And they were coming closer and closer together.

Scooped up the face of the first big storm wave, I clamped my jaw shut as my stomach made its way into the back of my mouth. Thank God I was on half-rations. If I'd been able to indulge in breakfast, I'd have lost it for sure on the skid down the wave's backside.

Sliding the cabin hatch open all the way, I stuck my head out and scanned the late-afternoon sky. It was churning, a whirlpool of greys and blacks.

It looked like a good one this time.

Grabbing the edges of the hatch, I hoisted himself to my numb feet and wiggled my shoulders through the tight opening, the effort rousing a groan from stiff muscles. Leaning forward, I yanked the jib sheets loose. There was no way I could face the storm with my sails up.

On a five-foot four-inch boat, you do a balancing act. If the wind caught us wrong, we might cartwheel, stem over stern.

But there is an advantage to a small boat. It has a proper human-sized dimension. You can stand in the hatch, your lower body still in the squat cabin below, and easily reach your arms from one end of the boat to the other.

A jagged spear of lightning knifed across the gathering gloom, its thunder only a heartbeat behind the searing flash.

I got the message. Hurrying in earnest now, I grabbed the boat's small mast, twisting the twin sails around it like a closed umbrella. Then they were furled.

I tied a line about them to keep them safe, readying my miniature craft for the war with the sea I knew was coming.

I glanced up — and wished I had not. Ahead, the gun-metal gray ocean darkened and boiled into clouds of black ink. Then the storm caught me.

For a few heartbeats, I was perched high above the ocean, balancing on the foaming ridge of the gale's leading edge, bubbles of froth tickling the boat's keel.

Then the world was snatched from beneath me.

Tossed from the summit into the yawning trough below, my toy-sized sailboat rocketed into the pit, a bright red speck of sand in a mountain range of two-story granite peaks.

I groaned, then reacted. Cramming my battered body into the tiny cabin below, I slammed the hatch shut just as the first crashing wave toppled onto the deck. *Father's Day* submerged under the sea's crushing weight.

Sealed inside the dark womb of the hull, I tried to brace myself between the cabin's ceiling and the floorboards. I felt like a man in a rolling barrel. The collapsing wave drove my boat deep under the icy surface, kicking the hull like a team of Clydesdales.

Father's Day reeled — punch drunk and dizzy — deeper into the black fathoms below.

For several eternal minutes, the wave held us motionless, pinned beneath the surface in a freezing headlock of death.

I glanced about, worried. Would we ever surface again?

And then I had another concern: How long will the air in the cabin hold out? The calculations flashed through my panicked brain cells. The boat's cabin wasn't much bigger than the inside of a refrigerator — barely tall enough for sitting and long enough for sleeping only if I curled my five-foot eight and a half-inch body into a fetal curve. The precious oxygen it held couldn't last for very long.

The noise was incredible, a bedlam of bangs, rumbles, booms and slaps. The hull was taking a vicious pounding. I prayed she was as watertight and buoyant as we intended her to be, for beneath her half-inch-thick hull was 15,000 feet of ocean.

A pounding tornado of dark water coiled around the boat's portholes. I was no longer sure which way was up.

The thought came to me that I'd finally pushed my luck too far, knowing all along if I kept playing with the King Cobra, eventually I'd get bit.

A floating coffin. That's what this boat amounted to.

For the first time, I noticed the resemblance.

The Atlantic unclenched its fist and *Father's Day* strained toward the surface. Wrestling free of the depths, she burst through a blanket of foam and popped to the top, water streaming from her deck.

Daylight flashed through the portlights.

Moments later, the next crashing wave caught us, and the cycle began over again. Down we went, corkscrewing wildly down the wave's side.

We canted to one side, and the portlights turned green with the water that covered them. We were underwater again.

I shook my head, trying to clear it. How did it all change so fast? Just a moment ago, the Atlantic had been serene. With cool, gentle breezes and following seas, it had scooted me toward my destination in England with tender hands.

But now the tortured ocean was trying to swallow me whole.

I glanced at my watch. There was worse to come shortly. What little daylight remained was fading fast. How would I face this battle in the pitch-black night, with no idea when or from where the next punch was coming?

I began to question my own sanity. What was I doing out here anyway?

Storms in the North Atlantic are treacherous for the biggest of boats. For God's sake, my bathtub back home was bigger than *Father's Day!*

Was I on an insane mission — trying to cross the North Atlantic Ocean in the smallest boat ever?

But it was too late for second guessing. Too late to turn back. Too late to call for help.

An icy shower of water found its way around the hatch seal as another wave let its overhand punch fly and *Father's Day* spiraled below again. I squirmed into my safety belt, struggling to control my frantic breathing. I had to make what little air the cabin held last as long as it could.

What on earth was I thinking when I defied all good advice and invested my time and a small fortune in this voyage?

Had I done it all for the purpose of coming out here — just to die?

Melrose Public Library
08/08/2018

You checked out the following items:

1. The stormy voyage of Father's Day : solo across the North Atlantic in the smallest sailboat ever
   Barcode: 39999031361130 Due: 9/5/18 11:59 PM

You may renew your items online at www.melrosepubliclibrary.org

CHAPTER ONE

A coward can sit in his house and criticize a pilot for flying into a mountain in fog, but I would rather, by far, die on a mountainside than in bed. What kind of man would live where there is no daring? And is life so dear that we should blame one for dying in adventure? Is there a better way to die?

— *Charles Lindbergh*

TWENTY-FIVE YEARS had come and gone since the last time I found myself alone in the middle of the Atlantic Ocean.

That was back in 1968, and I was pushing off from the steamy Moroccan coast of Africa, bound for the warm, sandy beach in Miami, 4,480 miles away.

There were those back home — and elsewhere I'm sure — who thought I was certifiably insane. After all, I was thirty six years old, had a comfortable life, a family and a well-mapped future. They just couldn't understand why I'd risk it all in a record-setting quest on the Atlantic. I wasn't even much of a sailor! And to make things worse, I really couldn't explain why.

I couldn't find the words, not even inside my own head. Of only one thing was I certain: It had nothing to do with sailing. As much as I loved the ocean, my favorite place to be was in the sky. The cockpit was my second home. In fact, up until now, sailing was only good for a weekend or two, a pleasant pastime I enjoyed a couple of times a year.

No, as near as I could figure, it all began in 1966, when I turned the first page of the book *Kodoku* and found myself transfixed by the tale of a young Japanese man's voyage across the Pacific Ocean. Alone in a nineteen-foot boat, twenty-year-old Kenechi Horie sailed from his homeland to California's Golden Gate Bridge in ninety-four days. Before Horie, no one believed an ocean could be mastered in a boat so small. His adventure astounded the yachting world and struck a deep chord somewhere inside my being.

The young man had left his mark. It wasn't an earth-shattering one, but a mark nonetheless. Like the vast majority of human beings, Horie knew he'd never be a king, a president or even a wealthy man. He would never solve the world's troubles. But he could do one thing only a few before him had had the courage to do. He could conquer his fear and set a world record. And when he was gone, his name — and his accomplishment — would live on. Others would come along to break the record, but the milestone would still be left behind. It was something time couldn't erase.

Kodoku stayed with me, its moral nagging at the comfortable complacency that was moving into my life as covertly as the silver strands of hair now threading my normal black ones. I'd like to leave my mark behind, too. I could do what Horie did.

And if I could do it in an even smaller boat, it would be my name, Hugo Vihlen, that would follow Horie's into the pages of nautical history.

Two years of hard work, $15,000 I couldn't afford to spend, along with astronomical amounts of understanding on the part of my family, began to make it happen. Step-by-step, day-by-day, the voyage became a reality.

Launch time finally arrived, a windy evening in late March. For the next eighty-five days, I sailed across the vast belly of the Atlantic Ocean, alone in six-foot *April Fool*.

The adventure almost broke me — financially, physically and emotionally. When it was over, and all was said and done, my fantasy had indeed come true. My name appeared in the *Guiness Book of World Records*.

April Fool, my creation of plywood and fiberglass, was the smallest boat ever to survive an ocean crossing. That fact alone made the whole thing worthwhile.

It was a triumphant return to our hometown in South Florida, the little town of Homestead, near Miami. With news reporters and television cameras, speeches and parades, the hullabaloo was worthy of an international celebrity. A "Hugo Vihlen Day" even was declared.

It was the '60s, an era of social upheaval. The country's young men were dying in Viet Nam — a war no one could agree upon — and at home a restless new generation flexed its muscle, defying the old ways, making the rules as they went.

I recall well that the winds of change were approaching gale force when I crated up *April Fool* and flew to Africa to set sail for the United States. But even so, I could never have conceived all that would occur back home while I was negotiating with the moody Atlantic.

Somewhere on the far side of the Canary Islands, I heard about the murder of Martin Luther King Jr. I was eight days into the voyage when the clipped British accent of a BBC announcer leaped from my radio, the words of violence and death radiating across the lonely waves. I turned my face to the heavens, praying for the sake of my nation that King's killer wasn't a white man. The violence that would follow such an act would only compound the tragedy further. Spellbound by the radio, I was thankful when later broadcasts reported no massive rioting.

News of Robert Kennedy's assassination came to me when I was just off Puerto Rico.

For days, a terrible depression gripped my soul. Two of my country's greatest men were dead, dropped by the bullets of fanatics. They were visionaries — men capable of changing the future. Unlike the rest of my countrymen, I had no one to mourn with. So I carried the burden alone, an island of misery in a sea with no sympathy.

After nearly three months of solitude on the ocean, the clamor of my June 21st arrival onshore was almost frightening. But I soon found myself loving every moment of the enthusiastic reception, basking in the excitement and warmth of the welcome.

For months to come our telephone had a life of its own. Calls of congratulations, invitations to appear on TV shows, requests for interviews and autograph sessions — it all extended the moment of the triumph. Even the President, Lyndon B. Johnson himself, sent a hand-signed note of admiration.

And to top off the hero's welcome, a new performing killer whale at Miami's world-famous Seaquarium was given my name. I went to meet my 15,000-pound namesake, but even in the shadow of the impressive attraction, everyone made a fuss over the voyage. I didn't even mind too much that my new friends kept pronouncing my last name wrong. I just patiently corrected them. "It's Vah-len," I'd whisper in their ear.

But when the heat of the moment passed, when the crowds went home and the handshakes were over, it was possessing the world record that meant everything; more than I'd admit to anyone — even myself.

As a conqueror of the world's oceans, it meant immediate respect among men of the sea. As one human being among millions, it meant special distinction. It meant I had accomplished one thing in my life that no one alive had ever done. And that felt good in my bones. Real good.

For two and a half decades, I wore the world record proudly, but quietly, close to the vest. I found I was no longer just Hugo Vihlen. I was the man who sailed the ocean alone in a six-foot boat.

Blessed with a warm, loving wife, a fine strong son and good fortune in business, I went on to other successes in life. I enjoyed my job as a commercial airline pilot. I was comfortable at home. I sailed just for pleasure. But there was one thing that continued to needle me, though it seemed to bother no one else. In the back of my mind lived a gnawing feeling that tarnished the satisfaction I'd sought from the voyage.

Was it possible that I didn't really earn that world record?

I hadn't made it all the way to shore on my own. Against my will, the U.S. Coast Guard had dragged me the last few miles to shore.

Technically, of course, I knew that I'd done it. I'd crossed the western boundary of the Atlantic back north of the island of Hispaniola, when the color of the ocean faded to light blue and

April Fool nosed her way into the warm waters of the Bahama Straits.

But the bitter disappointment of those last few miles was still with me, as fresh in 1993 as it was twenty-five years ago.

I could still see the skyline of Fort Lauderdale. It was etched in my mind, just as it looked that day, about five miles off *April Fool's* bow. I knew I'd hit landfall a little further north than I'd intended, but my spirits were soaring. Miami, my destination, wasn't far to the south and by God there was land right in front of me — land I recognized. I'd made it! I was still alive!

It was then that my luck took a turn for the worse.

The afternoon wind shifted suddenly, blowing from the west, pushing *April Fool* back out to sea. The sock-like sea anchor, used so much on the voyage to stop unwanted drift, lay in tatters on the deck, its nylon straps rotted to useless, frayed strings by the harsh ocean sun. There wasn't much I could do as the long-awaited land began slipping away.

I tried tacking, a method of sailing at an angle to the wind. But *April Fool* was designed for stability and strength, not speed. With her heavy, high-displacement hull and small twin sails she sat too deep in the water, moved too slow to make much headway by tacking. The four-horsepower Evinrude engine had drowned out early in the voyage, but even if I could've convinced it to start, there wasn't enough gas left to motor into shore. There was simply no way to overcome the effects of the eastbound wind and northbound current.

I'd survived nearly three lonely months at sea by dreaming of the day of my arrival. The thought of that day made me go on when my body was near collapse and my soul begged for surrender. Helplessly, I watched the sun sink behind the tall buildings on shore as the Gulf Stream carried *April Fool* further and further up the darkening coastline and the wind beat her back to the ocean.

By morning, the land was no more. I now knew the best hope for landfall lay much further north than where I'd planned for it to be.

My mind did a quick inventory of the supplies that remained. After all the hard-earned miles, all the wringing days and especially the lonely, uncomfortable nights, there was no way I could give up now. And why should I? I still had food and water. *April Fool* was riding high and dry, and the wind had to change sooner or later. In reality, this was the safest position I'd been in since the start of the voyage. Help wouldn't be far away if I really needed it now. Hell, I'd come ashore in North Carolina if I had to. I wasn't about to quit now.

Adrift in the midday sun, I was about twenty miles offshore, a good thirty miles north of Miami, when a sixty-foot cabin cruiser hove into sight. *First Edition* was a sleek, plush, beautiful boat, belonging to the Gore family, owners of the *Fort Lauderdale News*. Her crew, heading from the Bahamas to Ft. Lauderdale, spotted *April Fool* and came alongside.

I was delighted to see them. Communications from sea hadn't been as easy as I'd hoped. Getting through to anyone on the radio had proven near impossible. Weeks at a time had gone by when no one knew of my whereabouts or if I remained alive. Breaking off an antenna in a collision with a submarine, just north of the island of Cuba, had ended what little transmitting success I'd had.

I spotted the surfaced submarine in a cloud of black diesel smoke, looking more like a boat in flames than a cruising sub. In need of supplies, I'd sailed *April Fool* right for her. But when I drew alongside the mammoth cigar-shaped vessel, the pitching waves slammed the dwarf-sized *April Fool* into the massive steel hull, snapping my radio antenna in half.

I hadn't crossed paths with a single ship or airplane since the collision. No one knew if I was still afloat and on course. Now, so close to home and overdue, I was anxious to end my family's ordeal of worry.

Little did I know, concern for their peace of mind would turn out to haunt me for the next twenty five years.

For days, I'd been picking up radio broadcasts from shore. WGBS, a 50,000-watt station in Miami, was coming in loud and clear. On several occasions, I heard my wife's voice over the airwaves, that soft Carolina drawl unmistakable. It seemed people back home were pretty excited about this world record quest. In my absence, my wife had been thrust, somewhat reluctantly, into the spotlight, and the station jockey was interviewing her for updates on the voyage. The sound of Johnnie's voice inflicted a searing crush of homesickness.

In addition to the interviews with Johnnie, the Miami station was keeping in touch with the Coast Guard, broadcasting my location whenever *April Fool* was spotted or I made contact with a passing ship or overhead airplane. Unfortunately, the Coast Guard, using coordinates radioed to them by the same submarine I literally ran into off Cuba, had miscalculated in estimating my time of arrival.

The last progress report I'd heard over the radio predicted a landfall in Miami days before I'd ever be able to get there, even if I managed to stay on an arrow-straight course.

That one mistake, coupled with the changing wind, meant my greeting party had already been scouting for days, searching miles away from where I actually was, held tight in the grasp of the northbound Gulf Stream.

Johnnie would be on one of those search boats. I could picture her standing on the deck, the sun glinting off her hair, eager eyes scanning the wave tops, straining to catch a glimpse of *April Fool* and its captain. Our son, Dana, was only eleven years old, but I knew he was probably with her. Dana would be perched like a sparrow atop the rail, chattering with excitement and impatience by now. It would frighten them when I couldn't be found.

But the fully equipped *First Edition* could fix all that. At my request, they radioed my position to the Coast Guard. Now everyone would know I was all right. That meant I could quit worrying, too, and enjoy the rest of the voyage. I was accepting the crew's generous offer of supplies when the cruiser's radio crackled to life again.

It was the Coast Guard calling back. They wanted to know if I needed a tow to shore.

"No thanks," I yelled firmly to the crewman who relayed the offer. I wasn't about to take a tow now, not after coming this far. I was going to make it all the way in, all by myself, just as I said I would do. Pushing *April Fool* away from *First Edition*, I resumed my voyage.

But the Coast Guard had other plans.

I was wondering what was up when the cabin cruiser circled back and caught up to *April Fool* once again. The Coast Guard had radioed back a second time, requesting the *First Edition* stay with and keep an eye on me. Moments later, a seaplane came roaring overhead, dropping a dye marker into the ocean nearby. Two more boats materialized on the horizon, making their way steadily toward the gently rocking *April Fool*.

After eighty-five days and nights of isolation, it looked like I was in for an awful lot of company. The next few hours went by in a haze.

One of the approaching boats carried my wife and son. As *Sea Wolf II* drew near, I could see the familiar forms of Johnnie and Dana, standing at the rail next to a whirring TV camera. My heart ground in my chest, my eyes traced their welcome outlines.

Pulling alongside *April Fool*, the crew tossed a line and I clambered aboard. Thin, weather-beaten, my body fell into Johnnie's encircling arms. We had only just started to talk, our words stumbling over each other, Dana clamped tight around my waist, when the second of the two boats, the Coast Guard cutter *Shoalwater*, chugged up alongside.

The cutter's skipper hoisted his megaphone and pointed it to where I stood with my family.

"Do you want us to hoist her aboard or tow her behind?" he yelled.

"Neither!" I shot back. "I intend to sail her on in."

Then the skipper's orders, issued by some desk-jockey admiral back on land, boomed across the gap between the two ships. The steel rod of authority gave bite to his words. "So, as you can see, my orders are to pick you up, sir," the skipper summed up after the reading. "And that's exactly what I'm here to do."

My stomach felt sick. I could feel my face go pale beneath the voyage tan. Why were they insisting on towing me in? Did they really think I needed rescuing now? This close to shore, after finding the way — all alone — across nearly 4,500 miles of wide-open ocean?

Defiance momentarily surged through my veins. "Go to hell!" formed on my lips. In fact, to hell with them all! I was ready to take on the skipper, the admiral, the entire damned Coast Guard if I had to.

But the reality of the situation sank in. Could I make it back aboard *April Fool* with the Coast Guard trying to stop me? And even if I did, could I possibly outrun the cutter?

Fatigue was a poisonous barb, driving deep into my aching muscles and back. No, I couldn't escape the skipper's orders. They'd just arrest me if I tried. Exhaustion settled on my body like a shroud. A huge, unseen thumb was pressing against my chest. Frustration gleamed wet in my eyes.

Slowly, I pushed Johnnie away, lifted feet suddenly made of cement, and made my way down to *April Fool*. I knew what had to be done. At least this way, no one would board her but me. Once crouched upon the familiar deck, I attached the lift rings at her bow and stern.

Back aboard *Sea Wolf II*, I watched dejectedly as the *Shoalwater's* giant crane went to work and *April Fool* was plucked from the ocean, swung high into the sky and left dangling over the side of the tall cutter.

"I guess I'm supposed to thank the Coast Guard," I said to no one in particular. "But I won't."

By now, several small planes were buzzing overhead. I could see photographers at the windows, clicking away as the two big boats and the hanging *April Fool* began the two-hour trip to Fort Lauderdale. The word was out. Everyone who cared to, knew I was coming in.

At that moment, it didn't seem anyone in their right mind could consider the voyage a success. The next few days would show just how wrong I was. I found myself a returning hero, despite my own self-doubts.

By the time Fort Lauderdale's Pier 66 loomed on the horizon, our convoy had attracted a small flotilla of horn-blaring boats and circling airplanes. People were gathered along the bridges and coastal roads, waving and shouting. A welcome home banner trailed behind a passing plane. A three-cannon salute, fired by the *Brigadoon*, an old sailing vessel-turned-tourist attraction, echoed across the bay in a triple puff of acrid smoke.

And waiting at the pier, jockeying for position to jump aboard *Sea Wolf II*, was a pack of reporters, each hoping to be the first to interview the man who crossed the Atlantic alone in the smallest boat ever.

Standing by the rail, with Johnnie tucked under my arm, I

was in awe of it all. "This kind of thing doesn't happen to many people," I whispered in her ear. "Not in their entire lifetime."

I was starting to feel a little bit better. And as the years slipped by, the accomplishment of the solo voyage in the world's smallest boat overshadowed what I considered to be a failure to finish it to the very end.

But the nagging feeling of incompleteness stayed with me. And I knew one day I'd have to set it right. That's what I was doing out here now, at sixty-one years of age, when I should have known better.

I was trying to set it right.

CHAPTER TWO

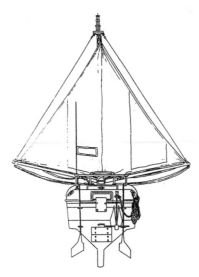

All of you that would be seamen must bear a valiant heart.
— Martyn Parker, 1656

IT WAS THE FALL OF 1991, nearly two and a half decades later, when the urge hit hard to go again. I decided to announce my decision over dinner to my son:

"I'm sailing across the Atlantic again next summer," I said in a low voice. I hastily added, "Don't tell your mother."

Dana nearly inhaled his mouthful of food, then leaned closer. "But Dad, you don't even have a boat!"

"It doesn't matter," I said, dismissing his well-founded point. "We'll build one."

I knew I already possessed a winning formula that had been proven in *April Fool*. With a little adaptation and use of today's technology, the same basic design of small boat that carried me across the ocean nearly a quarter of a century before should bring success once again.

I wanted a different route for the second voyage. The first time I'd followed the trade winds passage, a far-flung arc that traced the lower edge of the North Atlantic from east to west. This time I planned to head in the opposite direction, taking on the icy, often vicious and always unpredictable North Atlantic.

My planned northern route would be shorter than my

southern voyage from Casablanca, Morocco, to the U.S. mainland had been — as much as two to three thousand nautical
miles less.

A lot depended on which launch site we chose in the west
and how far the winds and currents pushed my boat off its
course. But without the trade winds to speed me along, as
they'd done in *April Fool*, the shorter distance would likely take
as long or longer to sail.

It would also be a much greater challenge.

The first trip had been accomplished under the gun, fretting
the entire voyage about returning late to my flying job. Now, at
least, I'd have time to properly plan the record attempt. For
thirty-five years, I'd earned my payday in the sky, working my
way up through the ranks at Delta Airlines, landing in the
captain's seat at forty years of age. As a pilot I'd known some of
the great cities of the world: Moscow and London, Paris and
Frankfurt, Copenhagen and Rome. Learning to fly had been the
passport to a glamorous, uncharted new world, a universe
away from my hard-scrabble roots, sunk deep in the dusty, red
soil of South Florida.

I grew up rough and ragged, the last child of seven for Edwin
and Sadie Vihlen. Life was rugged in the sparsely settled back-
woods of 1930's deep Dade County. The bustling city of Miami,
only twenty-five miles or so to the north, might have been a
continent away for all we Vihlens saw of its pleasures. Miles of
mosquito-infested Everglades, tall forests of pine and roads little more than ruts kept us from venturing too far from home.
The grandson of immigrant Swedes, mine was one of the
founding families of the isolated settlement of Homestead, a
tiny dot of civilization at the southernmost eastern tip of the
mainland.

My pioneering grandfather was a bold and independent
man; a college-educated horticulturist who fled Sweden to
avoid military conscription. Claus Sigfried Vihlen landed in
Central Florida in the late 1800s, where he fell in love with
Clara Enroth, married and became the father of five children.
He planted a citrus grove that prospered, until the hard freeze
of 1895.

The killer freeze drove Claus down to Miami, where he found

land available for homesteading further south in the wilds of South Dade County. Claiming 160 acres of inhospitable but fertile land, Claus built a log cabin and set about rebuilding the citrus business he loved, clearing and chopping, digging and watering acre after acre of orange, grapefruit and lime seedlings.

In time, Claus's groves thrived in the steamy tropical heat of South Florida, and by 1903 the family started building a larger house, near the settlement of Silver Palm. But the house was barely begun when Claus suddenly died of a heart attack. Clara found herself alone with five young children and an unfinished homestead. Now the sole breadwinner, my grandmother went to work outside the home, earning $1 a day in a nearby tomato packing house. Her talent for nursing brought in extra money now and then. She tended sick neighbors and delivered babies.

Trips to town were made by the four Vihlen sons, usually on rickety bicycles, down the long, muddy trails. When rainy season came, and the surrounding Everglades were flooded, water ran three-to-four-feet deep on the trails. During those times, it was Edwin, my father, the second to the youngest child, who made the supply run in a small sailboat.

Edwin was a jack-of-all trades, skilled in carpentry, hunting, crop farming and citrus production. From the seat of his motorcycle, he successfully courted my mother, Sadie Gossman, the daughter of an old family friend. They married, built a ramshackle wood house on the western edge of the family property, and settled on the homestead to raise children.

By the time I came along as Edwin and Sadie's last child, the year was 1931, only two years after the legendary nose-dive of the New York Stock Exchange. The nation was in shock, paralyzed in the stranglehold of the depression.

I learned early what it was to work hard. Everyone had to contribute if the family were to survive. I endured it like we all did, but there was a yearning inside. I fantasized a life of excitement, one that would carry me far, far away from the poverty and the dream-dulling toil of life in a pioneer family.

My first sailing experience came at the helm of *Smoocher*, a twelve-foot sailboat I built with my high school buddy, Roy Runken. Luxuries such as indoor plumbing, electricity and expensive toys were unknown in our family, but education was a priority. I was in my junior year of high school, when I figured out a way to finagle the boat.

It was time to order high school rings, an expense I knew my parents would consider worthwhile. I'd been dreaming of a sailboat, mooning for weeks over an advertisement for building plans in a dog-eared issue of *Popular Mechanics* magazine.

I approached my Dad cautiously. "I really don't care much about getting a high school ring," I said. "They're kind of dumb. How about if I get a sailboat instead?"

I was astounded when my father agreed.

Weeks later, when the eagerly anticipated blueprints finally arrived, Roy and I disappeared into his work shed. When she was complete, our boat was a thing of infinite beauty to my eyes; whenever we could escape our chores, my friend and I whiled away summer days, sailing up and down glistening Biscayne Bay.

We had high hopes for romance in that boat, as was evident by the ambitious name *Smoocher* we painted on her side. Much to our disappointment, though, the girls just weren't as impressed as we were. We soon discovered that *Smoocher's* rough, modest hull would never be the scene of much longed-for passionate courting.

By the time I came of college age, life was a little easier at home. The year was 1949, and my father had done well at his latest venture, a tiny grocery store in the countryside. Each year of college tuition would run my folks $130, but with the other children grown and on their own, it was an expense they felt able to shoulder.

Though I was the first Vihlen child born in a hospital, I wasn't the first to go to college. Brothers before me had gone as well. I would, however, be the first who wouldn't have to work to survive while attending. My parents were adamant on that point. They figured they could scrape up an extra $15 a week. That would have to suffice for my living expenses.

At age seventeen, I enrolled in the University of Florida in Gainesville, fresh off the farm, as green as the young oranges back home. At the country school I'd attended on the outskirts of Homestead, twenty-six kids had been in my graduating class. Dropped in the midst of a freshman college class of almost 2,000 students, I felt lost in a sea of human faces. The small, tightly knit community I'd known all my life hadn't prepared me for this sprawling campus, anchored by imposing buildings, crawling with smooth, sophisticated kids.

Eventually I made friends with some of the guys in my dorm, a long, stuffy Quonset hut that was my first home away from home. Campus life became a lot more fun after that.

But when the time came to choose a major, I was hard pressed to name any field that truly interested me. With no one to counsel me and little knowledge of my options, I made a stab at being practical and studied the construction trade. But neither my heart nor interest were in it. My grades were average at best.

One year later, North Korea declared war on her sister to the south, and my college days were numbered. By 1951, my junior year at the university, notices from the draft board began arriving. There was little hope I'd finish college before my draft number came up.

A recruiter from the Jacksonville Naval Air Station, just northeast of Gainesville, changed my destiny forever. Giving a speech at the college, he told the assembled students of an aerial training program at the station that, if we had the talent, would give us a shot at becoming a military officer without a college degree. It was a lot more appealing than being drafted as a foot soldier. If I could learn to fly, I'd be able to get an officer's commission.

Wide-eyed and sticky with sweat, I'll never forget my first time in a cockpit. Poor boys from the country didn't have much experience with flying. I'd never even been close to an airplane before.

But I found I had a touch for it, and it wasn't long before I was as comfortable at 10,000 feet as I was at the dining table back home. After eighteen months of additional training at the Florida Panhandle's Pensacola Naval Air Station, I accepted a commission in the U.S. Marine Corps.

Years later, after sharpening my aerial skills in the menacing skies of Korea, I was snapped up by Delta Airlines as soon as I came home. I never even missed a single paycheck.

When I ventured on my first transatlantic sailboat voyage, I had just received co-pilot's wings at Delta. I'd taken a leave of absence, but the sea trip took longer than I calculated. Reporting back to work three weeks late almost cost me my job.

Despite my new-found celebrity status, my superiors at Delta were fuming. Not only was I AWOL, they had serious doubts about my sanity. An airline pilot is expected to be of sound mind. He or she must exude stability and I wasn't exactly fitting into that mold.

I had to bite my tongue. If they could only imagine the mental stability it took to sail nearly 5,000 miles alone. A less stable man would have died out there.

Unimpressed, Delta officials wanted to suspend me. But, in the interest of public relations, they settled instead for extending my leave long enough to cover my absence.

But I wouldn't have to worry about any of that on this voyage. I'd said good-bye to Delta several months earlier when I reached retirement age.

All those years of flying across the Atlantic, I'd gazed for hours at the steely vastness below. In all that time no one had seriously challenged my world record. Oh, some had done it faster and in different ways. One had used a paddle boat, several had rowed, but no one had crossed the Atlantic in a boat smaller than six-foot *April Fool*.

So why was I hankering to go again? As far as I knew, my record was safe. What was it about that ocean that called to me so? It just wouldn't leave me alone.

By now Dana was a grown man of thirty-four and eager to be part of the adventure. Too young to be of much help with *April Fool* in 1968, his sharp mind, enthusiasm and companionship would prove invaluable this time around.

Together, my son and I built a one-of-a-kind boat. Smaller than six-foot *April Fool*, but nearly identical in form, the red and white *Father's Day* was a miniature marvel. Built of rugged fiberglass-enclosed Airex foam, she could carry myself and just enough provisions in her cram-packed five-feet six-inches to make it across the ocean.

That's if I were frugal and blessed by the winds.

There was no doubt, though, that some aspects of this trip would be much harder than the first one. For starters, my body was now almost sixty years old. And Johnnie was vehemently opposed to my going again.

But some things had changed for the better. I'd invested our money wisely over the years and I wouldn't have to cut corners on this trip. Now I could afford the best equipment and materials money could buy, and I intended to put that advantage to good use.

Better equipment meant an increased safety margin. I would need every edge I could get to survive the hostile, frigid waters of the North Atlantic.

Little did I suspect the first battle of wills wouldn't be fought with the ornery Atlantic after all, but with my old adversary, the U.S. Coast Guard.

Only days away from launch time, on June 19th, 1992, I received the first message from the Fifth U.S. Coast Guard District that forbade the voyage. Someone in the Fifth had gotten wind of my plans and a rude-voiced Captain Melvin called our house with the orders.

"We consider your boat manifestly unsafe, Vihlen," the captain said. "You won't be allowed to leave from our district."

We'd planned to launch from Nags Head, North Carolina, smack in the middle of the Fifth's territory. I tried to argue with him, tell him all we'd done and prepared for. But the captain hadn't the time or the interest to hear me out.

"You didn't succeed twenty-five years ago," he said. "What makes you think you'll make it now?"

I slammed down the phone, my brain awash with fury. The old wound was apparently still raw.

That captain really believed the Coast Guard had saved me last time! No doubt their records had it described that way. He had sounded young — so young he was probably still muddling through toilet training when I was facing off with the Atlantic.

They had nearly robbed me with their forced rescue offshore and now they threw it in my face, like a cold slap of seawater.

Resentment growled in my belly. "Manifestly unsafe, my ass!' My voice boomed to the rafters. My tightly knotted fist smacked the kitchen countertop.

That was enough! I would take no more. Sure, I'd play the

game. I'd try the legal route. It would be nice to get their permission, real nice, because if this Coast Guard edict held up, we'd have to revise all the launch plans.

But with the Fifth turning me away, chances were the other eastern Coast Guard districts would too. That meant no port on the U.S. Eastern Seaboard would be immune from their order.

Canada was the only other option; a choice I hadn't wanted to consider. It was nearly 2,000 miles from South Florida to Canada, an inconvenience that would add considerable cost to an already expensive undertaking. Financing this adventure had already topped $70,000. Every penny had come directly from my pockets.

World-record seekers usually find sponsors to underwrite their adventures, but I didn't want anybody else's name splashed across our beautiful little *Father's Day*. It was our dream and our accomplishment — not that of some slick corporate sponsor in a three-piece suit.

Relocating the launch to the north would strain the family coffers further. But much more important than the money, a launch from the Great North meant prolonged danger from lethal cold, jagged-edged icebergs and near-instant death should I wind up overboard in the freezing waters.

Before I let that happen, I had to exhaust all the proper avenues first. I offered to arrange a "ready for sea" inspection, so the Coast Guard officials could see *Father's Day* for themselves. Maybe if they'd just take a look at her, they'd see how much thought and planning had gone into her design, how much research and preparation had gone into equipping her.

But the Coast Guard wasn't interested in inspecting the boat it was condemning. They were satisfied doing it sight unseen.

So I sent plans and sketches to the Admiral in charge of the district. When no response came, I hired a high-priced maritime lawyer. But nothing I or my lawyer could say or do made any headway with the Coast Guard. Their opinion was apparently unchangeable.

Eventually, a letter arrived from the commander of the Fifth. The order and the consequences for defying it were detailed in unmistakable black and white.

U.S. Department
of Transportation

United States
Coast Guard

Commander
Fifth Coast Guard District

Federal Building
431 Crawford Street
Portsmouth, VA 23704-5004
Staff Symbol: (bb)
Phone: (804) 398-6204

16752
JUN 17 199.

Mr. Hugo Vihlen
15255 SW 268th Street
Homestead, FL 33032

Dear Mr. Vihlen:

It was reported in the June 16, 1992 issue of the Virginia Pilot-Ledger Star,
that you intend to attempt a voyage to cross the Atlantic Ocean in a five and
1/2-foot long boat, departing from the Eastern United States. If that is your
intention, then I hereby inform you that I designate such an attempted voyage
to be a manifestly unsafe voyage due to the unsuitable design and
configuration of such a vessel for such a voyage, the improper construction
and inadequate material condition of such a vessel for such a voyage, and the
lack of demonstrated proper operational and safety equipment for such a voyage
by such a vessel.

My authority for making this designation is Title 33, Code of Federal
Regulations, Section 177.07(g). Pursuant to the foregoing regulation and to
Title 46, United States Code, Section 4308, I find such a voyage to constitute
an especially hazardous condition and I hereby formally direct you not to
undertake such a voyage. Violation of this directive is a criminal offense
punishable by imprisonment of up to one year and by a fine of up to $5,000.00.

The Coast Guard does not wish to stifle the traditional American spirit of
adventure. However, the Coast Guard does not wish to witness an adventure
with a very low probability of success when there is a very high probability
that such an adventure will seriously threaten human life as well as visit
substantial costs on the American taxpayer. Attempting to cross the Atlantic
in a five and 1/2 foot boat without an adequate sea going support craft, is an
adventure with a very low probability of success. The failure of such an
adventure has a high probability of threatening life and of resulting in a
search by the Coast Guard for a small object in a huge ocean space. Such
searches can result in hundreds of thousands of dollars in costs that must
often be borne by the American taxpayer. The statute and regulation cited
above were designed and intended for the humanitarian purpose of protecting
the boating public. The statute and regulation were also designed and
intended to protect the taxpayer from being put to the hard choice of either
paying for very expensive search efforts or passively watching a fellow human
die. This action by me is taken to carry out the public policy expressed
through the above cited statute and regulation.

The contents of this letter constitute a regulation, effective immediately,
issued pursuant to Title 33, Code of Federal Regulations, Section 1.05-1(d),
(e), and (f), and constitutes your notice of regulation. The regulation is
effective immediately because it has been reported to me that you intend to
depart on your attempted voyage eminently.

You have the right to petition for reconsideration and repeal of this
regulation. If you wish to do so, your petition should be directed to me at
the address on the letterhead. Such a petition should contain: (1)
identification of the regulation you wish to have reconsidered or repealed,
(2) a statement of the action that you want taken, (3) whatever arguments or
data that are available to you to support the action that you seek, and (4) if
the date by which you wish for me to act on your petition is of significance
to you, so state, and give your reasons for the significance of such date.

Sincerely,

W. T. LELAND
Rear-Admiral, U. S. Coast Guard
Commander, Fifth Coast Guard District

Copy of the letter dated June 17, 1992, from the United States Coast Guard

The Coast Guard considered *Father's Day* unsafe because it was small. If I went on the voyage I could spend a year in prison on top of a $5,000 fine. They said it was their duty to spare the taxpayers the expense of having to come out and rescue me.

All along — ever since my sail in *April Fool* — I had known I'd one day go again. And I knew I had to do it before I was too old.

I was aware of changes in my body. Oh, I was still in pretty good shape. Staying active saw to that.

But it was a strange occurrence, this aging thing. Inside my head and heart and soul, I continued to see myself as I did in my earlier years; the same youthful image came to mind. Inside, nothing had changed. But the framework was starting to rust away.

Somehow, I never thought it would happen to me. I just kept waking up every morning, trying to enjoy life. But one day I looked down at my hands. Overnight, it seemed that they had turned into the hands of my father, dried and freckled with age. It was then that I felt the pangs of panic. The years were passing by with blinding speed. What was I waiting for?

This special year, 1992, celebrated the spirit of one of the greatest mariners of all time. Five hundred years ago, Columbus discovered America. He wouldn't have let the Coast Guard stand in his way. Still, convincing the skeptical crown heads of Spain may have been a breeze compared to navigating the wilderness of the modern bureaucracy. No matter. I would not be dismissed as easily as they thought.

It was time to go underground. The voyage took on the air of an espionage operation.

I pretended to continue the battle for permission, but instead revised our plans in secret. Hiding the truth from my mother, now age ninety-three, as well as the majority of my friends, I packed up my support crew on the afternoon of June 18, 1992, and snuck away for the distant Canadian border.

With me were Johnnie and Dana, Dana's wife, Nancy, and our boat builder, George Carroll. George and I trailered *Father's Day* behind my silver Chevy El Camino; everyone else piled into Johnnie's green Jaguar.

I'd developed a deep respect for George during the months we'd spent working together on the *Father's Day*. It was George who was the real genius behind the construction of my unique boat. An expert at working with fiberglass and Airex, the latest in super-strong, moldable, lightweight building materials, Dana and I could never have built her without him.

Despite our intention of going unnoticed, word of our adventure had traveled well ahead. People along the way took notice of the odd-looking little red boat. Some approached and asked if it was the boat they had heard about. We'd been encouraging publicity up until now, even broadcasting the clashes with the Coast Guard to the media. But since the decision to go undercover, I'd been lying low. When cornered by a couple in New Hampshire, who insisted they'd seen *Father's Day* on television news, I swore them to secrecy.

We tried covering the boat with a tarp, but the wind kept whipping it back and slowing us down, so we packed it away.

Our nervous caravan finally arrived at the Canadian border, four days later, tense and crabby, trying our best to resemble an all-American family on vacation. The last thing we needed was a hassle from Customs or Immigration.

I had no idea how the Canadian Coast Guard would feel about this voyage, but after my encounters with their U.S. counterparts, I couldn't afford to take any chances. If they turned us back now, I was finished, so the less they knew about our plans the better. I wanted to get far offshore before anybody was the wiser.

But one of the border guards instantly recognized *Father's Day* and our hearts sank into the floorboard when he asked, "Is this the boat I saw on CNN?"

No, I answered quickly, but the young man continued to press. "You aren't going to cross the ocean in this, are you?" he asked incredulously.

"No, not in this one," came my all-too-speedy reply.

"I *swear* this is the same boat I saw on TV," the guard insisted. "It even says *Father's Day* right on the side. Didn't I hear something about the Coast Guard saying you can't go?"

Feeling like the biblical Peter denying Jesus the final time, I stuck to the lie I disliked having to utter. "This is a different one," I maintained with eyes fixed to the ground, ears waiting for the cock to crow.

At last, we were allowed to pass through, but as we pulled out of the border station the guard yelled at our taillights, "Good luck!" We wondered if he'd known all along.

By the next day, our unconventional motorcade made its way up to Nova Scotia, where we found a suitable spot to launch *Father's Day* — the Ballast Docks in the heart of the little town of North Sydney.

Hoping to launch in secret, we'd covered the boat when we came into town, but it wasn't long after the yellow tarps came off that a steady stream of the curious stopped by for a look.

As it turned out, Ballast Docks was only about three hundred feet from the offices of the local newspaper, and in less than ten minutes a reporter arrived on the scene. So much for launching with no fanfare.

With few options left, we took reporter Wes Stewart of the *Cape Breton Post* into our confidence on the condition that he hold his news story until I made it offshore.

Inquiries along the dock hooked us up with Gordon Howell and his weathered, thirty-five foot work boat, *Rhonda Lynn*. For a small fee, Howell agreed to tow *Father's Day* out past the first channel marker and into the open sea at dawn's first light.

Rigging the boat ate up the rest of the day.

In the misty, damp cold of the Canadian dawn, almost a week after slipping out of Homestead, my support crew and I christened the tiny boat with a twenty-four-year-old bottle of cognac saved from the first record-setting voyage. But when we tried to drink a small toast before splashing the cognac across the bow, the brittle cork broke off in the bottle.

We should have known it was a bad omen.

My crew and our reporter were on board the dilapidated old *Rhonda Lynn* as it chugged steadily eastward into the deepening black of the North Atlantic. On a tow line, *Father's Day* followed obediently behind, with myself at the helm.

When I cast off to begin my voyage, we yelled our good-byes across the rapidly widening gap.

For an hour or so the *Rhonda Lynn* hung nearby, her passengers fishing for cod, watching my struggle to coax *Father's Day* further offshore. But the fickle wind refused to lend a hand. Even with both sails spread-eagle, it toyed with my boat, blowing strong and then waning. *Father's Day* floundered helplessly in the five to six-foot swells.

Finally, out of time or patience, tow boat skipper Howell cranked up the *Rhonda Lynn* and moved off, my family at the rail, their waving arms fading into the boat's dark silhouette as it merged into the deepening gloom.

When the sun ducked behind the craggy Canadian shoreline, I hadn't gone very far — only a couple of miles from where I'd said farewell to the *Rhonda Lynn*.

Getting clear of the swirling currents just offshore would prove to be one of the greatest challenges. The wind blew from every direction so the sails weren't much help. Darkness fell swiftly and I tried to get some sleep.

I woke every half hour throughout the night to check conditions. When the wind began to blow steadily to the west, I threw out the sea anchor, hoping to slow the drift back to shore.

Sometime during the night I heard whales nearby; the eerie sound from their blow holes was so close it scared me. What would I do if they decided to ram the boat? Or unintentionally surfaced underneath us?

I wasn't carrying a life raft, and it wouldn't matter anyway. Without a special immersion suit, I wouldn't last more than a couple of minutes if I capsized in these icy waters. And I wouldn't last much longer with one. It was a choice of dying quickly or dying slowly. Choosing the faster method, I had decided not to bring a suit on the voyage.

Dawn finally broke, leaden and drizzly. My mood was a perfect match. The rugged Canadian coastline unfolded just off the bow. I hadn't gone more than half a mile all night.

My eyes traced the water until I spotted the whales, their huge dorsal fins slicing effortless, flowing arcs in the surface nearby. One rose farther out of the water than the others, and I got a glimpse of what lay beneath the fins. Their sheer size was stupendous! How could any living creature be so big? *Father's Day* was a thimble in the water beside them.

But I was too downhearted to think about the whales for very long. Once I saw they were keeping their distance, I returned to my other problems. I needed an outboard engine to get off-shore. Without one, I'd never make it around Newfoundland. The huge island lay just to the northeast, and to get to the east-bound ocean currents, I'd have to clear its southern tip first.

Last night I'd made a call on my single side-band radio. As far as I knew, Johnnie, Dana, Nancy and George had headed south to Miami right after the launch. Not knowing where to reach them, but knowing I might need them, I'd raised a marine operator on the radio and placed a call to Dana's answering machine in South Florida, just like we'd agreed to do. It had been smart to register my AT&T long-distance credit card number with the marine operator before I went to sea. It saved the hassle of having to repeat a string of numbers every time I made a call.

I left a simple message on Dana's tape: "Having a hard time getting offshore. Stand by for a pick-up."

I could only hope my son would retrieve his messages before they got too far from Nova Scotia.

I berated myself for not bringing an engine this time, though having one along on *April Fool* hadn't done much good. Waves over the stern had quickly drowned it out. But I had used it successfully to get away from the African shore, after two at-tempts with only sails had failed miserably.

Maybe we could have modified an engine for this trip, like we did everything else that went on and into *Father's Day*. We probably could have figured out a way to keep an engine run-ning in heavy seas. But I'd mistakenly thought it would be easier in this direction. I figured the prevailing currents would whisk me offshore into the waiting arms of the Gulf Stream.

It was a costly miscalculation.

By the time Dana and the *Rhonda Lynn* found me that after-noon, I'd sailed only nine miles north of where they'd left me. I was also only half a mile from the wicked boulders that littered the coastline.

The sight of the beat-up old *Rhonda Lynn* chugging toward me brought comfort as well as resignation. The answering-machine message system had worked, but this voyage was over.

On the long tow back to port, I began revising plans once again. It was futile to try to launch from North Sydney. The local weather bureau predicted the same wind conditions for the next five days, and even if we managed to buy an engine and find a way to mount it without ruining the boat's delicate balance, it would never provide enough power to clear Newfoundland, not without perfect wind and seas.

But, if we found a port in Newfoundland itself, I just might be able to get offshore from there, even without an engine. We'd come too far with this thing not to try.

That night I slept soundly, snuggled next to my warm, sleeping wife in a hotel bed in North Sydney. *Newsweek*, the *Miami Herald* and two television stations left messages at the front desk. The world we left behind had found us way up here. In the morning, I returned the calls, realizing it was too late to be coy any longer.

Then George and I hired what had to be the biggest crane in Nova Scotia to lift *Father's Day* out of the North Sydney harbor, back to the security of her trailer.

For Dana, it was time go home to Miami. He'd followed in my professional footsteps and became a commercial pilot. He was due back at work in four days. Once again it was hugs all around, and Dana, Johnnie and Nancy drove southward for home.

George and I pulled my truck with its heavy burden in tow onto a massive ferry bound for Newfoundland for attempt number two. Our launching destination was St. John's, a bustling port town on the eastern edge of the island.

After a five and a half-hour ferry ride, it was a long, sleepy ten-hour drive across the island to St. John's. A light misty rain was falling. Neither of us felt much like talking.

With the wipers beating a steady drum, we fell into the drowsy, companionable silence of old friends. Outside the warm, dry car, the majestic terrain of Newfoundland slipped by. Along the way, we saw two magnificent moose, grazing boldly on the side of the solitary highway.

Neither of us could have imagined what surprises awaited us in the remote waterfront of St. John's.

CHAPTER THREE

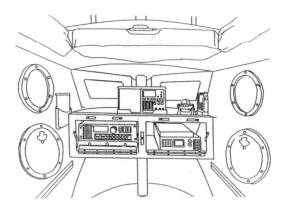

He was a true sailor, every finger a fishhook.
— R.H. Dana Jr.,
Two Years Before the Mast, 1840

THE MOTEL CLERK in the St. John's waterfront district cast a doubtful eye over *Father's Day*. "Why, it's just a tea cup, it is," she commented as she stood, a log of a woman, in the doorway of a faded, little inn.

"I can't imagine anyone crossing an ocean in this," she added, shaking her head.

We didn't need her sympathy or comments. George and I had been on the road for a week and a half now and the long drive across Newfoundland had just about finished us. Then the last words we wanted to hear came out of the clerk's mouth: "Sorry, fellas, but we're full."

That was that. As we wearily dragged ourselves back to the rig, I noticed a stranger standing next to *Father's Day*, watching our approach. Tall and lanky, fiftyish or so, his shock of brown, rumpled hair, thick bushy mustache and wrinkled, paint-spattered clothes drew my attention. He had the at-home look of a local.

"Hey buddy," I asked tiredly. "Can you tell us where we can get a room for the night? This place is booked full."

"That depends, mate," the man answered in a distinctively British accent. "Why don't you tell me what the 'S' stands for?"

I stared at him blankly, with the growing awareness that this wasn't a real good beginning for launch number two.

"What are you talking about?" My voice was short with impatience. "What 'S?'"

We were tired and we needed a place to rest. This nut needed to move out of my way.

"The 'S' in Hugo S. Vihlen," he said, pleased to drop his punch line. A playful grin hiked one corner of the overgrown mustache.

My eyebrows shot up. How could anyone way up here in St. John's know my name just by looking at the boat?

I responded slowly, suspiciously. "It stands for Sigfried."

For a moment of silence, he considered my answer, then tried the full name out on his tongue. "Hugo Sigfried Vihlen. Hmm." Apparently satisfied with the sound of it, he extended one grubby hand. "Well, Hugo, I'm Tom McNally, your competition."

I grasped his proffered hand cautiously, bringing us eye to eye.

An animated glint shone in his as he announced, "I've got a little something you just might be interested in seeing."

He pointed in the direction of the town dock.

George and I swapped quick glances. We really didn't have the time for this. OK, so he knew who I was. A lot of people did. And despite what he said, he sure didn't look like much in the way of competition.

But we fell in line behind him anyway, more out of curiosity than anything else.

There it was, bobbing gently in the oily water of the harbor — the one thing on earth that had the power to send me scurrying home to rethink the entire adventure.

In twenty-four years, there had been no real attempt on my world-record crossing. Now, in the run-down waterfront of secluded St. John's, stood two boats within one hundred feet of each other that were poised to do just that.

Mine and Tom McNally's.

Only McNally's boat, at five feet four and one-half inches, was a full one and one-half inches shorter than mine.

That night, after McNally directed us to the Battery Hotel, the three of us sat down to dinner together. And despite my sunken spirits, I became an instant fan of the rascally, free-spirited adventurer from Liverpool.

McNally had crossed the Atlantic successfully seven times already, and each time his boat had gotten progressively smaller and smaller.

He was a paradox of human nature — an artist, a poet, a hard-drinking, hard-loving, college-educated man who scrambled through just about every day of his life. McNally lived by the seat of his pants; a total contrast to my own methodical ways. But time and time again he'd been successful in the Atlantic. He was a seasoned sailor who didn't mind the hardships of constantly living on the edge.

His inspiration came from the heart and my 1968 world record.

Born and raised near the docks of Liverpool, McNally had been obsessed with the sea all of his life, even though he never learned to swim beyond a dog paddle. His poverty-stricken youth was spent scuffling among the rubble piles of an England left in ruins by the bombs of Nazi Germany.

A rebel by nature, he was always into mischief. For adventure, he and his childhood friends sailed homemade rafts of lashed-together cardboard down the meandering open-sewage of the Liverpool canals. Until the day one of his "crew" took a slip over the side and drowned.

As a teenager, he lied his way into a berth aboard a British cod fishing vessel. He'd never been on a real ship before, a fact that soon made itself embarrassingly apparent. The minute the big ship cleared the relatively smooth waters of the channel, he was retching over the side. But eventually a sailor emerged from the boy, and saltwater has flowed through his veins ever since.

McNally's first real daydreams of crossing the Atlantic alone in a world-record boat began in his early twenties. Englishman John Riding held the record at the time, with his twelve-foot sloop *Sea Egg*. But that was the same year I shattered Riding's accomplishment with a boat half the size of *Sea Egg*.

For fifteen years, McNally shelved his world record ambitions. His first attempt was made in 1983, a low-budget affair with no sponsors. My six-foot *April Fool* was still the un-disputed world record holder for ocean crossings in small sail-boats, but there were lesser records to be had — records for specific routes. For the northern Atlantic route, traveling west to east, Irishman Tom McLean held title in the seven-foot eleven-inch *Giltspur*.

It was his record McNally was gunning for.

He had chosen St. John's as a launch point, just as McLean had, and I would nine years later. Freighting his six-foot ten-inch *Big C* to St. John's thoroughly depleted his nest egg, but fortunate-ly for him, a kind grocer back home had stocked the boat with donated, unlabeled "mystery cans." Offering all of the voyage proceeds to cancer research pumped up publicity for the ven-ture. Of course, those plans hinged on whether he made it across and became famous enough to make any.

One thing after another went wrong, from *Big C* being "tem-porarily misplaced" in shipment to fierce gales hounding him at sea.

Nearly two months into the arduous voyage, *Big C* collided with a Russian super trawler after the astonished crew pulled alongside to investigate the small boat. Knocked into the trawler by pitching seas, *Big C* slid helplessly down the ship's massive, rusting side, heading straight into the churning blades of its enormous propellers.

McNally crouched on his tiny deck, kicking desperately at the ship, trying to free his boat from her seemingly magnetic pull.

The knot of crewmen peering over the rail scattered as a handful ran below to stop the engines powering the twin screw props. In less than a minute, the roaring diesels fell silent and the boiling white water at the props calmed to a harmless foam.

But *Big C*, sucked tight to the ship's side, made a beeline for the sharp metal blades anyway. As the stormy waves slapped them together, one prop ripped into the hull of *Big C*, splinter-ing her port side.

With the little boat taking on a geyser of water, and the Rus-sian crew hollering for him to jump clear of her before she sank, McNally scrambled around his wounded craft, tying ropes on wherever he could.

The Russians launched a life boat, its crew hell-bent on taking him on board until they finally realized he was more interested in saving his boat. More rope was then sent over. A bulky lift hook and boom creaked out over the trawler's towering side.

With a coil of the just-arrived rope clutched in his hand, the dog-paddling McNally dove into the bitter-cold ocean. Up and down, up and down, gasping for air between dives, he wrapped the rope around and around the hull of *Big C*.

By now, the lowered lift hook dangled just above the water's surface. McNally maneuvered its point under the wraps of rope just as the wave they were riding fell away, and *Big C* was snatched from the ocean, its captain still attached by his lifeline.

The exhausted McNally, weakened from the icy water, lost his grip on the side of *Big C*. With a violent jerk, he dropped to the end of the ten-foot lifeline, cracking a few ribs and scuffing up his body.

His dignity was taking a bashing too. His trousers were lost in the haul from the ocean. Completely naked from the waist down, he flailed helplessly beneath the ascending *Big C*, exposed to all, the taut lifeline dangling his bare butt in lazy circles. The trawler's boom lifted its load forty feet above the deck before setting the bleeding, self-conscious Englishman and his gashed-up boat down in the midst of the gathering coed crew.

Someone offered a blanket, which he quickly wrapped around his shoulders. His first step deteriorated into a stagger, then a stumble. The blanket fell in a heap around his ankles.

A muscular Russian fisherman stepped forward, scooped McNally into his beefy arms and carried him below deck to the sick bay. After a little tending, a hot bath and some fresh clothes, he was standing before the trawler's captain, insisting he be allowed to repair *Big C*. Once accomplished, they were to drop him back into the sea at the exact coordinates where the collision occurred.

The horrified captain, convinced it was all madness, argued fiercely. When rationale failed miserably, the Russian switched to bribery. "Just stay on board and we'll drop you in the Canary

Islands," he promised. "You can take a holiday, courtesy of the Soviet Union." The captain wanted no part in McNally's probable demise. Exasperated by the refusal of the splint-wrapped, bandage-covered Brit, he rolled his eyes upward. "Now I know why they call the English crazy!" he muttered.

Eventually, the obstinate Englishman triumphed. The reluctant captain gave in to his wishes — on the condition that he remain on board long enough for his injuries to heal.

His first night on the *Yuri Kostikov*, McNally was summoned to a solemn meeting of the ship's officers. The grave-faced captain began. "We have something important to tell you. It concerns our two countries."

For a moment McNally feared the worst. "My God!" he burst out. "Are we at war?" He'd been at sea without communications for almost two months. Anything was possible.

"No, no," the officers hurried to reassure him. "It's not that bad.....not yet anyway." The captain went on to explain that Soviet fighter jets had shot down a Korean Airlines jumbo jet that strayed into Russian airspace. Flight 007 had plunged into the Sea of Japan with two hundred sixty-nine passengers on board — mostly civilians. There were no survivors.

The captain added that his countrymen believed the commercial airliner was a spy plane, but now, relations between the Soviets and the Western allies, tense in the best of times, were understandably strained. No one could be sure what would happen next.

But if Soviet-Western relations were uneasy back on land, on the ocean they were friendly and warm. During the next few weeks, McNally was free to roam the length of the ten-thousand-ton ship, scavenging materials to patch *Big C*. Sometimes he took a turn on watch. Other times he holed up below with the crew, talking politics over cloudy glasses of illicit "bragger"; the discussions heated to a boisterous din by the strong, whitish brew that was covertly distilled in the bowels of the ship.

To show his appreciation for their hospitality, McNally scrounged up a few color markers and drew a portrait of the *Yuri Kostikov's* captain. He certainly didn't claim to be much of an artist, but the flattered commander was so impressed with the rendering he began scheduling rendezvous with other ships in the Russian fishing fleet. The trawlers, each as long as a football field, would tie up next to each other, elephantine rubber bumpers between the heaving hulls, and McNally and the captain would ferry across to paint yet another captain's portrait. Vodka flowed freely during the visits, so the results weren't always his best. But everyone else seemed to be pleased.

He was enjoying his new status as the roving portrait painter of the Russian fleet, but he had a voyage to finish. Unfortunately, repair materials on board were limited. After a few weeks of healing and working on the boat, *Big C* was lowered to the ocean for a test.

But the patchwork didn't hold. She was heavy with water in no time and McNally knew he had to give up. He and *Big C* were hauled back aboard and deposited a few days later in Plymouth, England.

After that he had the sailing bug. Nearly every spring found him hustling around Liverpool, courting sponsors and donations for his next voyage. Summers were spent on the Atlantic, each homemade boat just an inch or two shorter than the one before.

And now he was back with his *Vera Hugh-Pride of Merseyside*, a full inch and a half shorter than my five-foot six-inch *Father's Day*.

McNally had already made one attempted crossing in the *Vera Hugh*, named for his parents back in Liverpool. He'd set sail from St. John's a few weeks before we arrived, but was forced to return when the rudder refused to cooperate.

We lingered over our dinner in St. John's, talking sailing late into the night. We spoke of the ones who had come before us, the men who had gone to sea in search of world records and had never been seen again: John Riding, who disappeared twenty years ago in the Tasman Sea; Bill Dunlap, lost somewhere in the Pacific; Dutchman Bas Jan Ader and William Willis — both missing in the Atlantic. The boats of Ader and Willis had been found empty, drifting hundreds of miles off the rocky west coast of Ireland.

What could have happened to their captains? Were they swept off the deck by some hulking wave? Knocked unconscious by a swinging boom and fell overboard? Capsized by some monster of the deep? Or were they seized by such abysmal depression that they willingly slipped over the side?

McNally and I were both intimately familiar with the terrible mental toll of these small-boat solo voyages. The deep loneliness, isolation and physical hardship could easily drive a sailor over the edge. Hallucinations were not uncommon and neither was rock-bottom despair.

"Ah, Hugo, we're a dying breed," McNally said with a sigh. I wasn't quite sure how he meant that.

Three days after our meeting, the last day of June 1992, the wind gave me its blessing and I shoved off from St. John's for my second attempt at beating my own world record.

The night before, at yet another dinner with McNally, I'd made no mention of my launch the next morning. But, despite my best poker-face and cavalier air, I was sure the Brit suspected.

Scanning the surrounding hilltops, I half expected to see him perched on top of one, watching my departure with amusement. Sooner or later, I knew he'd be right on my tail in a boat even smaller than *Father's Day*.

If he were successful and survived the transatlantic crossing in *Vera Hugh*, then the entire ordeal that lay behind and in front of me would all be for nothing. They don't give world records for being second at anything.

But there was always the chance that McNally wouldn't make it. Yes, he had all the experience and determination he needed. Seven successful trips attested to that.

But the word "homemade" sprang to mind when it came to the *Vera Hugh*. She had the look of being slapped together and hastily supplied. After three days with McNally, I wouldn't have been surprised to learn he'd built her in his kitchen.

Like ships in earlier days, rocks provided her ballast. His fresh water-making machine was five to six years old and he didn't even carry a repair kit or new membrane for it. An old car battery spewed toxic fumes into the *Vera Hugh's* cabin — and I warned McNally to no avail about smoking inside. His provisions were the cheapest to be had, and nowhere on board could a sea anchor be found. I wondered if the man had a death wish.

I decided to proceed with my plans and gamble on the hope that McNally's lack of preparedness would keep him on shore.

So far, it had been a rough morning. One delay after another pushed the launch nearly three hours behind schedule.

By early afternoon, when *Father's Day* cleared St. John's harbor, released her hired tow and hoisted her orange and white sails, the sea had worked itself into towering swells.

Normally, in seas like these, I would have been tucked in below with the cabin hatch firmly shut, but now I had to stay atop to steer clear of a long spit of land.

The boat, heavy with supplies, rode low in the water. With my upper body sticking through the hip-high hatch and my bottom half still in the cabin below, my torso filled most of the one-foot by one-foot hatch opening.

But seawater creeping up the stern still found its way inside. By the time I made it into the clear, the cabin was soaked.

I watched waves foam over the bow and thought of the danger of sinking. It was cold, the water only forty to fifty degrees Fahrenheit during the peak of summer.

It occurred to me that it was not without reason that the "Newfies," as Newfoundlanders are called, refer to their local waters as "acid." Just the week before, an older lady had fallen off a boat at the dock and died of hypothermia before she could be warmed up.

But for the next five hours, my luck and the wind held steady. I was eight to ten miles offshore when both suddenly died. *Father's Day* began drifting with the current.

I put out the sea anchor and tuned the radio to a weather station. The news was all bad. Tomorrow's winds were predicted to come from the east. If the forecast was right, I'd be washed up on shore in no time.

A thirty-foot tall iceberg broke the sullen, pitching surface about five miles to the north of me, a testament to the coldness of the water. I had seen many icebergs from the cockpit of a jet, but this was the first time I'd seen one at eye level.

It was a flawless white wasteland of absolute solitude. Nothing moved on its frozen, hushed surface.

Darkness was closing in fast, and I could do nothing but stay below and settle in as best I could in the packed, wet cabin. During the night I drifted north, bolting awake at 4 a.m.

A loud horn was blasting from somewhere nearby. A bright spotlight flashed across the small portholes. I yanked open the hatch and scrambled through, panic welling in my chest.

I was well aware of the dangers posed by big ships. *Father's Day* was so small they could easily run her over and never even know they had done it.

In the thick pre-dawn dark, I made out the shape of a large freighter, stopped no more than fifty feet away from *Father's Day*. Blinded by her spotlight, I waved my arms a few times and ducked below to grab the radio. But in the dim light of the cabin, in a hurry, I neglected to switch from high power to low, so the freighter couldn't pick up my signal.

A breath of relief squeezed from my lungs when I heard the Canadian Coast Guard on the radio, responding to my signal from somewhere on shore. It seemed someone on land had seen my strobe light, steadily blinking from high atop the mast. I'd turned on the strobe to warn other boats to steer clear. Instead, it had drawn a whopper right to me.

Worried that a boater might be in trouble, whoever had spotted the light from shore called the Coast Guard, who in turn radioed the freighter with instructions to check on the light.

I assured the Coast Guard I was fine, thanked them for their concern and asked them to send the freighter on its way.

But before we pulled apart, I requested a position check. When the response came back that I was only three miles offshore, I knew I had drifted dangerously close to the jumble of sharp-edged boulders that break up the shoreline of Newfoundland.

Uncertainty began chipping away at my determination. I'd eaten very little since the launch and I was feeling weak-kneed and shaky.

When the sun climbed out of the Atlantic, it was disheartening to see just how close to shore I still was. It was the first day of July, and the wind forecast over the radio confirmed yesterday's report. My spirits drooped even lower.

With winds from the east, pushing me back toward shore, there was no way I'd ever clear the massive pull of the inbound currents off Newfoundland. Determined to at least avoid rescue by the Canadian Coast Guard, I radioed a call for a commercial tow.

I was still hoping for a better wind when the tow boat arrived. Should I go back to port? Or ask for a tow further out?

The decision was made for me. The tow boat was too low on gas to haul me out any further. I had no choice but to allow them to pull me back to the harbor at St. John's.

George had left for South Florida after yesterday's launch, and I found myself stranded in St. John's with no transportation, no place to stay and only $50 in my pocket. I hadn't figured on needing much money in the middle of the Atlantic.

Thank God, I'd squirreled away a credit card. With it I secured another room at the Battery Hotel, high on a hill overlooking the harbor, and tried to place calls to both my home and Dana's.

But no one was there and too many messages had fouled up both answering machines. I couldn't get through. In desperation, I left a message with George's cellular answering service.

It was a thin hope, but one that paid off. That night, George checked in with his service from a road-side motel and by morning was well on his way back to St. John's. I needed the rig to get *Father's Day* home to Florida.

Home? Yes, I was headed home.

But it wasn't to retire and give up this adventure.

It was to shave another two inches off my boat.

CHAPTER FOUR

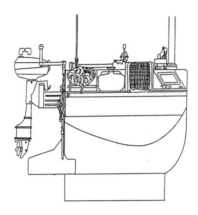

For who are so free as the sons of the waves?
— David Garrick, 1759

THE STRONG WINDS I'd been yearning for finally arrived. But they were too late, too strong and too far to the south. And I and thousands of others wished they'd never come at all.

The eye of hurricane Andrew passed over our home in South Florida on August 24, 1992. Home from St. John's for less than two months, we were hard at preparations for my third try at the North Atlantic crossing. McNally had failed in his second attempt in *Vera Hugh*. The same adverse winds that plagued me had forced him to give up, too.

The hurricane tore across the southern tip of Florida, cutting a swath of destruction so terrible and wide its brown, lifeless footprint could be spotted by satellite, twenty thousand miles above the earth. Thousands of tornadoes rode on its coattails, and the people of our hometown of Homestead knew a night like few alive could recall. Situated just twenty-five miles south of the sprawling metropolis of Miami, the quiet little farming town took the brunt of the killer storm, and we were plunged, along with the rest of our neighbors, into a trial of survival.

It would be days before help from the outside world arrived. The town and surrounding communities had been blown apart by the storm's 200 mph-plus blasts. In a single night, sixty-two people lost their lives to hurricane Andrew, one hundred and eighty thousand were left homeless, and thousands of businesses destroyed. Power and telephone lines lay in twisted, coiling heaps. Mile after mile of downed trees blocked roads. Andrew went down as the most costly natural disaster in the nation's history. Damage estimates would reach fifty billion dollars.

We weathered the hurricane itself as most in South Florida did, huddled on the floor of our bathroom, praying for salvation. Our block-and-wood ranch home groaned and popped, shaking from foundation to rafters, but in the morning it still stood, unlike many others.

The townspeople emerged from their battered shelters at dawn and gaped at the eerie, unrecognizable moonscape. Neighbors dug their way out of homes of rubble and ran to check on each other, to help in any way they could, to share the grief of loss and death. Getting through the next few months would be even harder.

I was more accustomed to hardship than most. I'd been trained for it by the military and had endured it in *April Fool.* But with no telephones, no electricity and few operating stores, the simplest of tasks took on a whole new meaning. Life quickly reduced itself to basic existence: filling the belly, a drink of water, and a dry place to sleep at night.

It would be five months before enough order returned for me to turn my attention and labor back to *Father's Day.* The tiny boat, backed up against the garage, had survived the hurricane. Trees had fallen all around, their limbs and leaves lying atop her, but none had done any damage — a testament to her solid construction.

By now, it was the tail end of February, and I was anxious to get back to my own adventure. I selected the end of May as the most favorable time for a launch, and that left only three months to prepare.

We drew a line around the bow of *Father's Day.* She'd have to lose two inches to take the world record. McNally may have failed in his latest attempt, but I knew better than to underestimate him. McNally would be back. So the only way to beat him was to do it better. And in this case, that meant smaller.

The necessary two inches came off pretty easily. I used a huge saw to cut the bow off flat while Dana climbed inside to make sure electrical wires and bolts weren't in the way. The chunk came off in a single piece, bow ring still attached. It was neat and triangular, heavy in my hand.

"I just might hang this on the wall," I said to Dana. "This little chunk of bow is going to keep my world record."

What was that saying I'd once heard? "A place in the Smithsonian or a place in the junkyard — that's the difference between finishing first and finishing second." I knew exactly which destiny I wanted for *Father's Day*. Now at five feet four inches, she was half an inch smaller than McNally's *Vera Hugh*. She was back in the Smithsonian league.

George Carroll flew from Chicago to build a new fiberglass bow. When it was done, the three of us stood back and surveyed the new look. We all agreed; it wasn't too bad. Aside from a little leg room, the only sacrifice was a single strobe light, and we had another atop the mast anyway. It was hard to tell we'd changed her at all.

Until the day came to put her in the water.

Father's Day had always been rocky, a little wobbly under my feet, much more so than *April Fool* had been. But now we'd shaved two inches off her already small size and added a brand new four-horsepower Evinrude outboard engine to boot.

The first sea trial after the renovations ended in humiliation. We trailered *Father's Day* to nearby Biscayne Bay and dropped her in the water. People were soon gathering along the docks, intrigued by the minuscule, brightly colored boat.

My son and I had done our calculations carefully before we mounted the small Evinrude right about midship, on a plank jutting over the starboard side. The addition of even the slightest weight had to be very carefully positioned.

We knew from our two previous attempts that *Father's Day* already rode dangerously low in the back. The rear porthole had been transformed into more of an underwater viewing window and on both attempts several waves had nearly made it into the hatch.

If that were to happen, I'd be a lot more than just wet. I'd be in deep trouble. Once the first wave fills the cabin, the boat sits lower in the water, making it that much easier for the next to follow. In a matter of minutes, I'd be sunk.

So the decision was made to position the engine on the side, instead of the traditional transom in the rear. With enough rudder compensation and ballast on the opposite side, we figured it just might work.

Now, in the water for the first time since her renovation, I cranked the Evinrude and Dana shoved *Father's Day* away from the dock, pointing her nose out to the open water beyond.

But all she would do was spin crazily in circles, like a one-legged duck in a pond. I glanced back at the docks. Most of the spectators had quietly disappeared. They must have been as embarrassed for me as I was for myself. Here I was, hoping to cross an ocean, and I couldn't even get my boat out of the marina.

Dana and I hastily loaded *Father's Day* on her trailer, not even bothering with the radio checks we'd intended to perform. We rode home in silence, stopping only to pick up an engine mount. We had no choice but to mount the Evinrude on the rear, even though the last thing the tiny boat needed was another thirty-five pounds on the transom.

The next sea trial was worse than the first.

Already resigned to a return trip to St. John's, we no longer concerned ourselves with secrecy. After all, the Canadian Coast Guard had shown no real interest in us last year, and all had been quiet from their U.S. equivalents. No doubt they were hoping I'd given up and gone away. They probably assumed the hurricane had blown our plans to bits.

So Dana had invited half a dozen reporters to our second sea trail. He even arranged for a chase boat to make sure they had an optimum view. Within minutes, we were wishing he hadn't, because even with the engine mounted on the back, *Father's Day* was alarmingly unsteady. And with the Evinrude running, she was almost impossible to steer.

The boat rode too buoyant; the center of gravity too high. When I tried using sail alone, her response to the rudders wasn't much better, the steering still erratic and over-controlled. Something was very wrong, very different from my first boat. *April Fool* had handled so well. And the two boats had been designed virtually the same. I'd used almost the same blueprints to build them both. But *Father's Day* was now a full eight inches shorter than *April Fool*. We'd have to find a way to compensate for that.

Several months earlier, while we were still wading through hurricane wreckage, my rival Tom McNally was shoving off from the coast of Portugal, intent on topping my record. This time, he was retracing the route I had followed twenty-five years ago, crossing from east to west on the lower edge of the North Atlantic. The trade winds route might be longer than the northern route, but it was much more charitable, and I knew there was a good chance McNally would make it.

If he did, it was the end of my long-standing world record. His *Vera Hugh*, at five feet - four and a half inches, was seven and a half inches shorter than *April Fool* had been.

After all these years, what would it feel like not to hold the record? It had become a part of my very identity. The only way to save it was with *Father's Day*.

I had no choice but to make it this time.

McNally was another good reason for choosing the northern route. Not only did I welcome its challenges, but once I made it, all would be settled. A crossing in the north is the ultimate sailing achievement. It would be enough to hold off McNally for awhile. And keep my world record safe for at least a few more years.

Knowing he was out there, I chafed at being landlocked, anxious to get on the ocean as well. But McNally was paying his dues. I should have known better than to envy him.

We had stayed in touch since our meeting in St. John's. Despite our rivalry and competitive natures, a friendship had flourished between us. When we parted in St. John's, almost a year ago now, I gave him my unneeded supplies, figuring he could use them on his next attempt. And when he wrote of his latest voyage plans, I mailed my original ocean charts from *April Fool* to England for him to use.

I marveled at the situation with a slight shake of my head. The Brit and I had come a long way since our first encounter. Here I was, making it easier for him to take my world record. But if anyone was going to take it — and sooner or later someone would — I'd rather it be someone who'd worked hard for it like McNally. Besides, I couldn't stand the thought of the likable Englishman disappearing at sea. I'd grown much too fond of him, and enjoyed our rivalry too much to see it end like that.

But despite my small contributions, McNally wasn't having an easy go of it. Operating, as always, on a non-existent budget, he'd arrived in Sagres, Portugal, flat broke. Scouting for sponsors, he hooked up with a watch company, which meant his sails had to be sent back to England for the appropriate logo to be stitched on. Whiling away the delay in Sagres, he was run down by a truck, a misfortune which forced him to postpone the launch even further so his wounds would have a chance to heal properly.

While he was on the mend, two locals wandered over to the docks to admire his boat. McNally made the mistake of being preoccupied when they asked permission for a closer look.

With one man in the cabin and one on the tiny deck, the boat began to tip. Water rushed into the hatch. Within seconds, *Vera Hugh* sank to the bottom, the man in the cabin now her prisoner. McNally jumped in and saved him before he drowned. But as he yanked the man free and pulled him to the surface, he was flirting with the idea of drowning him himself.

The sinking caused a load of complications. All of *Vera Hugh's* radios, equipment and supplies were drenched; rust would plague him throughout the long voyage.

When McNally was finally ready to launch, Portuguese officials "decided they were undecided" and withheld their permission for his departure. Ensconced in their opulent offices, they endlessly debated their responsibility toward this adventurous sailor, unconvinced of the soundness of his voyage.

Determined to get underway, McNally resorted to our old backstairs tactic. He informed everyone that he was taking the *Vera Hugh* for a sea trial. As proof of his intentions to return, he asked a government sentry at the dock to guard the valuables he'd be leaving behind. Feeling secure that McNally wouldn't forsake his possessions, the sentry cleared the way for the *Vera Hugh's* departure and watched as the tiny boat sailed out of sight, never to return.

Imagine the dock sentry's surprise when he opened the "valuable" boxes the wily McNally had left in his care and found nothing inside except rocks.

The next we heard, McNally was stuck in the Maderia Islands, about five hundred miles west of Casablanca. Two days out of Portugal, he'd been rammed by a large ferry, and spent the next fourteen days sitting in a swamped cabin, pumping the ocean by hand from the leaking *Vera Hugh*.

Two attempts later, McNally slipped out of the Maderias, and for seventy-seven days no one heard a word from him.

With each week that passed, I grew more concerned about the fate of my friend. And if I was worried, I knew that Edna, McNally's girlfriend back in Liverpool, must be frantic. More than once, I called her, trying to make comforting, convincing excuses for her boyfriend's tardiness.

"I'm sure he's OK, " I reassured her. "Don't worry. It's just the wind holding him up. The same thing happened to me."

But I couldn't stop thinking that Johnnie could soon be the one in Edna's unenviable position. People like Tom and I aren't easy to live with. Any woman who loves an adventurous man has her own little private hell to endure.

While I struggled at home with the abbreviated, uncooperative *Father's Day*, McNally finally came ashore in Puerto Rico, forty pounds lighter and weak from dehydration. Contaminated food had been the cause of his weight loss, but a cracked filter on his water-making machine had almost cost him his life. By the time he made port, he was urinating blood, his kidneys damaged from drinking salt-tainted water. He sailed into the wind shadow of El Morro Castle and paddled ashore from there.

Relieved as I was to hear he was alive, I had to hand it to my gutsy rival. The guy sure knew how to make a dramatic entrance. With *Vera Hugh* safely harbored in Puerto Rico, McNally was well on his way to nabbing the world record. As soon as he was able, he'd sail for the U.S. mainland — a short hop away for a sea dog like him.

I had to get going — and fast.

We added a twenty-inch keel to *Father's Day* for stability. But first, one hundred thirty-five pounds of lead birdshot loaded inside a compartment in the bottom of the hull had to be tediously spooned out by hand, poured into the hollow center of the keel and another twenty-five pounds added. Moving the weight to the newly installed keel would lower the center of gravity and add to the overall stability of the boat.

It was already nearing the end of May, our target launch date. With no time left for another sea trial, we readied for Canada.

The next few days were spent tying up loose ends. Friends and neighbors tossed a little bon voyage party. A reporter came by for an interview. But the best part was meeting Bill Butler, who looked me up to deliver a note from McNally, still recovering his health in Puerto Rico.

Butler was a sailor's sailor, a true hero as far as I'm concerned. He and his wife survived sixty-six days in an inflatable raft after their boat sank off the Pacific coast of Central America. The raft was designed to last no more than two weeks, and they were battered daily by sea turtles, nightly by sharks. Butler and his wife were the poster couple for the Survivor 35 reverse-osmosis water maker I was taking with me. I was glad to meet Bill. I was betting my life on that water machine, and it was good to meet a man whose life had been saved by it.

In the early morning light of May 26, 1993, my son and I put the finishing touches on our packing. I said good-bye to our dog, Sam, first. The big brown Weimaraner's saucer-sized eyes gazed steadily up at me.

"You're probably wondering what all the fuss is about," I said, talking softly as I scratched his favorite spot behind the ears. I added, "Hope you recognize me when I get home".

I gave the dog a final pat and turned to my wife, still rumpled from sleep, slightly shivering in the cool morning air.

No matter how many times we say good-bye, and there have been many in the course of our marriage, I've never gotten used to doing it. Tenderly, I crushed her small frame in my arms. There was little use for words.

Releasing her, I slid into the El Camino's cab beside Dana and we began our 2,000-mile trek northward, back to Newfoundland and St. John's.

Two days later, we found ourselves near Cape Cod, Massachusetts, with a Memorial Day wind howling out of the west. And what a wind it was. It was exactly what I would need to get *Father's Day* offshore.

The idea of leaving from the Cape blossomed in my brain. It was a long way yet to St. John's, and if we could manage to slip *Father's Day* offshore at Cape Cod, I could catch a ride on the Gulf Stream current much closer in than I could up north, where it meandered its way further away from the coastline. The northbound Gulf Stream, moving an average of two knots per hour, was my ticket to England. A Cape Cod launch would add over eight hundred extra sea miles to the voyage, but even with the extra miles, I could still wind up days ahead of schedule.

Each precious day we saved now meant fewer days I'd have to risk on the Atlantic during the dangerous fall storm months.

Dana didn't like the idea of a Cape launch at all. The U.S. Coast Guard had labeled *Father's Day* unsafe when she was five feet six inches. She was two inches shorter now. We'd really get reamed if we got caught this time. My son wanted us to continue on to Canada, but eventually I convinced him that a Cape launch had merits. The no-voyage order we'd received from the Coast Guard had come from the Fifth, whose district covers the mid-Atlantic sector of the east coast. But the Cape was in another district, and maybe, just maybe, these officials would see things a little differently than their counterparts to the south.

But I still wasn't willing to count on that possibility. I intended to make certain they never even knew we were here. Until it was too late, of course. Once I made landfall in England, I'd be happy to reveal our launch site to the world.

Dana had a long-time friend who lived nearby in Exeter, New Hampshire. Tim Bohan was a pilot and avid sailor also, so he was the one we called on for advice on the local waters. We combined his information with that gleaned from local charts, tide diagrams and weather reports. In the end, we decided a launch from Cape Cod might be difficult, but well worth the trouble.

We located a test site on the Bass River near Yarmouth, readying the boat in a nearby hotel parking lot for a sea trial. Both of us wanted to see how she performed with the new keel. But neither did we want a big fuss at the docks. If the boat was balanced right and riding well, I planned to just keep on sailing, right down the Bass River into Nantucket Sound and out to the Atlantic. The less attention we drew, the better our chances of eluding the Coast Guard.

We hired a forklift to hoist *Father's Day* out of her traveling cradle and place her gently in the water. So far, so good. Once again we were fortunate. A popular sailboat race was set for the same day, and the attention of most everyone in the harbor was turned to the hundreds of colorful race contenders. But that was the extent of our run of good luck.

Father's Day still wasn't right. She floated high out of the water like a fishing bobber, teetering and tipsy; very unsure of herself.

A round-faced little girl on the dock tugged her mother's hand and pointed at us. "Mommy, look!" she said. "That boat's going to tip over!"

My heart lurched as I looked at my boat, so high and unstable. Cautiously, I climbed aboard and dropped into the hatch. She felt like she was going to go over, even though the water in the harbor was flat and calm, nothing compared to what I'd be facing on the ocean.

How could I go to sea like this? It was scary just standing in her beside the dock. I kept leaning toward the center of the boat trying to steady her, but nothing seemed to help. The slightest shifting of my weight caused an exaggerated roll. Her nose rode high and her hatch, located near the transom, was only inches from the waterline. Dana was trying to film the test, but quickly dropped the camera to help me clamber back onto the dock.

We needed more ballast, lots of it and fast. Lead was the only thing to provide it. Charging over to a nearby gun shop, we made it through the door a spare five minutes before closing time. But a single twenty-five pound bag of birdshot was all they had to sell. It would never be enough. We were forced to call it quits for the day.

It was a long, restless night for the two of us. I was startled awake at midnight; my mind a muddle of depression. For hours I lay there, staring at the ceiling, wrestling with the problems of *Father's Day*. What had we done so differently this time? Why wouldn't she ride like *April Fool*? I was tired and frustrated, unsure of my next move. Should we return to

Homestead and try again next year? Or hang on at the Cape until we solved the problem? We couldn't expect the favorable wind to hold out much longer.

The sleep I finally found was troubled, haunted with un-answered questions.

In the morning, Dana and I began the search for more weight. The thought of giving up had evaporated with the darkness. But we'd already purchased the only bag of birdshot the Cape could offer. We headed for Tim's house in Exeter, boat in tow, our long-sought-after west wind whistling across the road.

By the time we made Exeter, green leaves and branches were tumbling all around. This was the wind I had been waiting for! If only *Father's Day* was properly ballasted! We backed into Tim's garage, and the three of us went to work. Dana and Tim scoured the town for weights, while I prepared the boat for the ballast.

I drilled two one and a half-inch holes in the side of the keel. Using a plumber's snake and an electric drill, it was two hours before I'd broken up and vacuumed out enough of the foam that filled the front keel section to add eighty pounds of the one hundred and seventy-five pounds of birdshot Dana and Tim had found in Exeter. After tilting the front of the boat trailer as high as it would go for even distribution, Dana and Tim poured the rest of the lead into the center keel section. As careful as they were, the round, rolling pellets spilled everywhere.

"My kids will be finding these things for years to come," Tim ribbed us.

The pellets from Cape Cod were dropped into the center sec-tion, too. With the keel and the added birdshot, *Father's Day* was now almost 250 pounds heavier than she was for her last launch. But would that be enough?

The next day we covered the two holes in the keel with fiberglass and headed for Mike's Marina on the Portsmouth River to see how she sat. Mike was in his mid-seventies, wear-ing worn bib overalls with more stains than blue. His rolled-up shirt sleeves were held in place with rubber bands and the grease under his fingernails looked like a permanent part of his anatomy.

His place was as full of character as the old man himself. The rust-encrusted crane had to be thirty years old, and looked as if it hadn't moved an inch in all that time. Everything from the storage house to the docks was dilapidated, and I was soon doubting the wisdom of entrusting my life's dream to such run-down equipment.

I held my breath as Mike hoisted himself behind the controls of the crane and went to work, lifting *Father's Day* from her cradle. Swinging her high into the air, he deposited her in the cold, muddy marina next to a row of old pilings rotted off at the waterline. Then he gently kissed the floating dock with her, so I could climb aboard.

Relieved that part was over, I saw she was floating level, flush with the waterline we'd painted on her sides the year before. Jumping onto the deck, I felt what had been missing. She was stable!

Confidence returned with a rush as I moved around the deck. The wobbly feeling was gone, and there was no threat of her flipping over. It was so obvious that we'd fixed the problem that we didn't even bother to unhook the crane's cables. I leapt back to the dock and Mike lifted her from the water. When *Father's Day* was snug in the comfort of her trailer, we headed for a New England lobster dinner and a well-deserved night's sleep.

In the morning, Dana and I were off to Cape Cod with an approaching cold front in the forecast. Tomorrow was the first day of June, one week since we pulled out of Homestead. The stability problem had cost us valuable time.

By 3 p.m., *Father's Day* was floating in the root beer-colored water of the Bass River. We hurried to attach the radio antennas and mast. Lying on my stomach, leaning out from the deck to work the screws that held the mast, I started feeling sick and threw up over the side. Embarrassed, I grabbed a beer from the cooler in the truck and washed the sour taste from my mouth, a furtive glance darting around the dock. Thank goodness there were only a few people watching. I was supposed to be an accomplished sailor, and here I was getting seasick in the harbor.

Dressed with her booms on, antennas bristling, sails reefed and multi-colored lines in place, *Father's Day* took on a whole new look. She really was beautiful, with only the grimy flotsam at the waterline to detract from her handsome lines. She was a thoroughbred, mingling with lesser stable mates for the night, but we knew her lineage. To get her out of the dirty harbor and into the clean ocean beyond was what I wanted more than anything. Tomorrow would be the day.

I savored my last night ashore. Only my son, myself and the tow boat captain we'd hired knew of my morning departure. It was a secret we had to protect for fear of being stopped by the Coast Guard. Dinner consisted of a tasty steak and two martinis, a fitting last supper. I placed a call to Johnnie and for the second time on this leg of the trip, we said our good-byes.

Once again, I awoke around midnight, the rain on the leading edge of the cold front pelting the hotel room window. From then on, the night was a sleepless one, as I lay thinking of what the next twenty-four hours would bring. Should I even be doing this?

My confidence lagged. I was having second thoughts.

The day dawned wet and drizzly with a west wind whipping across the land. Yesterday we'd made arrangements for a tow to the ocean with Bill Coughlan and his boat *Victorious*. Bill showed up at the docks late, and suggested we wait until the next day. With this kind of weather, he wasn't sure the *Victorious* would survive the rips that would be waiting at Monomoy Pass. We reluctantly agreed.

As gloomy as the rotten weather was, it was no match for the dejection that came with another delay. I spent the day with Dana, checking and rechecking charts and toying with our two new handheld global positioning systems (GPS). These little marvels would make navigation, and therefore life, so much easier than it had been on *April Fool*. No more sextants, no more star charts, no more complicated equations. All I needed was a few moments in the hatch, and the GPS would tell me exactly where I was.

The next morning, at 8 a.m., we were standing on the shore of the Bass River, anxious to begin launch number three. It took nearly five hours for the *Victorious* to pull *Father's Day* past the reefs and shoals, across the ten or twelve miles to the open ocean. When Coughlan threw the tow boat into neutral, I untied the rope and tossed it to Dana.

The first few minutes were touchy. The waves were three to four feet and choppy, rising ominously close to the opening of the hatch. But when I leaned forward to set the sails, *Father's Day* stabilized and leveled out.

We yelled a farewell across the steeply rising waves and the *Victorious* headed for shore. Twice we spoke over the radio before distance carried my son out of range and I was alone, surrounded by the swelling seas of the Atlantic.

It wasn't long before the waves were topping six feet and I knew it was time to batten the hatch. I tied the tiller in place, set the sails and went below. Crowded with gear and supplies, the cramped cabin didn't allow much room for comfort, but I rested as best I could. The anxiety of the past few weeks was taking its toll. I was exhausted.

Just before dark, I heard the buzz of a jet. It sounded so close. I slid open the hatch to see it circling back, low over the water, headed right for me.

On its underside were painted the words I dreaded the most: *U.S. Coast Guard.*

CHAPTER FIVE

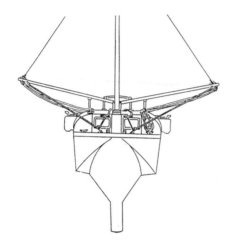

Above all, we must keep alive that courageous spirit of adventure...
— *Her Majesty Queen Elizabeth II, Christmas, 1952*

I DUCKED BELOW as the twin-engine Coast Guard jet circled overhead. "Damn! Damn! DAMN!" My curse disappeared into the uncaring gloom. This was definitely not a good development.

How had they found me? Only a handful of people knew we were up here and even fewer knew I'd launched from Cape Cod! But, I had to admit, the Coast Guard could have discovered what we were up to from any of a number of sources. The boat drew attention wherever it went, and we had dragged it up and down the Eastern Seaboard more than once.

Damn it to hell! Now I'd have to deal with them again.

Freeze-framed images of the day twenty-five years ago, when the Coast Guard had towed me to shore like a wayward child, flashed through my mind. I could still feel the anger and frustration. For years it had festered in my chest. And now they were back to do the same.

I flipped on the marine VHF and immediately heard *"Father's Day, Father's Day, do you need any assistance?"* So there was no doubt the jet's interest wasn't just routine. The Coast Guard was looking for me.

"Negative, Negative, I'm OK," I said firmly into the microphone. "Go away, go away!" The prayer was whispered fervently in the silence that followed.

But I knew better. They weren't going to go away, no matter how much I wished it. Why were they hounding me? I knew what I was doing. I'd done this successfully before! Why wouldn't they just leave me alone?

Twice more the jet carved circles above the bobbing *Father's Day*, until finally, I could stand it no more. Snatching up the mike, I ground out the words. "*Father's Day* to Coast Guard jet; do you have a problem?"

Then came the reply I least wanted to hear. "Roger *Father's Day*, please stand by. A boat will be pulling up shortly. I'll be staying on this station until they have you in sight."

Sinking back against the cabin wall, I stared at nothing, the mike still clutched in one hand. Well, that was that. They'd found me.

If they were sending a ship to intercept me, they wanted to do a lot more than just check on my condition. They could have done that through the jet. I wondered just how much trouble I was in. They could clamp me in shackles if they really wanted to. After all, a direct order not to sail had been defied.

The fact that we'd launched from a different Coast Guard district than the one that issued the order probably wouldn't summon a crumb of leniency. The Coast Guard was the Coast Guard, and if these guys coming after me didn't already know about the order from the Fifth District down south, it was only a matter of time before they did.

I figured I might as well keep sailing. There was still a slim chance they wouldn't make me turn back. I pulled out the GPS to see how far I'd come. It had been six hours since I dropped the tow from the *Victorious*, and I was curious to see what tricks the swirling offshore current had played.

Only twelve miles. At that rate I'd only make forty-eight miles a day, not the sixty I was hoping for.

Of course with the Coast Guard now on my tail, none of that probably mattered. If it was their intent, this voyage was doomed.

It wasn't long before the USCG cutter *Wrangell* appeared on the darkening horizon. Within minutes, the one hundred ten-foot ship from South Portland, Maine, was slowly circling the still-sailing *Father's Day*.

An inflatable boat dropped over the cutter's side, and its three man crew motored toward me. Oh hell, I deduced with dread, they're really going to put me through the hoops.

Reluctantly grabbing the line they threw, I proceeded to drag out all of my safety equipment, making quite a show of the entire process. I had every single piece they required.

Then they asked my destination.

Did that mean they didn't know? For a second I considered lying, but it went against my grain. They were probably only testing me anyway. If they knew who I was, then they probably knew exactly where I was going.

"I'm headed to Falmouth, England." I could feel my chest puff out a bit, like a father bragging on a gifted child.

The confession invoked no reaction. Their faces remained unreadable. More questions followed: birth date, citizenship, social security number and more. I fished a damp business card from my wallet and handed it over. After several shuttles back and forth, the inflatable's skipper instructed me to wait. He'd be bringing over some papers from the captain.

Perched tensely in the hatch, I wondered what would come next. When the inflatable finally returned, the skipper handed over a set of boarding papers. Tucked in the fold was a note from the captain.

Heart thumping, I unfolded the message. "Good luck and bon voyage from the captain and the crew of the *Wrangell*. Please call us when you make it home!"

It was a struggle to keep the relief from showing on my face. A few more questions followed and the inflatable returned to the mother ship. All was quiet from the *Wrangell*. As the night set in, I continued to sail, the hulking shadow of the big ship keeping pace alongside.

Why didn't the *Wrangell* move off? Wasn't I free to go? What was she hanging around for? The chances of the Fifth District Coast Guard's orders being discovered grew greater with each passing moment.

Then came the death blow over the VHF. What about the orders from the Fifth? Had I appealed them?

With a deep breath, I launched into the tale but I knew it would do no good. Then, silence reigned the airwaves as midnight came and went. Still under sail, I amused myself with visions of the stuffed shirts in Washington. I pictured them debating my voyage around a table twice the size of the boat they were discussing. I doubted any of them even had any small sailboat experience. The debate must be raging if they haven't handed a decision down yet. I hoped I was keeping them from their comfortable beds!

There was every possibility they were going to drag me back to port. I needed to be prepared. Placing a call to Johnnie over the single side-band radio, I asked her to reach Dana in Cape Cod to tell him to stand by. The next couple of hours would determine our fate. It was past midnight already. No use sitting in the hatch any longer. I went below and curled into a ball, but sleep only came in fragments.

At 2 a.m., I was notified that the Coast Guard was terminating my trip.

They'd be sending a boat in the morning to fetch me. In the meantime, I was to take up a heading for the nearest landfall.

I hung up the mike with a sigh and slid upward through the hatch, head and chest emerging into the night sky. The stars glittered like chips of shattered glass. A cool west wind billowed in the sails. Just off the stern, the *Wrangell's* black silhouette was dotted with bobbing lights.

I was twenty-six miles off a very tough shore to get away from and here was my wind. In twelve more hours, if the wind kept up, I'd be clear of the land's pull and well on my way. But I'd need a lot more than a good wind to outrun the *Wrangell*. There was no way to do it in the *Father's Day*.

I called Johnnie again and told her the latest. Her sleepy voice made me feel a little better. Gone less than a week and already I missed her. At least she'd been able to reach Dana. He'd be waiting for me back at the Cape.

With the *Wrangell* standing guard, I rolled up my sails and tried to get comfortable, watched over like a common criminal.

At daylight, I heard another boat approaching. The Coast Guard's newly arrived forty-four-footer tossed out a tow line, which I was expected to attach to *Father's Day*.

Five minutes into the tow, the circus began. The hookup wasn't right and the ornery *Father's Day* wouldn't follow behind properly. As I struggled to correct the problem, head under the icy water trying to retie the line to the submerged bow ring, an enlisted man on board the large boat grew impatient.

"Hurry up. We haven't got all day, " he snapped.

Having been a captain in the U.S.M.C., I barely muzzled the curse words on the tip of my tongue.

Then the debate started. Should they bother with another tow or try to lift *Father's Day* onto the *Wrangell?* Whichever it was to be, they wanted me off my tiny boat immediately. An inflatable was sent for the pick up. I was delivered to the smaller Coast Guard boat.

They finally settled on another attempt at towing. It reminded me of an Indian war party surrounding an Old West wagon train. The *Wrangell* and the forty-four footer closed the circle while the inflatable moved in for the kill. At last the proper hook up was made and away they went, dragging *Father's Day* four hundred feet behind, while I labored to get my teeming emotions under control.

I knew these men had nothing to do with the making of the orders they were carrying out. Their job was simply to follow them, as all good sailors do. Even so, it was hard to accept their hospitality. I slumped below in the forty-four footer's rough cabin, a shaking cup of coffee in my hands. Cold and wet, I grudgingly accepted a warm blanket extended by a crewman. They all looked so young. I hadn't noticed that when the Coast Guard hauled me ashore the last time. Of course, I had been younger then too.

It wasn't long before the tow operation hit another snag. *Father's Day* was trailing too far behind. Everything ground to a halt when she tangled in an unseen lobster pot line. An hour dragged by as the whole affair waited for a thirty-three foot rigid inflatable boat (RIB) to be summoned from shore. Once on the scene, the RIB's crew went to work with their knives. A few slashes later, the offending trap fell away and my little boat was lashed to their port side for the dreary haul back to land.

Apparently, someone with a bent toward compassion noticed

the forlorn look in my eyes, because I was soon ferried over to the RIB. It was small solace, but at least I could watch over my boat a little better from there.

The miles I'd fought so hard to conquer were quickly eaten up by the RIB's churning prop. And then, there it was, the blurry shoreline of Cape Cod. I had hoped it would be a long time before I saw that sight again. Funny, it looked a lot different from this angle. And from this state of mind.

Soon, the pier of Chatham became distinguishable; its weathered planks crowded with people. What was going on? I'd only been out for one day. It never occurred to me that the crowd was waiting for me. After all, I hadn't done anything worth waiting for yet.

But the Coast Guard had sent out a news release, detailing and defending their decision to end my voyage. I supposed it was a stab at damage control. This decision of theirs had all the ingredients necessary to brew into a public relations disaster — a classic tale of David and Goliath.

Drawing out the torture, the RIB made big circles instead of heading straight to the dock. They must be killing time, waiting for Coast Guard officials to arrive from Boston. When I finally stepped off the RIB and onto the Chatham dock, two Guardsmen in uniforms were approaching.

Guess these are the guys we've been waiting for, I thought grimly. Looks like I'm in the brig for sure.

After a cursory introduction, the lieutenant of the duo handed me a document, hot off the desk of a rear admiral. It stated that if I could manage to obtain a certificate of seaworthiness, signed by a marine surveyor or naval architect, *Father's Day* would be allowed to launch once again.

I was astounded! Could they really be letting me off so easy? No handcuffs, no penalties, no confiscation of my boat? It was probably the latter I feared the most. Dana and I knew intimately every hard point, seam and bolt on *Father's Day*. She had been our invention, our dream, our big adventure, and the thought of losing her to the Coast Guard had the power to scare me good. I'd grown to love her so much. She was my project, my pet. And my ticket to keeping the world record.

Reporters, photographers and sympathizers milled around

the pier. One group started clapping in a show of support, but I mistakenly thought they were congratulating me. "I haven't done anything yet," I protested. Confused at their meaning, I hid my face in the crook of one arm, shielding my watery eyes from the intruding cameras.

Finally collected, I raised my head to spot Dana, standing high over the crowd on the balcony of a commercial fish house that overlooked the pier. Dana shook his head and flashed a thumbs down. He was lying low with his video camera, filming the scene from his vantage point. Dana didn't know if the Coast Guard was going to arrest me or him, both of us or neither. Whatever happened, he figured he'd be of more help from outside the spotlight.

After a near sleepless night under guard at sea, the physical, mental and emotional drain left a vacuum. I tried talking to the reporters, but barely recognized the strangled voice that rasped from my throat.

The officers on the pier drew me aside, courteous enough to ask my permission before boarding my vessel. I accepted the token politeness in the spirit it was offered. They really didn't have to ask. I knew full well the power they could wield.

Cautiously, taking turns, the men climbed into the miniature boat, now tied to the dock, and took a look around. Boarding her was a lot harder than it looked. Finding a footing on the tiny, teetering, wet deck and getting through the tight hatch was like dropping through a moving manhole into a box the size of a coffee table. But each officer emerged admitting he was impressed with her design.

"Get the certificate," they urged. "Then you can sail her across the Atlantic." With that, they turned on their polished heels and retreated down the splintery dock.

When the crowd finally thinned, Dana and I managed to have *Father's Day* lifted from the harbor. It was a tight squeeze, since the only equipment available was a front-end loader whose main job was digging septic tanks — hardly a dignified recovery for our world-record baby.

With only an inch or two to spare between pilings, the operation was nerve-wracking. At the height of the lift, a huge glob of leftover sand dripped from the big scoop right into the hatch, leaving a real mess for us to clean up later. It was a dismal finish to an even more dismal day.

But by morning, we were recharged and working the telephone. Unfortunately, none of the marine surveyors we called were interested in inspecting *Father's Day*.

We quickly ran out of names on the Cape, and called Tim Bohan in Exeter for help once again. Tim knew of a guy who was supposed to be the best. But, after meeting the highly recommended inspector, I began to suspect his reputation came mostly from his own testament. Fielding a barrage of swaggering boasts, I arranged for the inspection. I was desperate.

By 2 p.m. the next day, it was obvious that the "cream of surveyors" wasn't going to show up. I stood alone on the dock, missing Dana's company. I'd dropped my son at the airport yesterday. He was due back at work in Miami. At thirty-six, retirement was still a distant day for him. I was grateful I didn't have to shoulder that familiar pressure on this voyage. It had taken a lot of the fun out of the last one.

But the time constraints I did have were, in reality, even more limiting. It was already June 5th, and if I didn't get underway soon, I'd have to wait until next year. Venturing on the North Atlantic during the stormy later months would be suicide in the diminutive *Father's Day*. That portion of the Atlantic was sailable for small craft only in the summer months. Winters were too vicious for any small boat to challenge.

The window of opportunity was closing fast. I couldn't allow the Coast Guard to waste another day of my time. They were pushing my arrival too far into September and arriving in a bad storm would be just as dangerous as leaving in one.

I knew we could fight it out in court, but I couldn't afford the time it would take to legally defeat such foolish bureaucracy. I called my son in South Florida to discuss our options.

There weren't really very many open to us. Once the decision was made, I began setting the stage for a reenactment of our great escape to Canada. Up there, I'd be beyond their reach once again.

I continued the cat and mouse game with the Coast Guard, only now I felt more like the cat. Fifteen pages of information and appeals went to the Coast Guard in a flurry of faxes. The next day, Captain Terry Hart called with the expected news.

They didn't have an answer and wouldn't for some time.

But, they assured me, once the decision was handed down, it would be an all-encompassing one. If they approved me, I'd be allowed to leave from any port in the U.S.

I also knew that if they didn't, the reverse would apply. There'd be no port in the country that would welcome me.

OK. That was it. If there was ever a time for a good lie, it was now. In even tones, I told Captain Hart on the phone that I'd decided to leave my boat in Cape Cod, and fly home to await their decision.

Alone, with only $65 and a well-used credit card to my name, I walked through a Cape Cod mall, picking up supplies for the drive north. Making my way through a strange town with a near-empty wallet added to the loneliness and frustration.

I could only hope the captain bought my story about going home. My family and I had put everything into this adventure. I'd be damned if I'd let anybody get in my way now.

That night I ate dinner alone, my credit card so worn the cashier had to enter the number by hand. I felt as worn as my "plastic."

In the pouring rain the next morning, I started for Canada and almost had an accident before I even got off the Cape. Three traffic lanes came together on a bridge under construction, and my stomach did a backflip as I slid helplessly toward the traffic jam, unable to stop my heavy load on the wet road. I came to a halt just inches short of the rear car.

Whew! That was close! With all the emphasis Dana, George and I had placed on safety during the planning of this voyage, we used to say the most dangerous part of the trip would be running around town doing errands. Here was a perfect example!

At Bar Harbor, Maine, *Father's Day* and I caught the 7 p.m. loading of the famed, ocean-going *M.V. Bluenose* for the six-and-a-half hour ferry ride to Yarmouth, Nova Scotia.

Everywhere the question abounded. "What is it?" Everyone was curious about the little red boat. "Is it a buoy? Is it a sub? Is it a shark cage?"

I just nodded my head and smiled. "You're pretty sharp,

aren't you?" I answered each different guess.

There was no delay at the Canadian border this time. After a couple of routine questions, I drove through the border station into the darkness of Nova Scotia.

After a night of hard sleep at the first hotel I came across, I set out for North Sydney, with *Father's Day* obediently trailing behind. It was a long way across Nova Scotia to North Sydney, some 450 miles, the fog and drizzle my only companions.

Sleep dragged at my eyelids. More than once I had to pull over, jump out of the car in the middle of the road and jog in place to wake up.

By 1 a.m., when the neon of North Sydney's North Star Inn materialized in the windshield, I was chilled to the bone from driving with the window down in an effort to stay awake at the wheel.

By 3 o'clock that afternoon, after too little sleep and a very busy morning, I had *Father's Day* secured aboard the ferry for Newfoundland. In the meantime, I'd made the most of my few hours in North Sydney.

First I contacted local reporter Wes Stewart. Stewart had been faithful about holding his story last year, when he'd discovered us at the Ballast Docks downtown. I knew I could trust him to do the same now. After a long interview with Stewart, I paid my respects to Gordon Howell, the grizzled old seaman who'd given me a tow out of North Sydney during last year's first attempt. It was hard to believe an entire year had passed since I'd last seen Gordon's weather-lined face. He'd suffered two strokes during the year, but I was relieved to see he looked good in spite of it, still full of tall tales of his adventures on the ocean.

This time, he told of how he used to catch swordfish by driving the boat right up beside the giants as they sunned themselves on the cold water's surface. On the business end of a spear, the thrashing swordfish were hauled aboard. A stout club usually ended the encounter before too much damage was incurred.

That old man was the damnedest fisherman I ever knew. Between snagging cod with big hooks and spearing the swordfish, he had little use for bait on his outings. We said good-bye with a firm handshake and little hope of seeing each other again.

Next on the list of things to do: two new trailer tires. Mine were balding rapidly, so I charged two new ones on my over-burdened credit card. Then I placed a call to my business partner in South Florida, my nephew, Richard Vihlen. We'd dabbled in a number of business ventures together. One of our money-makers was a billboard business. Richard told me he was putting up a special billboard on U.S. 1, one of the busiest highways in Miami.

It read "If the Coast Guard would have been here in 1492, Columbus never would have discovered America." Ouch! That should turn a few heads back home.

| U.S. Department of Transportation **United States Coast Guard** | Commander First Coast Guard District | Capt. John Foster Williams Bldg 408 Atlantic Avenue Boston, MA 02110-3350 Staff Symbol: (bb) Phone: (617)223-8311 |

16750
10 June 1993

Mr Hugo Vihlen
15255SW 268 Street
Homestead, FL 33032

Dear Mr. Vihlen:

I have reviewed your letter of appeal dated June 4, 1993 requesting review of the June 3, 1993 finding of manifestly unsafe for the proposed trans-Atlantic voyage of your vessel "Father's Day". The information provided in your letter of appeal was extensive, demonstrating that you have put considerable time and thought in the planning of the voyage. The fact remains, however, that none of the information provided convinces me that the design, configuration, and size of your vessel is adequate for such a voyage. Your appeal for removal of the regulation designating your vessel manifestly unsafe for the intended voyage is therefore denied.

Commander, First Coast Guard District Regulation: Unsafe voyage designation dated June 3, 1993 remains in effect.

Sincerely,

J. D. SIPES
Rear Admiral, U. S. Coast Guard
Commander, First Coast Guard District

Copy of letter dated 10 June 1993 from the U.S. Coast Guard

A phone call to Johnnie had confirmed what I'd expected. The Coast Guard had indeed turned me down for the final time. She was expecting the official letter any day. It was a good thing I hadn't waited any longer.

I had to get offshore before they found out where I was. If the U.S. Coast Guard contacted the Canadian Coast Guard, there was no telling what obstacles would arise. Dana was flying to meet me in St. John's.

Together we'd make this thing happen.

After sixteen hours on a ferry and another two on the road, I arrived in St. John's, weary but excited. I was as prepared as I could ever hope to be. I was here to cross the North Atlantic. It was now or never.

Scouting the town in a blinding rain, I finally arrived at the same fishermen's docks I'd launched from during my second attempt last year. Two years of closed cod fishing had taken its toll on the St. John's waterfront. What was weathered before was rotting away now; the place was deserted and dilapidated.

I drove around looking for some way to get *Father's Day* in the water. But the fisherman's dock didn't offer many choices. The lift we'd used the year before had barely handled the job, and this year the boat was nearly two hundred and fifty pounds heavier with ballast and keel. We'd have to risk using the old lift again.

Dana arrived on the 7 p.m. flight and we headed for dinner and catching up. A week had passed since we parted in Cape Cod. A lot had happened, and there was much to talk about.

The next morning found us standing atop historic Signal Hill, with the stormy Atlantic pummeling the rugged cliff face below.

Today was Father's Day, June 13th, the special day our tiny boat had been named for.

Father's Day had always been one of my favorites. That's why I'd stuck the name to my boat. It was the one day of the year when dads got to do exactly what they wanted. And right now this dad wanted to sail the North Atlantic. Actually, I had hoped to be far out to sea by today.

Far below and behind us, the sprawling waterfront snuggled

into the base of elongated Signal Hill and wrapped around the natural, U-shaped St. John's harbor. The two-mile-long, coal-black harbor churned in the best of weather, but it was worse directly below the cliff where we stood.

This was where Signal Hill and the opposite embankment compressed the harbor into the boiling Narrows, the deep, slender channel that would carry *Father's Day* to the harbor mouth and give me a straight shot to the wide-open Atlantic.

There was no need for a tow this time. We'd launch at the inner entrance to the Narrows and the new Evinrude should be able to power us through the half-mile long stretch to the ocean, providing the wind didn't object too strongly.

As far as the eye could see, wind-whipped white foam skidded along toppling wave crests. Spray shot up from the jagged rocks on the shoreline and a stinging east wind numbed our faces.

We shivered in our jackets. It was rough out there. And cold too. But it was more than the temperature that sent shivers down our spines. About two miles south of where we stood, a three-story iceberg was hard aground in one hundred twenty feet of water. We marveled at its immensity, knowing that most of it was hidden from view below the black water. The iceberg was as solid as a mountain of concrete; it would do plenty of damage if the waves knocked the boat into it.

Down at the docks, Dana and I met up with Dorman Leamond and set about getting *Father's Day* in the water. With the boat trailer backed perpendicular to the harbor's edge, Dorman went to work with the dock hoist. But as I had feared, the now-heavily ballasted boat was too big a load for the old rig. Dorman stopped cold when the cables groaned and a loud popping noise rent the air.

Gingerly, I climbed up and on board to toss whatever supplies I could down to Dana. When the load was somewhat lightened, the tired hoist was able to lift the boat, just enough for me to drive the trailer out from underneath.

Jumping out of the truck, I hollered "Push her clear!"

At least if the hoist gave out now, the boat would be over the water and damage would be kept to a minimum if she fell. But a bow line was tangled in the boat trailer, and the few seconds it took to free it limped by like an eternity; my expensive little toy dangling over the concrete seawall, at the whim of those corroded cables.

Once we got her over the water, *Father's Day* was lowered smoothly, until she floated like a little red duck on the murky water below. With the wind pushing into the dock, Dana motored her over to the protected side where we readied her for our fourth attempt at a new world record.

Once she was outfitted, my son and I headed back to the hotel. But neither of us could stop fretting over the equipment we'd left on board. What if someone came along and robbed the unguarded boat? St. John's wasn't a bad town, but work had been scarce in recent years, and I knew the desperation poverty could breed. To return in the morning to a vandalized boat could mean the end of our adventure. When Dorman agreed to watch over the boat in exchange for $40, we knew we'd sleep a lot better.

That night Dana and I sat in Trapper John's bar, toasting all we'd overcome and all that lay ahead. The path that led us to this waterfront had been a long and exhausting one. Most people would think of the voyage itself as the ultimate test, but getting here had been at least half the battle.

I looked around the bar, studying the customers, the bartender, the waitresses. What would they be doing tomorrow? Getting up as usual and driving to work? Mowing the lawn, watching a movie, making love?

It was hard to comprehend the world I'd be entering tomorrow. It would be a place of deafening solitude and determination; where life itself depended on the wind and the waves. Once I cleared the coast, it would be just me, my boat and the North Atlantic.

By 3 a.m., I was awake, listening to the moaning of the wind.

At dawn, after some last minute dockside preparations, I climbed aboard and motored into the middle of the harbor channel, setting the sails for the crossing.

Dana drove the truck along the southern bank of the harbor. High atop the rocky spine opposite Signal Hill, he could observe departure number four.

Fifteen-foot swells greeted *Father's Day* at the harbor mouth.

Wave action like that, this close to the rocky shore, was dangerous business. I could be dashed on the jagged shoreline in seconds.

Riding the outgoing tide, I decided to keep the small engine idling and ready, at least until I cleared Cape Spear, the easternmost point of the continent that loomed up ahead to my right.

A hard, southwest wind was swirling around the tip of Cape Spear, whistling by Signal Hill on its way to the northeast. *Father's Day*, packed with a full load of supplies, rode low in the water, waves lapping at the hatch.

Looking back to shore, I could see Dana standing with several others in front of a lighthouse that illuminated the south side of the harbor entrance.

Just outside the harbor mouth, hoping for more control, I twisted my upper body and reached for the engine to kick it into gear. However, the move caused the tiny boat to jibe, spinning around. Now she faced the wrong direction. With the blustering wind on the wrong side of the sails, the boat careened crazily.

I suddenly found myself in grave danger. If the boat heeled over too far with the hatch open, I was sunk. As weighted as she was, it wouldn't take much water in the cabin to do it.

Abandoning the sinking ship wouldn't do much to save me. I couldn't swim for more than a few minutes in heavy, saturated clothes, and the water was close enough to freezing to kill me anyway, long before help could arrive.

As I struggled to roll up the sails, the ferocious wind caught a loosened boom and slammed it full force into the mast. It knocked the wood-and-fiberglass box to which both booms were attached loose from the deck.

For an instant I refused to accept my situation. But I knew that without booms I couldn't sail.

Crazy thoughts shot through my head. If I could just get away from this harbor, maybe I could rig some kind of emergency repairs at sea.

But as much as I longed for the open ocean, common sense prevailed. This was no way to start an already perilous voyage. It was time to cut my losses and get back to shore alive.

From his vantage point a mile or so behind, Dana had seen *Father's Day* spin around and the sails collapse. He saw my wildly waving arms and knew I was in trouble. Taking off at a run, he headed for my truck. He had to reach the safety boat we'd hired and get to me as quickly as possible.

In the meantime, I had more trouble. A huge freighter was bearing down on the harbor entrance, blaring her horn.

Giving gas to the outboard engine, I struggled to get clear of the mouth, booms dragging the water like broken wings. Thank God, my engine hadn't been swamped.

To avoid the freighter, I had to maneuver dangerously close to the shoreline rocks, the swells pushing the boat ever closer. I could still see tiny figures standing next to the lighthouse.

What was Dana doing? Couldn't he see I was in trouble?

The treacherous rocks were luring me in. Not knowing what else to do, I kept waving my arms.

Suddenly, I saw a blue-and-white fishing boat heading toward me. It was with great relief that I saw Dana hanging off its rail, video camera in one hand — and a tow line in the other.

Three prior failed attempts, two the year before and one in Cape Cod, had taught us well the value of being prepared. With the safety boat standing by in case I needed rescuing from the vicious bay and a tow line already in place, the hookup to *Father's Day* was made fast.

I had always tried to reserve certain words for certain occasions, and this was a four-letter occasion. I vented my frustration to the heavens on upraised arms as the fishing boat towed me to safety ashore.

Just what would my fortune be now? Would it be another year? A few days? A few weeks?

No. There was no way I was waiting any longer. It must be today. Today, I had the wind. Tomorrow, I might not.

This was the fourth time I'd tried to get offshore and all four times had ended in defeat.

Today was the day. Come hell or high water.

It looked like it was going to be both.

CHAPTER SIX

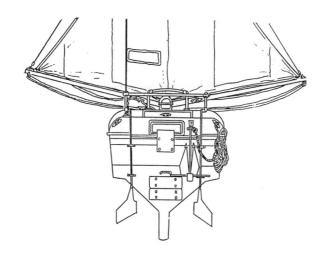

Being in a ship is like being in a jail, with the chance of being drowned.
— Samuel Johnson, March 16, 1759

June 14, 1993
Day 1

GOING UP AGAINST the cold, pounding harbor twice in the same day took every ounce of courage I could muster.

Planning the repairs before even reaching the docks, I leapt from the boat onto the warped wooden pier, grabbed Dana and hustled him into the truck. The only way to fix the boom box, and fix it quick, was to patch it as best we could. For that, we needed something strong.

The groggy shopkeeper was just opening his doors when we charged into his machine shop in search of two pieces of stainless steel angle iron.

Anxious to help, the metalsmith went right to work, cutting and drilling the steel pieces to order. When the first set turned out to be too small, he double-timed it on another.

And since regular screws would rust to a nub in no time, the search was on for stainless steel screws, a hunt that led us all over town. Chilled and wet from the drizzly morning, I stayed in the truck, the heater on full blast, while my son ran in and out of nearly every store in St. John's.

Once the screws were located, the quest turned to the proper screwdriver, since the only stainless screws to be found weren't the standard Phillips or flat-heads, but some other foreign animal known only to Canada and not compatible with the tools we had brought.

Back at *Father's Day*, Dana used our old hand drill to make the repairs. Wrapping my fingers around the familiar old tool, I was glad we had brought it along. It had crossed the Atlantic with me once already, on board *April Fool*. We looked everywhere for a new one for this trip, but the only replacements to be had were plastic modern-day versions, and I didn't trust them to hold up on the North Atlantic. After twenty-five years, the gears on the old drill had petrified to a standstill. But a good coating of oil coaxed them until they spun like new.

The work on the boom box proceeded cautiously, both of us aware that one dropped piece into the muddy water below could mean another year of postponement.

We were already two weeks behind schedule, making the tail end of the voyage that much more risky. Each day I spent on shore now meant one more day spent on the ocean during the early winter storm season. The danger grew greater with every delay.

The repairs were done, but the safety boat wasn't ready to stand by yet, so Dana and I grabbed some lunch and returned to the hotel.

Lying down for a few minutes' rest, I thought to myself that no one should have to face something like this twice in a single day. The morning in the harbor was scary, with its surf-battered rocks, pounding waves and angry swells, each coming right on the heels of the last.

It sure would be nice to start fresh tomorrow. But the wind was right today. Who knew what tomorrow would bring? Tom McNally had waited a month for these winds last year.

I wasn't waiting one more day.

I hauled myself up. "It's one o'clock. Let's go."

Dana didn't look convinced. His blue eyes canvassed mine. "Are you sure you want to do this again today, Dad?"

I must have looked pretty whipped. A step to the bathroom mirror revealed the tired face he saw. Running a hand through my wild hair didn't help much.

"I have to, son," I said, turning away from the weary reflection. "Come on. Let's go do it."

We shrugged into our winter gear and stepped outside. The sky looked a little lighter, the wind a little less fierce.

Maybe it wouldn't be so bad this time.

On the ride to the waterfront, our talk turned to other concerns. The repairs to the boom box had eliminated one safety feature and that had us both a little worried.

Father's Day, designed to ride rough seas, was more like a miniature submarine than a boat. When the hatch was closed, the sailboat was almost watertight, capable of taking quite a dunking.

But along with that security came an invisible, deadly danger. Sealed inside the cabin, I could kill myself simply by breathing. With no fresh air from the outside, the carbon dioxide from my own lungs could quickly reach lethal levels. Dana was afraid I might fall asleep one night and never wake up again.

To solve the problem originally, we had drilled a hole through the boom box and inserted a tube to act as an air shunt. But the repairs we made this morning had blocked off the tube. Closed up for long periods, the cabin would be a poisonous place — more dangerous than a feverish ocean outside. I realized that cracking the hatch open for fresh air would be crucial.

One deep sleep could be my last.

The harbor had settled down a little, and Dana didn't even say good-bye when I motored away from the dock for launch number five. We parted as if I were running down the block to the neighborhood store to pick up a carton of milk.

As *Father's Day* made its way toward the mouth of St. John's harbor, I thought of my last phone call to my wife. After our morning failure, I hadn't wanted Johnnie to worry about *Father's Day* being unfit, so I told her a fierce rain had delayed the morning launch. It bothered me that I'd been whittling away at the truth so much lately.

And I wasn't even out of the harbor.

The great expanse of the North Atlantic fanned out before the jaws of the inlet, gray and rough, rolling into the horizon. Behind, Dana faded to a tiny dot on the cliffs, his waving arms bidding good-bye and good luck.

Ahead beckoned nearly 2,000 miles of wide-open ocean. I was on my own. From this moment on, survival and success would depend entirely upon me and my boat. And on my ability to do everything just right.

This fifth attempt was going smoothly. The iceberg, still grounded about a mile away, posed no threat. Even from this distance, I could see how much its shape had changed in the span of a single morning. The wind and waves had a dramatic effect on the ice. Broken-off chunks of it floated in the water nearby and dotted the shoreline with nuggets of dirty white.

With that big ice cube melting so slowly in the bay, the water couldn't be too much above the freezing point. The air temperature wasn't much above that. This was the middle of June, and it was with a distinct pang that I realized that air conditioners would be humming back in South Florida.

But South Florida was 2,000 miles to the south. And I was headed to Falmouth, England — in the opposite direction from home.

My course would be north northeast and then directly east for 1,876 nautical miles, as the sea gull flies.

Unfortunately, I also knew, that winds and currents could make the final tally much greater.

With swells pushing into the lee shore of Cape Spear, I depended on the small motor to clear the jut of land. A healthy wind hooked around its point, mushrooming the spread sails. I felt its added thrust beneath my feet.

Oh, what a beautiful wind! If it would just keep coming for a couple more hours, I could put some distance between my boat and these ungodly shorelines. Around here, you don't just wash up on a beach and step ashore. Between the rocks and a wicked surf, your boat winds up shredded into a hundred unrecognizable pieces. I'd be lucky to escape with my life.

The Evinrude's steady hum helped calm my frayed nerves. Cape Spear slid into the distance. After an hour or so, my confidence had built enough to cut back on the throttle and depend on the sails more. Surely I'd make it this time.

The wind died down around dusk, a development that brought thoughts of last year's failure. That had been attempt number two in these same waters.

Memories came back to haunt me again.

I went to sleep with no wind in my sails; just the forlorn fog horn of St. John's in the distance and the waves splashing on rocks I couldn't see.

June 15th
Day 2

I was awake before dawn. It was hard to tell how far I'd come. I couldn't see land anywhere, but a haze hung in the air, making it impossible to separate sea, sky and horizon.

With no wind to speak of, I cranked the outboard and motored east until high noon. I'd have to use the engine with prudence. With only twelve gallons of fuel split between two plastic gas tanks that were strapped to the deck, I could only afford to motor for a limited time.

I'd have to save the fuel for when it was needed the most, like avoiding big ships and staying clear of the giant rocks that guarded the other side — the mouth of the English Channel.

Twenty-four hours after I left the dock behind, it was time to break out the GPS for an anxious calculation of my position. Moments later, I had the results: we were twenty-one miles from St. John's.

It was nothing to celebrate, but at least we were on our way.

I wanted to call Johnnie to let her know I was all right. I also had a message for Dana. It looked like this time was the charm, and there was no use in him hanging around St. John's any longer. He might as well start the long trek home with the empty boat trailer.

It took more than three hours of button-pushing and dial twisting on the single sideband radio to get through, and when I did, Johnnie was not at home. Gene Klein, a family friend, was staying at our house during my absence, and it was he who answered the phone. According to Gene, reporters from all over had been hounding the house, news that set me worrying for Johnnie.

She hated dealing with the press. A reporter had embarrassed her once by portraying her as a chain-smoking, nail-biting, neurotic who paced the floor and waited endlessly by the telephone during my first transatlantic voyage.

Throughout *Father's Day* preparations, the rest of the family had agreed to shield Johnnie's privacy as much as possible. The reporters must be driving her crazy right now.

I relayed my position to Gene and signed off, disappointed that I hadn't caught my wife at home.

In a dead calm wind, I motored until dark. With an alarm set to go off every forty-five minutes, I tucked in below and tried to get some sleep.

The chances of crossing paths with a big ship were much greater this close to shore. If I slept too long or too hard, I'd never hear it approaching. And as small as *Father's Day* was, I sure couldn't depend on them seeing me. It was easy enough to be run down by a big ship in the daylight. In the darkness of night, the risk was even greater. I'd heard of small boats being sucked into their giant propellers, sliced up and sunk in a matter of seconds.

Haunted by the image, I turned and tossed in my tiny bunk. Sleep did not come easily. Each time, I was awake before the alarm.

June 16th
Day 3
24 miles offshore

The dawn found me so tired that it was an accomplishment just to move. Grateful for enough wind in the sails to keep me from having to motor, I struggled my weighty body through the hatch at 7 a.m. and took a GPS shot. Only twenty-four miles from St. John's.

Disheartened, I spent the day trying to regroup and get organized. The noon position fix wasn't much better. It had taken five hours to sail a single mile! Only twenty-five miles in forty-eight hours at sea. It would be a long way to England at that rate. I could only hope the wind would improve.

At $800, the handheld GPS was an expensive piece of equipment, but one in which I was glad I had invested. Its advanced technology wasn't available when I set my original world record. I did my navigation on that trip with a sextant, just as centuries of sailors had done before me. For this voyage, I carried two GPS units, the spare in case the first one malfunctioned. The North Atlantic was a rough environment, capable of ruining even the finest equipment.

All I needed to make a GPS shot was an unobstructed view of the sky. That meant seas had to be calm enough to allow standing in the hatch for the few minutes it took to work. The walkie-talkie-sized GPS communicates with passing satellites, reading their signals, comparing them with its own and giving a position report on its LCD display. It reads signals from at least three satellites, orbiting 10,900 miles above the earth. If the satellites are directly overhead, the GPS latches onto strong signals, and calculations take three to five minutes. If signals are weak, it takes longer — too long to keep the hatch open when the cold waves are taunting.

I tried to call Johnnie on the radio, over and over, but couldn't raise a marine operator. Staying in touch might not be as easy as we thought.

June 17th
Day 4

I awoke during the night, fretting about Johnnie, longing to hear her voice. We hadn't talked since right before the launch. That was only two days ago, but it seemed much longer. I was in another world already. All by myself.

I'd have to get used to that. The solitude would probably be the toughest part of the voyage. I knew from experience: this caliber of loneliness is hard to endure.

April Fool had been a lonely, tortuous voyage, but the beginning was probably the worst. The tail end was pretty bad too, though. I suppose it's the closeness to shore that intensifies it. Proximity to others is tantalizing. It makes one more aware of being alone.

Somewhere in the middle of the Atlantic, I knew I would get used to it, grow accustomed to my own company and find small ways to salvage my sanity. It would be easier then.

I was up with the first pale showing of dawn, fiddling with the single side band radio, hoping to pin down the problem. I tried every trick I'd ever learned, but still couldn't reach an operator.

Eyes closed, I rubbed both temples, trying to stave off a headache that was blossoming in my skull. Agitated, I tossed the mike down and pulled up through the hatch.

This was going to be frustrating. I'd worked my butt off to earn an advanced ham radio operator license before the first launch last year. All that schooling wasn't doing a bit of good now — and it looked as if my call letters, KI4WL, would remain silent.

Calm winds forced me back to the motor. A noon position fix registered fifty-three miles east of St. John's. In our cruising waters back home that's equal to a crossing between Miami Beach and the Bahama Islands. That thought made me feel a little better.

Another problem arose. Not threatening, but a real aggravation. The all-band radio bit the dust in a cloud of smoke.

Salt water dripping through a crack in the damaged boom box must have found its way into the radio rack. The dead all-band meant I'd have no news, no music, no company at all. Radio had eased the loneliness a great deal on my first trip. Hours had flown listening to BBC broadcasts. After awhile, the announcers began to feel like old friends. I even started to like cricket, looking forward to gameside broadcasts, rooting for a favorite team.

And the news. I'd really be isolated now, with no idea what went on in the rest of the world while I sailed across the ocean in solitude.

Anything could happen in the two or three months I'd be gone. And unless I gleaned the information from a chance communication with someone at sea, I'd never know a thing about it until I made England.

Whenever that might be.

June 18th
Day 5
75 miles from St. Johns

I woke up in a fog, both mentally and literally. It was eerie in the smothering grayness, suspended in the middle of a cloud. Like a miniature ghost ship, *Father's Day* sailed on, gliding silently through the damp pea-soup mist. The world was reduced to a few undulating feet on all sides.

I had to find a way to get through on the single sideband radio. If I couldn't use it to communicate, this voyage would be a much hotter hell for Johnnie and Dana. With everything depending on the whims of the wind, an educated stab was the best I could offer for an arrival date in England. It could be off by any number of days. Weeks even.

With no way to tell the family of my progress, they'd be counting on that date. And every day I didn't show would be a miserable one for them.

I pulled out the tool box, no small feat in the tightly packed storage compartments of *Father's Day*. Everything had been carefully inventoried, vacuum-sealed in labeled, color-coded plastic bags, then fitted into the compartments like pieces of a three-dimensional puzzle. Carrying enough supplies and equipment for a three-month journey on a boat five feet four inches long had turned into a real science.

Each morsel of food had to pass tests of longevity, nutritional value and ease of preparation. Each tool and piece of equipment had to serve more than one purpose. And all had to have a storage place, somewhere in the eleven tiny, watertight compartments inside the cabin or strapped on the deck outside, where there was always the chance they'd be ripped off by a clawing wave. I was grateful we'd drawn up an inventory list, showing which compartment held what. It saved me from having to search the entire boat for a needed item.

The tool box was stowed in the aft bilge compartment in the bottom of the hull, directly underneath where I stood or sat down, right below the cabin's entry hatch. To get to it, I first had to move all loose supplies to the front of the cabin, peel back the cushions we'd installed for comfort, lean against the radio rack in the front and pry up the bilge hatch cover.

Once I gained entry, I had to remove dozens of items, food rations and other supplies and pile them all around the sides of the opening, my spread legs buried beneath the mound.

Then I wiggled the heavy plastic box containing the tools from the very lowest point of the boat, up between the two big, 100 amp, gel-cell batteries and the bilge hatch rim and finally to the top of the surrounding supply pile.

Water had seeped in from somewhere, forming a small puddle in the bottom of the bilge. Locating a sponge, I soaked it all up before shoving enough of the compartment's contents back into place to at least move around the cabin. Then the hatch cover went down with a slam. The cushions were jammed back into position.

What a hassle! Just getting the tools was enough to exhaust a man!

I'd have to repack it all correctly when the radio repairs were finished. Thank God, the fog-blanketed ocean was relatively calm today. I never would have attempted the project in rougher seas.

The next chore was finding an entry point to the base of the single sideband radio antenna, where I suspected the problem lay. I dug into an eye-level hatch reserved for emergency supplies. Out of the compartment came flares, epoxy kits for repairs and fishing gear should I need it. With no way to cook, I hadn't planned on fishing for food, but if worse came to worst and I was out of supplies, I could always eat the fish raw. Not too appetizing but at least I'd survive. If I thought of it as sashimi, told myself that a lot of people pay big bucks for the pleasure of eating it, maybe it wouldn't be so bad. At least I was assured of its freshness.

After several alterations to the antenna, I still couldn't raise anyone on the radio. So I decided to troubleshoot with an emergency antenna. Again, easier to decide than to do. The spare antenna was snugly attached to the cabin ceiling, the necessary allen wrench tied around its four-foot mast. That was the easy part.

The other needed parts, the wavelength resonators, were in the bottom of a portside compartment. Everything from that compartment landed atop the mess already in the cabin. I had to admire Dana's packing. My son had worked on each compartment, organizing them over and over, trying several different ways, each time managing to fit one more item inside. I doubted I'd ever be able to get it all back where it belonged.

With the spare antenna measuring eight feet assembled, I had to stand it up through the hatch to work on it, knowing the tiniest dropped piece overboard could render the entire thing inoperable. Sure enough, with all the antenna appendages sticking out, I knocked my favorite pair of eyeglasses over the side. At least it wasn't part of the antenna. I had a spare pair of glasses. But this antenna was my only hope of communication.

With the emergency antenna assembled, wrenched into place and wires attached, I ducked below to try the radio. Silence. All that effort for nothing.

By noon, the weak North Atlantic sun had burnt away most of the fog. A GPS shot placed *Father's Day* eighty-five miles off St. John's. At least I was making some progress.

Sixty or seventy sea birds, big, white gull-looking creatures, had deployed in the water behind the boat, a flotilla of bobbing cotton balls easily keeping pace. Where had they all come from? I hadn't noticed that many flying in. In pairs or alone, they appeared from nowhere, settling gently in my lazy wake, calling back and forth to each other. I wondered what attraction this tiny boat held for them. Were they hoping for a morsel of food, one I couldn't afford to share?

A whining noise came to my ears, not much more than the buzz of a mosquito above the chatter of the gulls. There it was! An aircraft was passing high overhead.

I snatched up the mike to the aircraft VHF radio, calling several times. But no response came from the pilot. Now what could be wrong with this radio? Frustrated, I yanked everything out of the compartment located above the VHF radio antenna. For protection, the antenna was mounted horizontally inside a compartment in the hull. I removed the sea anchor from the deck area over top and anything else that could possibly interfere with transmission.

When the next set of wispy contrails appeared, I was back at the microphone. Damn! Still no answer.

Radio wave propagation is a science, but it's also an art form. Perhaps the spare single sideband radio antenna I'd just mounted was now interfering with the VHF transmission. Too many antennas too close together can be a problem. And on the Lilliputian-sized Father's Day, there was no way the three different fixed antennas couldn't be close together.

Down came the spare, back into storage. It wasn't doing any good anyway. And it wasn't sturdy enough to leave up all the time.

With the cabin in shambles and Dana's meticulous organization in shreds, I sat before the soundless radio, running out of ideas. The batteries were strong enough, so it couldn't be that. Dana and I had researched extensively, choosing two marine gel-cell batteries and placing them in the watertight aft bilge compartment. Well, it was almost watertight. I was already realizing that nothing was really watertight out here.

Each battery fed separate pieces of equipment and both were capable of being recharged with two flexible solar panels attached to the deck. The stingy North Atlantic sun didn't give much in the way of recharging power, contributing only about thirty-five amps per week. But it was certainly better than nothing. Without it, I'd be out of juice in no time.

Throughout the day, the seas intensified. Just before dark, with the cabin hatch still open, a large rogue wave crashed over the boat, soaking everything inside. Grabbing a sponge and a small bucket, I wiped up as much as I could.

It would be a long, cold, wet night.

**June 20th
Day 7**

Finally! The prayed-for wind arrived. The day before had been shrouded in fog, just like the one before that; the flat seas barely ruffled by a breath of wind.

Motionless, downcast, I couldn't even spare enough spirit to write in my log. Today I awakened to more of the same, but by mid-morning the hand-held wind gauge read four to six knots, by noon twelve to fourteen. Father's Day lurched to life beneath me, sails straining at the seams. Blow baby, blow! I could take plenty of this! It was the first real west wind I'd gotten.

The unnerving part was watching the front portholes dip half under water with each passing wave, sometimes completely submerged by swells that now came from another direction.

But she seemed to be holding her own, as long as I kept the sails and boat carefully balanced. A wind this strong could push her head over heels if the two triangle sails were fully spread.

I was still wearing the clothes I'd left the dock in six days ago, and was beginning to feel rather ripe. But with the temperature hovering at forty-five degrees Fahrenheit, it was no time to consider a bath. It would be a long time before I could enjoy that luxury, if one could consider a dip in freezing salt-water a luxury at all.

I considered my ensemble: a "Polar cloth" jacket, wool shirt, long johns, t-shirt, Levi's, two pair of wool socks, leather boat shoes and foul weather pants and jacket.

And I was still cold. I'd only been out of the jacket for about three hours all week.

It's amazing what a little underarm deodorant can do for a guy's morale.

Especially if that's all he has.

June 22nd
Day 9
240 miles from St. Johns

The past few days had fired my resolve. I checked and double-checked today's reading on the GPS.

At last the winds had been good to me. One hundred and thirty-five miles had slid by since my last position check four days ago.

And most of it accomplished in the past two days.

Hallelujah! I was finally making headway. I hummed that old mariner's ditty, "Sailing, sailing, over the Bounty Main...."

But good luck celebrated prematurely has a way of evaporating instantly.

June 23rd
Day 10

My favorable wind abandoned me. In its place, a surly north wind howled, and with the sails wide open as I'd left them during the night, I was not only losing ground, but was actively sailing in the wrong direction.

All day I sat at sea anchor with the sails rolled up tight, trying to salvage what I could of my hard-earned headway.

A sea anchor isn't a real anchor at all, at least not the kind that drops to the ocean floor to hold a boat's position. Only eighteen inches wide, it resembles a big open-weave bag, fashioned from thick, intertwined nylon straps. Its function is merely to slow unwanted drift.

With the sails rolled up and the north wind still pushing to the south, I deployed the sea anchor forward, where it acted as a drag, helping hold onto at least some of the miles I'd gained.

At one o'clock I spotted a blue and white freighter on the horizon to the north. No one responded to my calls on the ship-to-ship VHF.

By the next day, I'd lost fourteen miles.

Standing in the hatch, looking over the bow, I surveyed the tossing gray ocean before me. A new wind was blowing right in my face, tickling its way through my hair.

An east wind. Definitely a turn for the worse.

CHAPTER SEVEN

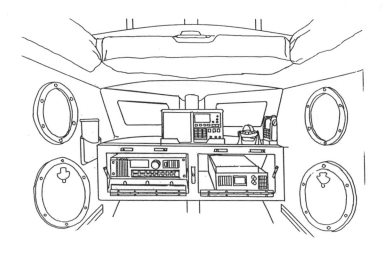

How little do the landsmen know of what we sailors feel,
When waves do mount and winds do blow!
But we have hearts of steel.
— The Sailors Resolution, Traditional from the 18th century

June 25th
Day 12

FINGERS OF FOG crept across the ocean, enveloping *Father's Day* in a thick drizzle of smoky white. With seas hopping at twelve to fifteen feet, I stayed crunched up below, entertaining myself as best I could.

My back was already feeling the effects of the tight quarters. When waves mounted higher than four or five feet, the hatch had to remain shut. That meant a whole lot of time spent below in the cabin.

If you could call it a cabin. Only thirty-two inches from side to side, five feet long, and twenty-seven inches tall at its highest point, it was much smaller with padding and gear. Two inches of sky blue canvas-covered foam padding lined the cabin floor, one inch on the walls and ceiling. It was a custom-made luxury that greatly increased my comfort, though my sore backside now told me it should have been a little thicker.

Even so, with the regular banging I was taking inside the bucking boat, I'd have been immensely more miserable without it.

The buoyant floor padding, like nearly everything else in the boat, served multiple purposes. Its underside was covered in dayglo international orange material. If I needed to signal for help from the air, I could float it behind the boat, greatly increasing the chances of being spotted.

I had Johnnie to thank for my cozy little sleeping bag. Originally, I'd planned to bring a regular sized sleeping bag, maybe goose down or some other cold weather type. I was glad that was one of the ideas we'd improved upon. A bulky bag like that would have taken up way too much room and most likely been constantly wet. But nothing more suitable could be found in any store, so Johnnie created one for me.

It was made of a silky feeling, teal blue, polyethylene fabric, resistant to water and remarkably warm for its light weight. More of a flap than a bag, it was stitched together only along one side and the foot seam for fast escape. There were no zippers to rust away, or jam up and hold me captive.

Only five feet long, it was perfect for sleeping curled up in a tight ball. Thin on the bottom, thicker on top for warmth, the tiny sleeping bag was stuffed into a compression sack each morning, and squeezed down to the size of a loaf of bread. Not only was it out of the way then, but compressed so tight no stray wave could soak it.

A flotation life vest served as a pillow — otherwise the most useless item on the boat. I'd brought it along to comply with U.S. Coast Guard regulations — downright humorous considering I'd defied all their orders in the end. If I wound up overboard, I was dead anyway in these cold waters. The vest would only keep my lifeless body afloat.

Supplies that wouldn't fit in compartments rode loose in the cabin, stealing more precious stretching room from the captain.

For maximum light and visibility, the five rectangular windows and twelve-inch by twelve-inch overhead cabin hatch were made of clear, bullet-proof lexan. Dana had used a three-pound sledgehammer to test the security of their installation. The toughness of the lexan meant we could risk more and bigger windows than I had allowed in *April Fool*. With mood so dependent on the weather, I would need all the sunlight available to keep my spirits up in the dismal North Atlantic.

Even so, the windows were miniature, averaging only one foot across and five inches from top to bottom. Two tiny mini-mag flashlights, velcroed to the overhead padding, provided interior light at night.

The radio rack occupied the front width of the cabin, right below the two bow windows. Seven inches deep, it held the single sideband, ship-to-ship, ship-to-aircraft and hand-held VHFs, headsets, mikes, a spare antenna and whatever else could be stuffed behind its two see-through, oblong doors.

Bolted to its top was a gimbaled compass and the now useless all-band, the radio I was counting on for companionship. How I missed the music and news.

Underneath the rack, the cabin dropped to only nine inches tall, and stretched for another foot or so to the front of the boat. It was here that I crammed most of the loose supplies, sacrificing valuable leg room in the deal.

To sleep, I had to curl into a ball on my side. Sitting was done hunched over; the cabin was too squat for me to sit with my back straight. To stand up, I had to open the cabin hatch, something I could not do in rough seas.

The confinement was starting to gnaw at me. Claustrophobia was closing in, choking off my lungs.

"My God, it's only been twelve days!" I grumped to myself.

Cracking the hatch just a little, I gulped in a sliver of cold ocean air before the next wave crashed on the deck and the Atlantic came sloshing through the inch-wide opening.

Slamming the hatch shut, I found a sponge and scrambled around mopping up the cabin, squeezing the water into a small bucket. Most everything was really soaked now and gritty with the salt the ocean left behind.

It was everywhere, on everything, causing tools to slip from my hands and the skin on my wrists to crack at the folds where the insidious salt caked like powder. My clothes were stiff with it, my hair dried to straw. The cheeks of my butt, chafed raw by it, were erupting in oozing saltwater sores that made sitting in the cabin a torment.

Propped against the back wall, I pried open a side hatch and reached into a compartment for some distraction. With no room to spare, entertainment items had fallen low on the list of supplies. But we had found space for a few books, carefully chosen for their small type and long-winded subject matter.

I purposely avoided bringing along certain sailing adventure stories. These were filled with tales of capsizing and demasting in shark-infested waters. I didn't need anything else to scare me. The North Atlantic was doing a fine job by itself.

My library consisted of an atlas, a dictionary, a world almanac, nautical almanac, *First Aid at Sea, Guiness Book of World Records* and three nonfiction books. If I could settle down and read a little, I might be able to take my mind off the suffocating, water-logged surroundings.

Fishing out *Paddle to the Amazon,* I leaned back and opened the cover. A rivulet of water dribbled out.

I put the book down immediately.

June 27th
Day 14

The west wind started yesterday, just after midnight. Blowing steady and strong at eighteen to twenty knots, *Father's Day* skimmed fifty miles in twenty-four hours. And, more importantly, it was in the desired direction.

Spirits soaring, I braced myself in the padded hatch, heedless of the wind-whipped spray, and surveyed the stormy thrusts of the ocean.

Up ahead! A ship! At one o'clock off the bow. She disappeared as *Father's Day* dropped into a deep trough between swells, and was visible once again when I reached the summit of the next wave.

For a few minutes I watched her, unable to place her lines. She didn't look like a freighter and didn't seem to be following the shipping routes.

Then it hit me: a fishing trawler dragging a net.

And she was on a collision course with *Father's Day.* Visions of my tiny boat entangled in her long net, dragged under water for hours, vaulted into my head.

Calling on the VHF brought no response from her captain. He'd never spot me in this kind of seas. No one would be expecting to see a small boat way out here.

I reefed the sails in an attempt to slow down. It was hard to keep track of exactly where the fishing boat was. I kept losing sight of her in the swells. Then she'd pop up unexpectedly, closer than before.

I crossed her trail about 100 yards behind her stern, wincing as *Father's Day* cut through her wake, unsure of how far back the deadly net dragged.

I couldn't relax until the waves swallowed her for good.

June 28
Day 15

There it was again! That roaring in the sky!

Bloodshot eyes striving to pierce the thick cloud layer, I tried to track the source of the noise. It had to be missiles. Nothing else makes a sound like that.

There must be a submarine in the vicinity, conducting firing exercises. I'd heard it three times yesterday, each about three hours apart. It sounded like two missiles at a time, one fired just a second behind the other. They sounded so close, rocketing right overhead.

I hoped they were long range. It'd be ironic to have one land on my head. No one would ever figure out what had happened to me.

My attention returned to the radio problems. I had to find a way to communicate with the outside world. The single sideband was receiving ok. I could hear people talking in a full house of languages. It was frustrating to listen to them chatting while I sat in isolation, calling over and over into the mike, never to hear a response.

Troubleshooting, I removed the antenna once again. Perhaps the radio wasn't properly grounded. Disassembling the connection, I reinforced the ground and put it all back together. Hunched over the radio, I anxiously tried again.

Still nothing.

June 29th
Day 16
340 miles from St. John's

The sun made its first appearance, its tenuous, fragile rays a beautiful sight indeed. For more than two weeks, I'd traveled through a world of grayness, blanketed by fog more often than not.

I couldn't believe the comfort the pale warmth carried. It still wasn't much above forty-five degrees, but the damp fog had penetrated to my skin, making it feel a lot colder. The first time I'd seen the North Atlantic fog rolling in across the surface, I ducked below and closed the hatch, mistaking the heavy vapor for rain.

Shedding my outer gear for the first time in over a week, I felt amazingly thin without the bulky polar jacket. Slipping a hand under my waist band, I tugged out on my jeans. I was thinner. Sixteen days at sea had taken a few pounds.

But that was to be expected. I'd lost fifteen pounds on *April Fool*. Eating voraciously in the months before the final *Father's Day* launch, I'd added ten extra pounds to my normal one hundred seventy-five-pound frame — extra insulation against cold and starvation.

Digging in a compartment for a snack, I fished out a bag of dried dates and relished their sweetness. Dana and Nancy had dried and vacuum-bagged an assortment of fresh fruit, and sealed portions inside ziploc bags. It was a lot of work for them, but the fruit was a real treat for me, already weary of the bland voyage menu.

As in everything else that concerned the trip, our voyage team had painstakingly researched this important aspect too. The nutritional needs of a human body at sea were carefully calculated. Only foods high in nutrients, low in salt, long lasting and simple to store could be brought along.

Cooking was too risky on a boat the size of *Father's Day*. Flammables on board were dangerous, and besides, there wasn't a clear spot of room big enough to risk any type of fire.

So everything in my diet had to come ready to eat. Lord, how I craved a cup of hot coffee.

Each day's caloric needs were tabulated in a daily menu, the backbone of which was military-issued food rations and high energy drinks.

Water was the most crucial of all my supplies. I could go without food for a month or more if I had to, but without water I wouldn't live more than a few days.

Twenty-five heavy-duty plastic, one gallon jugs with locking tops, stashed mostly in the forward bilge, held the precious clear liquid and provided more than 200 pounds of ballast. If I regulated myself to a quarter of a gallon a day — four priceless cups of water — I'd have enough to last a little more than three months. If the voyage went slower than expected, I'd have to do with less and less every day.

When it was gone, the reverse osmosis kit could be used to make fresh water from seawater, one drop at a time.

Human nature being what it is, bodily functions must go on, despite adverse conditions. Urinating was done over the side in fair weather; in an empty water jug in high seas.

As might be expected, bowel movements were more difficult, but I would become ill in no time if the need weren't regularly attended to. On gentle days, I crouched over the side, safety harness securely in place. During rougher weather, when I couldn't leave the cabin for long, a cut off plastic jug, emptied quickly over the side and thoroughly rinsed, served the purpose.

Last night, I switched gel batteries and tried to call Johnnie again, but the spare wasn't holding its charge. An amp meter revealed it only held ten volts. I needed at least fourteen to transmit. So today I hooked both batteries to the radio, hoping together they'd have enough. With no sun before today, the solar panels couldn't do their job, and both batteries were abysmally weak.

I waited, knowing the best time to try was around dusk, when the Europeans weren't crowding the airwaves and radio wave propagation was at its best. I couldn't afford to waste one amp of power.

When the sun melted to red wax on the horizon, I turned on the power and called into the microphone. I was startled when someone answered back.

Fumbling with the dials, I pursued the faint voice. It was a marine operator, but my transmission was too weak to be clear. The operator asked if I wanted to call back in an hour, when my signal might be stronger, or if they should try to patch me through to another operator. Thinking my radio problems must be solved, I foolishly answered that I'd try again later.

An hour later there was no answer at all.

June 30th
Day 17
368 miles to date

The fog returned with a vengeance, stealing across the ocean under the cover of night, waiting for me when I arose in the morning. Four to seven-knot winds accompanied the gloomy weather, keeping *Father's Day* moving. But it was the current that really carried her along. For the first time it was with me. I was making good time.

But I couldn't stop worrying about Johnnie. She'd been so opposed to this trip. Anguished, I thought about all the grief and distress I'd caused her over thirty-six years of marriage. She was a simple girl from North Carolina, who really wanted nothing more than a life of peace and harmony.

I, despite good intentions, had supplied her with exactly the opposite.

I'd met her as a young marine, in 1954, stationed at Cherry Point, North Carolina. Johnnie sparkled with a zest for life that drew me to her immediately. She had that all-American girl look — clean, athletic, sexy.

She joined the Marines to see something other than the small Carolina mill town where she was born. It was ironic that she wound up stationed at Cherry Point, only a few hours drive from her home town of Cramerton. Our romance was swift, passionate and secret. She was a private and I an officer. A relationship between us was against Marine Corps rules. But three months later, despite the disapproval of our superiors, we were married in a clandestine ceremony in the quiet dusk of the base chapel. We told no one about our marriage until it was too late for interference.

But the Marine Corps has its own methods of dealing with

those who ignore the rules. Twenty days later we were torn apart. I was off to Korea, the only one from my squadron to receive the combat orders. Later, I would learn that it had to do with my frowned-upon marriage to Johnnie. Korea was my punishment.

That was ok with me, though. A tour in Korea, scary as it was sometimes, turned out to be a small price to pay for a lifetime with a woman like Johnnie.

Seven months in Japan followed the seven in Korea, and I came home to my young wife a stranger. Our twenty days of marriage seemed like a mist-shrouded fantasy.

Who was this woman known to the world as my wife?

But it didn't take long for it all to flood back. The forces that drew us together in the first place flared stronger than ever. She had the best personality of any girl I'd ever known. And still does.

I felt like an ass. I'd sworn to her, promised her, pledged to her that I'd be able to stay in touch this time.

"Don't worry, hon! With modern electronics, it's no problem!," I'd said confidently.

She'd lost twenty-five pounds worrying about me during the *April Fool* trek, when weeks went by without anyone hearing from or spotting me. Back then, I'd had little enough to leave her, if anything had gone wrong. Aside from a decent job with Delta, I was half-owner in a small package store and billboard business, but both ventures were new and not worth a whole lot.

With a rented house, an eleven-year-old boy and an old car and truck to her name, her future wasn't very bright if I hadn't made it home from the sea.

She was fishing alone at a bridge near our home in South Florida when a neighbor came to tell her I'd been spotted off Cuba. Fishing was a pastime she found soothing and enjoyed often. Dana was raised with a pole in his hand.

But having more assets to leave her now hadn't seemed to bring her much comfort on this trip.

My fist banged on the clear hatch overhead. "I've got to get to Falmouth by August 14th!," I vowed. "I've got to be there for our thirty-ninth wedding anniversary."

Isolated in my lonely quest, I had no way of knowing that at that very moment, Tom McNally was guiding *Vera Hugh* into Bahia Mar Marina in Ft. Lauderdale, seizing my twenty-five-year-old world record for himself.

July 1st
Day 18
398 miles to date

I was having a lot of trouble sleeping. Each time I dozed off, I'd startle awake with both feet numb and tingling. Jumping up and down in the hatchway, jogging in place — nothing seemed to help.

Unwelcome thoughts of gangrene and amputation filtered into my mind. In two and a half weeks at sea, I'd only seen two ships. Getting help wouldn't be easy out here. Especially with my radios on the blink.

Searching my memory for the little medical knowledge it possessed, I reckoned I could make it to England before blood poisoning got me, should the worst prove true. With about seven weeks to go, I should be able to beat it. If not with my legs, at least with my life.

An early morning position check put me nearly four hundred miles off St. John's — I had accomplished more than thirty miles of sailing in one day.

If that pace continued, I might see England in the next forty days.

By late afternoon the southwest wind was screaming, slamming into the sails at twenty-three knots. The mutinous ocean, whipped into a rage, tossed twenty-foot waves to the torturing wind.

I rode the purgatory in between.

Unable to stay up top to tend the sails, I twirled line around the mast, afraid the powerful wind might cartwheel the boat head over heels. With the sails securely closed, I settled below, stuffing flying gear wherever it would wedge.

My small craft labored up the side of one monstrous wave after another, only to reach the crest and corkscrew wildly down the other side. Up and down. Up and down.

Over and over, I completed the circuit, an unwilling rider on a runaway roller coaster. Water pounded the deck, its massive weight shoving *Father's Day* under the surface, holding her down like a bully at the beach.

As tightly as we'd sealed her, water dripped in around the cabin hatch. I double checked my safety harness and seat belt and tried to brace myself better. Not that either would do me any good if the boat fell apart. *April Fool*, made of fiberglass-covered plywood, would never have survived this kind of beating.

I had to hold back a grin as I remembered my demonstration to Johnnie. Trying to convince her I would return in one piece, I'd escorted her out to the garage, placed a square of hardened Airex on a cinder block and hit it hard with a hammer.

Secretly relieved when it stood up to the pounding, I had turned to her, hands spread wide. "See? I told you it was strong."

If the Airex had shattered, I had a Plan B prepared. I could have told her that was the stuff we had decided not to use.

It looked like I was in for a long, rough ride today. A loose can of Nutriment drink left out for lunch rocketed across the small cabin, hitting me square in the knee cap. I felt the pain all the way down to my foot, momentarily piercing the numbness that was always there now.

That was it! The problem in my feet wasn't gangrene!

With relief I remembered how my thumb had felt the same way after hurricane Andrew. I'd worked for weeks putting up a new fence to contain the horses. Constantly bending the wire damaged a nerve, causing one thumb to go temporarily numb.

"It's probably just nerve damage in my knees," I comforted myself. They were always pressed against something in the cabin.

Why is it we humans obsess over the worst possible scenario? Maybe it's a way of staying prepared. I remembered a co-pilot I'd known when flying DC-8s. He'd lost feeling in his left leg from constant pressure on the gustlock.

If that were the case here, I almost wished it would work its way up my legs. While my feet were strangely numb, my knees stabbed constantly with needles of fire.

Too scared to be seasick in the crazily swirling seas, I bounced across the ocean, wrapped in a dark, wet cocoon.

June 2nd
Day 19
460 miles to date

The seas had calmed down around sunrise, but rain spattering on the tiny deck kept me below. Peeling back two layers of heavy socks, I checked the color of my feet. They were a little shriveled and peeling, but their color looked fine. I put aside worries about gangrene for good.

It was warm enough in the cabin to shed the polar jacket again. Slipping through the hatch opening during a pause in the rain, I leaned over the back of the boat to check water temperature with a thermometer.

Sixty five degrees Fahrenheit seemed impossible. If the reading was accurate, it meant I'd finally reached the swift, slightly warmer waters of the Gulf Stream. Curling around the southeastern tip of the U.S., shooting up the east coast and heading for Europe offshore of Newfoundland, the powerful ocean current turned into the watered down North Atlantic Current for a straight shot to Europe.

It was the fuel that would carry me to England. My being in the Gulf Stream would explain the great distance we covered yesterday.

The rain resumed and I holed up again, carefully turning the damp pages of *Maiden Voyage*, a book about the first woman and youngest person ever to circumnavigate the globe in a sailboat. Tania Aebi spent two and a half years alone on board her twenty-six foot *Varuna*. Like me, she found the first days at sea the loneliest.

But Aebi had ports of call on her journey. My first and only stop would be England. At least, I hoped that's where it would be.

Hating to turn the last few pages, I was lost when the book was done. Reading was a fabulous escape. Immersed in a good book, I was in another world.

I wished I'd had room to bring more.

I'd travel as many miles as I could standing up in the hatch. I couldn't face the confinement of the cabin unless I had to.

As I stood there, ignoring the now lightly falling rain, I spooked when something broke the surface near the boat. It was a porpoise! Three more appeared, traveling with the first.

I watched them frolic for a moment of delight, then ducked below to grab my camera.

But when I pulled myself topside again, they were gone. Aside from the sea birds, who returned to shadow me regularly, it was the first sign of life I'd seen.

July 3rd
Day 20
483 miles to date

The timid North Atlantic sun made a tantalizing appearance today, then coyly ducked behind another patch of clouds. The heavy gray and white mantle, perpetually pregnant with rain, was finally breaking up. The west wind kept the sails full.

The first aircraft I'd seen in days skimmed across the sky between clots of clouds. Maybe I'd get lucky on the radio today. A second one came overhead. I knew I was near the heavily traveled commercial flight latitudes — the same ones I'd traveled so often myself. I used to look out the cockpit window, way, way down at the ocean below and imagine myself down there, a tiny dot in its rippled vastness; a smudge, breaking the perfection of its endless marching rows.

I must have crossed it two hundred times, insulated in the cockpit, warm and dry, the wind and roaring engines muffled to a dull, constant drone by the skin of the airliner. But down here, riding the tossing crests from ridge to ridge, cold waves spitting in my face, boat tilting and rocking, icy wind screaming across the heaving surface, it was anything but the quiet picture I'd admired from 30,000 feet.

I knew the commercial flight schedules. It was too early in the morning for the aircraft above to be U.S. carriers. By the size of the contrails they had to be 747s, probably belonging to Air India, possibly out of Cairo. Making myself understood to a pilot from India could waste my already dwindling battery power. I'd wait.

Scanning the skies, I bided my time. An hour slipped by, then another.

With the clouds rapidly closing ranks once again, I prepared for the optimum transmission. Removing my flare gun and all metal from the glove box over the built-in aircraft VHF antenna, I cleared away anything that might interfere with the radio waves.

My battery system was down to little more than twelve volts. I knew it normally took fourteen to transmit. But it would only dwindle more. The next one was it.

There it was. A third aircraft materialized in the heavens to the east.

Headset in place, mike in hand, power on, I sat motionless in the cabin, timing the transmission to the perfect moment. The airplane had to be in just the right position if I were to have any chance at all of getting through.

When the airborne target was at just the right distance, I pushed the button on the side of the mike.

"Aircraft approaching 40 west," I said. "Do you hear the sailboat *Father's Day*, just below you on 121.5?"

Releasing tense fingers from the button, I waited, unable to take a deep breath.

"Yes, this is TWA 843. I hear you, *Father's Day*."

At the completion of his record-breaking 1993 voyage, Hugo Vihlen stands triumphantly atop his five-foot, four-inch sailboat *Father's Day*. He battled the Atlantic for 105 days.

On his 1968 voyage across the Atlantic Ocean in his six-foot sailboat *April Fool*,
Hugo meets the U.S. Submarine *Grenadier*.

April Fool arrives June 21, 1968, in Fort Lauderdale, Florida. The tiny sailboat set the world record for the smallest boat to cross the Atlantic Ocean.

Hugo christens
his namesake,
"Hugo" the
killer whale.

Home at last: After the 1968 voyage, Johnnie and Hugo reunite.

In 1992, the hull of Hugo's new record challenger *Father's Day* takes shape. The hatch measures twelve inches by twelve inches — just wide enough for Hugo to get in and out.

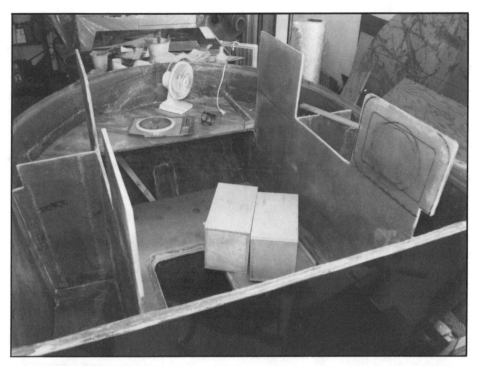

Father's Day's strong construction is of Airex foam covered with fiberglass. View is aft to forward. The cabin 's inside width is between the two upright sections of paneling (note starboard side marked for a portlight.)

Father's Day undergoes sea trials near Miami in 1992 .

In Sidney, Nova Scotia, George Carroll readies *Father's Day* for its first attempt to cross the North Atlantic Ocean.

After the first attempt fails, *Father's Day* is hoisted out of the water. Note that the boat does not have the deeper keel added later.

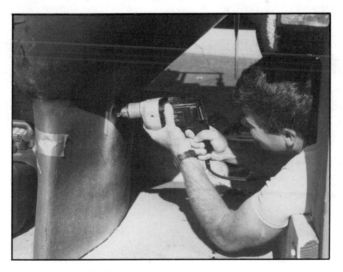

An extra length of keel section has been fiberglassed on and Dana prepares to add 275 pounds of lead.

Amid broken trees in Hugo's back yard, the little boat sits unscathed after Hurricane Andrew paid a visit to Homestead, Florida.

A few dockside spectators gather as *Father's Day* is hoisted to take to the water. The embarkation point this time is from Cape Cod. Note the addition of the new and deeper keel, which made the tiny sailboat more seaworthy and maneuverable.

The close quarters are evident inside *Father's Day*. View is from the stern, looking forward to the bow portlights.

In the mid-Atlantic, the French ship R.H.M. *Centaure* graciously provides the solo sailor with gas and food.

The Spanish Navy Boat *Chilreu* let Hugo make a call home to Johnnie. The written message on the photo is from the Patrol Boat's commander.

For Hugo S. Vihlen with our admiration and respect as memory of his short but intimate and historic stay on board of Spanish Patrol boat "CHILREU"

On board at sea August 31th 1993 L.C. Comander

Hugo's rival and good friend from England, Tom McNally, under full sail in 1993 aboard his five-foot, four and a half-inch record-holding boat, *Vera Hugh, Pride of Merseyside*.

Off the English coast after 105 days at sea, Hugo jubilantly waves. He now has earned the world record for crossing the North Atlantic Ocean in the smallest boat ever.

As a British press boat pulls alongside *Father's Day*, Hugo and Johnnie have a joyous reunion.

Dana, Johnnie and Nancy join Hugo in a toast. The voyage. took three years, five attempts and an outlay of approximately $87,000, most of which was for costs of the boat and its equipment.

Because of his unexpectedly lengthy voyage, Hugo found he arrived in Britain with an expired passport. At Falmouth Dock, an immigration officer discusses Hugo's problem.

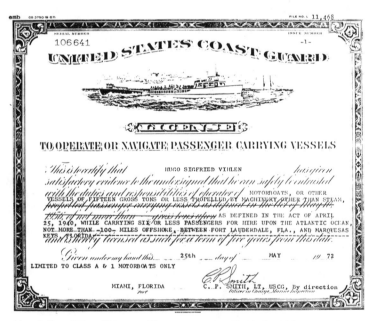

Hugo's Coast Guard License. The same agency that judged his voyage in *Father's Day* "manifestly unsafe" had earlier licensed him to carry passengers in other vessels.

CHAPTER EIGHT

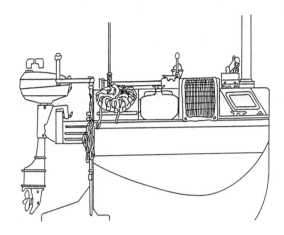

Water, water everywhere
Nor any drop to drink.
—Samuel Taylor Coleridge,
The Rhyme of the Ancient Mariner

EUREKA! The pilot could hear me!

"TWA, can you switch to 131.8?" We'd be able to communicate better on that frequency. My voice, rusty from silence, was trembling with excitement.

"*Father's Day*, this is TWA 843," the words sprang to life in my headset. "Do you need assistance?"

"Negative 843!", I managed to choke out. "But I'm running late. Could you call my wife for me?"

"No problem," came the comforting reply.

My beard-stubbled face split with a grin as I eagerly relayed the two phone numbers where I was sure a message would reach Johnnie, our home in South Florida and her mother's in North Carolina. I instructed him to call collect. This was one bill I looked forward to paying.

"Please tell her I'm ok and the boat's ok. Tell her I should be in England by August 6th! Oh yeah, this is Hugo Vihlen," I added lastly, along with my current coordinates.

Reluctant to let go of the human contact, I tried to strike up a conversation. "I'm a retired Delta pilot. Where are you headed, TWA?"

"New York," the voice replied with no embellishment.

"Ok, well, thanks 843!" I was practically yelling by now. "I really mean it. Thanks a lot."

Heart hammering, mike left dangling at the end of its coiled cord, I wiggled my upper body through the hatch and stared after the jet until it vanished into a tall, billowy stack of clouds to the west.

Had I told the pilot enough? I should have said more!

I should have asked him to tell Johnnie that the solar panels weren't working, and that's why I couldn't call myself. I should've said for her not to worry and that I loved her. That might've been my last chance for a long, long time. It might have been my last chance forever.

But at least now she would know I was alive, and after all we'd been through together, she already knew I loved her. For a few minutes of ease, my family and friends could relinquish the millstone of worry. I could picture their faces, lit with relief. The message would make them very happy.

And that made me happy.

"YES!," I yelled across the waves, toasting my good fortune with a little jig in the hatch. I'd said enough in my message.

The pilot hadn't been too talkative anyway. We'd crossed paths just east of the imaginary forty degrees west longitude line, one of the points on the North Atlantic route where all pilots radio a mandatory position report to Gander Radio.

"Guess he didn't have time for my whole life story," I mumbled sheepishly. "I sure hope he has time for that phone call."

I'd have to assume he'd take care of it. It was the only way I could stop worrying for a little while too. And settle down to my adventure.

I was tidying up below when I noticed the forward motion of the boat slowing. I was getting pretty good at this sailing.

Stale in the beginning, my sea legs and instincts were second nature by now. Popping my head out the hatch, I saw the two orange sails hanging limp in their rigging. My west wind was gone. And chasing its tail was the enemy from the east, exacting an immediate toll on the miles I'd attained.

Down came the sails and out went the sea anchor. A sudden squall accompanied the east wind, raising hell with the ocean it clawed, stroking the waves until they rose above the transom and tickled the cabin hatch.

I rushed to relocate the sea anchor line, hoping to make my *Father's Day* ride more level. Settling on tying it midship, I let out a bit of sail and adjusted the twin rudders. With the boat now more stable, I shut myself below as fast as I could.

As quickly as it came, the squall moved on and the ocean settled down in its wake.

Drained and disbelieving, I leaned in the hatch in its aftermath, staring at the now placid ocean.

Everything changes so fast out here! Just a moment ago this ocean had scared the hell out of me. Now it was peaceful and innocent, like a colicky baby at long last asleep. It seemed impossible that it was even the same one.

July 4th
Day 21

Happy Fourth of July.

I wondered what everybody back home was doing. Barbecues and fireworks were undoubtedly on the schedule. Johnnie would probably spend the day with Dana and Nancy. My stomach growled at the thought of a charbroiled steak.

Never a fan of fast food fare, I was slipping into fantasies that involved a grease-flecked bag of burgers coming at me on the outstretched arm of a surly drive-through window waitress.

Still at sea anchor, I pulled out the pilot chart to study the prevalent conditions for July. The pilot chart is the Bible out here, predicting month-by-month the winds and currents, conditions and storms a sailor could expect to encounter on the North Atlantic.

According to the chart, I could anticipate an east wind only an average of four percent during July. Locating a vacuum-bagged calculator, I translated that figure into twenty-eight and eight-tenths hours for the entire month. Well, I'd already had twenty-eight hours of an east wind with no sign of a change. I could only hope this July would be an average one.

An unfamiliar species of sea bird attempted a landing on the twelve-foot mast, but the whipping five-foot VHF antenna, mounted to the top, scared it away.

I miss the gulls that used to trail me; I'd welcome the company of their raucous chatter now. For whatever reason, they'd disappeared entirely, the only evidence of their existence an occasional feather floating by.

Nearly five hundred miles from St. John's, the ocean is very clean, the only trace of humankind a few bobbing plastics. It bothers me to see the floating trash. The plastic will outlast generations to come.

It's strange. A lot of people believe anyone who enjoys the sport of hunting is a ruthless killer, a spoiler of the innocent beauty of nature. But hunting and fishing are part of everyday life in the South Florida countryside where I was raised. And I care deeply about the environment and the future of the earth's creatures. So do most of the hunters and fishermen I know.

Ten years ago, out of love and respect for the sea, I founded Fish and Game Unlimited in my hometown and have been a member and officer of the Florida Conservation Association for years. Made up of others who share my concern for the future, both organizations work to purchase or create wildlife habitat and lobby in the state capital for closed fishing seasons, pollution controls and bans on commercial netting.

I would throw no trash overboard on this trip. Empty water jugs would be refilled with seawater and replaced in the forward bilge to maintain ballast weight. Food wrappers were shoved back into compartments. I refused to add my litter to what was already polluting the ocean.

A light rain sent me below. Several days ago, much to my delight, I discovered a new book on board, one Dana had squirreled away without my knowledge. I'd savored the anticipation of reading George E. Day's *Return With Honor* ever since. Now seemed like a good time to enjoy it.

Tears blurred my vision as I read Dana's scrawled inscription, written inside the front cover of the book:

To Hugo:
Fighter pilots frolic where men dare not travel.
Fighter pilots push the envelope and set the standards by which others must judge themselves. Thanks for being the role model that set such high standards.

Return with honor,
Dana

Love for the little skinny boy who'd grown into such an exceptional man surged in my heart. Taller than his dad, Dana had inherited my blue eyes and, to the endless frustration of Johnnie, my love for adventure too.

I was fortunate in Dana. We were just enough alike to make time spent together enjoyable, but different enough so that Dana was his own unique person. I wouldn't have had much in common with a less adventurous son. Thank God, Dana turned out to be strong and daring too.

I wondered how much credit I could take for that. My flying career had often kept me far from home. I'd missed so much when my boy was growing into a man. Johnnie had been both mother and father in my absence. Dana was proof of the fine job she'd done.

Ironically, though, it was flying that drew my son and me back together. Dana loved it as much as I did. Cutting his teeth as my co-pilot on excursions over the Everglades, he was flying before his legs were long enough to reach the foot controls of my J-3 Cub.

Between my "toys" and those of friends, Dana had plenty of airplanes to play with. Infused with the brashness of youth, acrobatic flying became his specialty. At twenty-three years old, fresh out of college, he won the 1979 National Aerobatics Championship. I'll never forget the sight of his happy face lit with pride, the first place trophy clutched tightly to his chest. The U.S. Air Force Reserves offered Dana a crack at the ultimate flying machines, the F-4 and the F-16 fighter jets. Rocketing across the sky in maneuvers across the globe, Dana thrilled to the power and capability contained in the multi-million dollar military jets. It was a natural progression to commercial flying, just as it had been for me in the days following my return from Japan.

After several years spent hopscotching around the world with three or four different flying outfits, Dana settled with Piedmont Airlines in 1987, surviving the buy-out by USAir that came later. The cumbersome 737 he flew felt like a bus after the cutting-edge flying of the fighter jets. But it was a living and a good one, for a man who loved the sky.

My son couldn't have picked a more inspiring novel to stow away on *Father's Day*. George Day is the United States' most highly decorated hero, holding more than fifty combat decorations and awards. Held as a prisoner of war for more than five years by the North Vietnamese, Day never gave up, managing to escape once for fourteen days, crossing into South Vietnam before being recaptured by the Viet Cong.

His courage and strength stirred my blood. If Day could survive all he'd overcome, I could best the North Atlantic.

July 5th
Day 22

Forty-six hours at sea anchor, and still no wind from a decent direction. According to the GPS, *Father's Day* had lost nearly eighty miles in the past two days, the northeast wind pushing her forty miles to the south and forty to the west.

With waves only inches from splashing in the cockpit, I was forced to keep the sails up, giving the wind added assistance at shoving me around. The constant wind pressure on the back of the sails kept the stern from bobbing up and down so much, so I sacrificed miles in the interest of safety.

July 13th
Day 30

For ten straight days, the erratic wind played Ping-Pong with *Father's Day*, sending her north, south, east and west. Miles gained one day were quickly lost the next when the wind unexpectedly swung around and came from a new direction.

With amperage dwindling quickly on both batteries, I disconnected them from everything in the boat, hoping to conserve what little power was left for one more chance at communicating with the one or two overhead airplanes that broke through the thick cloud cover each week.

Tomorrow would mark one full month at sea since I sailed out of St. John's. One month to sail fewer than five hundred miles.

I ran the calculations once again: my journey would take nearly three more months at this pace.

That would be a problem. *Father's Day* only carried enough food and water for about seventy-five days, and a good chunk of it was already gone. What would I do when it all ran out?

In thirty days I'd seen two ships, and neither had answered my calls on the ship-to-ship VHF. If the wind didn't cooperate soon, I'd have to go on half-rations. With my daily food allowance already cut to the bare bones, that was not an appealing prospect.

For more than a week I had moved in circles, just east of the forty west longitude line. Winding up due north of where I'd made contact ten days ago with the TWA pilot, I'd zigzagged in frustration, unable to cross the next longitude line to the east. Last night the fickle wind changed again, blowing to the north, a direction I'd already gained enough headway in. From this point on I had to head due east or wind up missing the mouth of the English Channel, hitting the rocky coast of Ireland instead. If it blew north long enough, I could miss Europe altogether, ending up in Iceland and the forbidding Norwegian Sea.

There was only one thing certain. Every day I spent meandering around out here now, I'd pay for dearly later. The North Atlantic, moody in the best of months, becomes downright ill-tempered in the winter. And winter comes early at these latitudes.

It was only mid-August when a gale force nine storm killed eighteen people during the 1979 Fastnet yacht race. Overwhelmed near the South Irish Sea, twenty-three yachts were either sunk or abandoned.

Father's Day was the size of one of their dinghies.

But there was a lot to be said for the way we had built her. The design was deceptively simple, but brilliantly efficient. Like the underappreciated egg, her smallness was one of her greatest assets.

With bulkheads only thirty-one-and-a-half inches apart, *Father's Day* was actually much stronger than a larger boat. As anyone who's tried to crush an egg in their fist can attest, collapsing a compact object isn't easy, no matter how thin the walls. And the walls on this floating "egg" were as thick as most sea-going sailboats.

But most people couldn't see beyond how tiny she was. Not only wouldn't the U.S. Coast Guard look beyond it, but Johnnie was having a hard time as well. When I first broached the subject of another record-breaking voyage to my wife, my palms were sticky with sweat. I wasn't surprised when she exploded with objections. The conversation ended with me swearing to forget the whole thing.

But somewhere along the line it became apparent that I was going. Johnnie sought support from our son.

"Dana, you have to convince him not to go!," she had pleaded. "This is crazy! He'll die out there! You've got to talk him out of it!"

Dana, his own adventuresome soul intrigued by my dream, found himself caught in a tug-of-war. He was worried about me, too, but stop me? No, he didn't think so. I knew what I was up against and I was determined to go. That fact was obvious during the few times we'd talked about it.

In Dana's opinion, it was far more productive to be a partner in the adventure. That way, he could put his two cents in and make sure his old man didn't take any unnecessary risks. What better way to make sure I came home alive? It was also a lot more fun.

"He'll be safer if I help him, Mom," he persuaded Johnnie. "You know I'll make sure he's all right."

Eased by her begrudging approval, Dana jumped into the project with zeal.

April Fool's design was the key to transatlantic success. I was convinced that with modifications, it would hold its own in the North Atlantic.

For nearly a quarter of century, my aging *April Fool* had sat in a hangar, gathering cobwebs and dust, her gold and white paint peeling off in ripples. Now, Dana and I attacked her, armed with screwdrivers and tape measures. Measurements were scribbled on a pad; pieces that must be copied, like the rudders, were stripped from the six-foot hull.

Dragging out the original plans for the boat, we modified the design down to five feet six inches. Six inches off my still-standing world record should be plenty of leeway to hold off any challengers, I had thought. Of course two more inches would come off later after we ran into Tom McNally and his five-feet four and a half-inch *Vera Hugh* in St. John's.

But this new boat had to be more than just smaller than *April Fool*. It had to be stronger as well. Conditions were a lot tougher in the north, so we chose Airex as a building material. Not only was it incredibly strong, it was moldable, non-flammable and buoyant. Sandwiched between two layers of fiberglass, it should do the trick. But to work with it we needed an expert.

A series of inquiries led to George Carroll. George had already built two boats out of Airex, though none with the miniature dimensions of *Father's Day*. Carroll was sharp, likable and knowledgeable, and an instant rapport was born among the three of us.

George was between jobs and anxious to get started on the new project. Moving into a spare bedroom in our home, he quickly became part of the family.

From March until June, six days a week and sometimes seven, one, two or all three of us could be found out in the work barn, heads bent together over the emerging *Father's Day*. Lively discussions considered and discarded a multitude of methods and ideas, finally settling on acceptable solutions. Every possible scenario had to be examined and prepared for.

How would I handle it if this happened or if that broke or this tool didn't work? How would I sleep? Eat? Use the bathroom? Brush my teeth? How would I communicate? Know where I was? Stay sane?

I knew that organization, experience and foresight were crucial. The trials of my first journey were invaluable. My tiny *Father's Day* would have to carry the same equipment and supplies one might find on a boat five times its size. Anything left behind that was needed could turn out to be a big mistake. And with space such a valuable commodity, anything I brought that wasn't needed was a big mistake too.

Each piece of equipment, every tool and supply item was the smallest, most compact to be found and nearly all had to serve double duty. Just about everything had to be customized somehow, edges ground down or cut off, waterproofed or preserved, or repositioned. Nothing remained as we bought it.

Survival was our number one goal. Attaining England was number two.

July 15th
Day 33

A zombie-like state settled over me, veiling my misery and impatience in a cloak of apathy.

Nothing mattered anymore. England was a fuzzy dream, my family an out-of-focus still-life. I was reduced to wondering what the hell I was doing out here.

If a boat came along today to offer rescue, would I go quietly? Would I be ready to give up? If I could erase the last few years of my life, probably.

But I couldn't. Two years of planning and thousands of dollars were invested in this adventure. Not to mention my reputation. People expected Hugo Vihlen to do exactly what he set out to do. No, I couldn't go back. I realized I was in this too deep.

July 19th
Day 36

Sixteen days since the wind turned on me.

More than one hundred miles of ocean had passed beneath the tiny hull of *Father's Day* since then, but most of it had been in the wrong direction. The past five days had shoved her fifty five miles back to the west. And today brought another southeast wind.

A dozen times a day I told myself it had to change. According to the pilot chart, this should not be happening.

More than 1,300 miles left to go. Fewer than five hundred miles sailed in five weeks. If this keeps up I won't see England until November. I'll have to take a food inventory sooner than I planned. What was left might have to last for a very long time.

The least the beast could do was calm down a little. If the ocean wasn't going to give up any miles, at least it could stop tossing me around so badly. Day after day, the Atlantic surged and heaved, never still, never, ever quiet or motionless. Like a thing possessed, she moaned and tossed, some humongous demon trapped beneath a liquid blanket, endlessly wrestling to get out. Yesterday, it was so rough I didn't dare eat. Not only was I dubious about the stability of my stomach, but using the bathroom was a real chore in rough seas like this.

Growing up with an outhouse came in handy now. I still retained the skill of getting a good lung full of air, taking care of business and getting out the door, or in this case the cabin, before needing another breath. I had to hurry in the task to empty the "latrine," timing my careful squirm through the cabin hatch, the open container of waste held above me, to the perfect moment between waves.

Every time I opened the hatch door, I exposed the vulnerable jugular of the boat to the beast. If it got in the cabin, it could kill me. By eating and drinking less, I could slow my digestive system and minimize the need to eliminate.

Three sips of water is all I will chance.

July 20th
Day 37

It changed. I could feel it in the slant of the boat, in the tempo of the rocking. A west wind!

Fully awake now, I peered out the salt-encrusted window to my left. Still gray, but I could definitely feel a change. And yes! The compass on the radio rack read east. Slipping back the door, I popped my head out of the hatch. The barely open sails were puffing toward the weak, early morning sun, silhouetted just above the horizon, diluted by the ever-present clouds.

The square hatch opening being smaller than the width of my shoulders, it usually required a little wiggle to squeeze myself through. But this morning I shot through it like a greased arrow, and in seconds I had both sails open wide.

It wasn't much, but the wind was from the west. I'll take it.

July 21st
Day 38

Yesterday was spent at the tiller, milking the slowly-strengthening west wind for every grudging mile it would give.

Fairly calm seas allowed me to spend twelve hours standing in the hatch, gripping the bar between the twin rudders, working them for all they were worth. By hand-steering the rudders, instead of tying them into a fixed position, I could keep a truer course and tighten the sails even more.

A ship appeared to the north, just before dark.

I went for it. Ducking below, I flipped the door down on the radio rack and pulled out the mike of the ship-to-ship VHF. Untangling the cord, I turned on the power and called to the distant ship, barely visible in the swells and gathering gloom.

Nothing. No reply.

I turned the squelch knob all the way over. Silence. The batteries must be too dead to transmit. The ship vanished in the waves.

Johnnie thinks I'm coming in on August 6th. That's the message I gave the TWA pilot. That's only sixteen days from now!

I need at least another five or six weeks. That means I'll be considered missing for at least three weeks. Unless I can reach her, she'll be waiting for me in England.

She'll have a fit when I don't show.

July 22nd
Day 39

I can't believe it. A northeast wind again. It's time to take stock of my dwindling supplies.

Digging through the compartments, I tallied up the inventory. Forty-eight military meals-ready-to-eat, thirty-three cans of Nutriment, thirty-five small cans of fruit cocktail, a couple of cans of corned beef, a gallon jug of M&M's, some assorted dried fruit and a handful of health bars. It doesn't look like much.

Heading nowhere, I took advantage of the flat calm sea. It was a good day for housekeeping. The small tasks would distract and make me feel more secure.

I pulled out my camera and gave it a thorough cleaning. It was just too rough too often to use it like I'd intended. Several attempts to take it topside had ended with the camera doused in seawater.

Next, I reworked a boom line, removing the two heavy jackets that had become second skin to work in the comparative warmth of midday. My safety harness and lifeline were refastened securely in place. Even with the tiny, plastic footholds Dana attached to the back of the hull, climbing back into the boat wouldn't be easy if I fell overboard. Not only would my winter clothes be impossibly heavy after a dunking, the water had turned colder again. At fifty-five degrees Fahrenheit, it would paralyze me in minutes.

The last three gallons of gas were sloshing around in a dangerously worn container, lashed to the top of the deck. I fashioned a funnel from an empty water jug cut in half, and transferred the remaining fuel into the not-so-worn second container, spilling a quart or so in the process. I figured it was better than losing it all. That worn container wasn't going to last much longer.

The second gas container, now half full, was tied in place atop the sea anchor, so the nylon strap bag could take the constant chafing against the rocking boat instead. Compartment after compartment was checked, emptied, cleaned and repacked. An inch of saltwater was discovered under the canned food, a third of the cans badly rusted. Those were the ones I'd have to eat first, before they had a chance to spoil.

"I guess food poisoning isn't as bad as gangrene," I told myself, mentally ticking off the list of things to worry about.

Taking up two notches on the wristband of my watch, I continued my work.

I couldn't afford to waste anything.

CHAPTER NINE

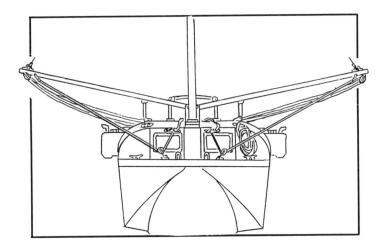

It is part of a sailor's life to die well.
—Stephen Decatur, 1779-1820

July 24
Day 41
560 miles from St. John's
1,316 miles to go

TODAY WAS THE FIRST DAY of half-rations.

Cooped up below by a driving rain since yesterday, I tossed and turned, trying to sleep away the wasted hours, the east wind still holding me at bay.

Pinched between the pain in my left shoulder and the one in my right knee, I wasn't finding the escape I sought. Caged inside the tiny cabin, fighting down the urge to pound my fists on the underside of the raindrop-spattered hatch, I realized this was the worst part of all.

It was so much better when I rode in the hatch, the wind blowing in my face, clearing my head, the ocean and horizon fanning out before me, an endless play of motion and change.

My eyes, with little else to amuse them inside the compressed limits of the cabin universe, knew intimately every detail of the four absolute dimensions of my floating prison. I'd counted and memorized every mole on her complexion, every seam in her padding, everything in her possession.

Even the crazy times, when the ocean was going ballistic, seemed better than this interminable, rocking waiting. Being stuck below when the heat was on was a lot different than this kind of confinement. In times like those I was too damned scared to get cabin fever.

Keeping the five-foot four-inch boat balanced was a constant vigil. The placement of any item over a few pounds took major consideration. I rearranged compartments as supplies were consumed.

But the biggest ballast weight of all was my own body, though it too dwindled in size at a steady rate. My Levi's, snug at the beginning of the trip, now hung loose around my hips. I must have lost ten or twelve pounds already.

And now I faced the reality of half-rations.

To keep the boat balanced, my sleeping positions were limited. In spite of the methodical shifting of supplies, the wind and waves had a tremendous effect on how the boat rode. If on one day she leaned to the left, I had to sleep on the far right on my left side. If on another she leaned to the right, the reverse rule applied.

Sleeping on my back was impossible, unless I was willing to sleep with my bent knees in the air.

The saltwater sores on my butt still hadn't healed, despite repeated applications of antibacterial ointment. To try to heal them I was reduced to sailing naked from the waist down, unnerving even way out here.

My toenails and fingernails were steadily receding in the constant dampness.

And now, for the second time on the trip, a sore was erupting on the same spot on my lip. I'd had several sun cancer melanomas removed in the past. If this was another one, I'd deal with it when I got back.

Lets see: Gangrene, botulism, sores that wouldn't heal, an aching back and now concern about cancerous melanomas.

Beriberi and scurvy couldn't be too far behind.

July 25th
Day 42

Another tabletop calm day.

I was up before dawn, unable to wait another moment to escape the stuffy cabin. The rain was over. Stretching my legs in the hatch, I noticed three good-sized fish had taken up residence in the shadow beneath the slowly drifting boat. They looked to be sea bass, about six to eight pounds. The bird flocks had returned now and then to follow me, but I was starved for new company and these fish were welcome.

The sea bass would swim about ten feet out from the boat and then dart back under its cover. I pulled the camera from a compartment in the cabin, removed its plastic bag and tried to take some pictures. When the shutter button wouldn't work, I resorted to the owner's manual, which was wet from one too many waves, its pages stuck together in clumps. After quite a bit of time spent trying to pry the pages apart, an effort that resulted in them mostly ripping in half, I gave up without finding the solution.

The day's food allotment consisted of one can of Nutriment (three hundred sixty calories), one can of cold Franco-American spaghettios (three hundred twenty calories) and fourteen mixed nuts.

I savored every nut, eating them slowly, one by one.

July 26
Day 43

A light west wind, no more than one to three knots, had moved me eighteen miles toward England in twenty-four hours. At least it was something.

With rain once again drenching the deck, I holed up below and examined the pilot chart for the hundredth time. According to the chart, I could expect episodes of number four or five gale force winds before this trip was through. That's thirty-eight to forty-knot winds! Twice the strength of what I'd encountered so far.

The worst I endured in *April Fool* was one gale with twenty-five foot seas, and that really wasn't all that bad. The wave action to the south, even when kicked up, isn't near as violent as it is in the north. Up here the ocean is much more confused, with bigger waves, closer together, and monstrous rogues that follow no pattern and come out of nowhere to knock the crap out of you.

At 4 p.m. the biggest, darkest, ugliest cloud I'd ever seen lay in wait on the eastern horizon. Oh Lord, had I jinxed myself by checking the pilot chart for storm information?

I'd better get prepared. Straightening and securing the lines on deck, I brought in the water jug and tucked loose cabin items away. Washing down a dry MRE entree with a few sips of water, I hurried to brush my teeth and use the bathroom in preparation for a long night of captivity below.

But when the menacing cloud crept closer, finally hovering overhead, there was blue sky behind it. Just a scare tactic of the Atlantic, I realized with relief. The worst I would get was more rain.

That night the sky was clear and the waxing moon shimmered down from a chorus of pinpoint diamonds. I stood in the hatch, filling my lungs with the cool night air, trying to stamp every detail of the black-velvet panorama into memory.

I was so very alone out here. One tiny raft of human life, traveling across a triangle of reflected moonlight, floating in a colorless world of gently swelling water and endless night sky. In the absence of light and clouds, the curtain over the firmament was gone, and I craned my head back to look up, up, up. It seemed I could see into the depths of creation.

It was one of those moments in life I knew I'd always remember: the way it looked, the way it smelled, the way I felt. Like a man of adventure. Free, daring, anything but ordinary, and lucky—very lucky—to be here.

**July 27th
Day 44**

My sights had lowered. The twenty-four miles I'd sailed to the east since yesterday were looking pretty good.

I was an idiot to think I could average forty miles a day out here. I was lucky to get twenty-four.

Last night the dream returned, the one about the airplane crash. At least once a year, for the past five or six years, I tussled with the dream, waking up in a cold sweat, my breath coming hard. Last night's version had me flying into Atlanta at the controls of a fully-loaded L-1011. We were coming in too high and too fast.

Pulling back on the throttles didn't slow the plane one bit. So I dropped the landing gear, an emergency move that reduced our speed just enough. But my relief didn't last long. When it was time to add more power to level our descent, the engines didn't respond to the controls.

I crept the throttles forward a little more. Still nothing. No answer from the engines. No prayed-for surge of power.

Then my co-pilot started yelling, barely-controlled panic lacing his voice. "All three engines are dead, Captain! They're dead!"

In this dream, our crew was missing its engineer, and for this episode the engineer was the only one with the emergency procedure manuals that would guide us through what lay ahead. And without him, we couldn't dump fuel to lighten the load.

It came to me! An airstart! That's what I was supposed to do next! Now low enough to pick out the leaves on the treetops, I bellowed to the co-pilot, "Start number two!"

Number two roared to life and I milked her for all she had. But it just wasn't enough power. I was yelling into the intercom, "Emergency landing! Emergency landing! Ready the passengers! Get everybody ready!"

We were too low. We were going to crash. What could I do? I was powerless to stop it. I heard the horrible screech of tree branches on the jet's metal belly.

It was too late. Everyone would die.

Bang! I was awake, mouth dry, pulse racing like I'd just run a marathon.

There had been plenty of close calls in my life as a pilot. I'd set down more than one airplane on a wing and a prayer.

But I could swear the nightmares were even worse than the real thing. In them I was gripped with fear and panic, my limbs heavy and uncooperative, my mind sluggish and muddled.

Sometimes — in real life — I surprised myself. I supposed it was all the military and pilot training, but there were times I was amazed by how cool I was in emergencies.

Of course, there was that episode in Korea when I almost soiled my britches.

At age twenty one, the ink still wet on the transfer papers, I was assigned to night missions in war-torn Korea. Though most of the fighting was over, stragglers were out there and tensions remained high. Flying a Marine Corps F3D fighter jet through the muddy darkness of unfriendly foreign skies, I had only my radar observer and ground crew to depend on.

That night, ground radar radioed up a dreaded message: "There's an unidentified bogey on your tail! At six o'clock!"

It had to be a MiG. Nothing else could keep pace with my jet. The enemy was after me.

A couple of steep turns failed to dislodge the MiG, now a closing green blip on the radar screen. A mountain range snaked below, its tallest peaks, tipped in white snow, were barely visible in the weak moonlight. It was dangerous, but it was the only way.

Slamming the throttle forward, I dove straight for the pitch-black cover of the winding mountains below. Leveling out just below the highest summits, I weaved through the valley at more than six hundred miles per hour, tilting and rocking, wingtips almost grazing the rocky outcroppings.

When my jet shot out the end of the mountain range, I hightailed it for the base, the white-faced radar observer silent beside me.

Yeah, that had been scary. I was fortunate to lose the MiG, lucky I didn't wind up with enemy rounds up my butt. I'd been jumpy for days after that one.

Over the years there had been others. A pilot doesn't get through nearly forty years of flying without his share of dead engines and touchy landings. I still remember my first aircraft emergency.

It was at Cabiness Naval Air Station in Corpus Christi, Texas. Flying a World War II Hellcat propeller-driven fighter, I was attempting my first take-off as I gunned the 2800-horsepower radial engine to maximum power. But as I neared the midpoint the engine began backfiring and stalling. As I pulled the power back, I saw that I was runnning out of runway and would not be able to stop the tail-wheel fighter. Panicked, I jammed on full power and watched, horrified, as my aircraft sliced the barbed-wire fence at the end of the landing strip. My mind numb with fear, I bounced into the air and began slowly climbing. I was aware that I was screaming into the mike.

Then I heard a voice in my headset, calmly telling me what to do. As I looked to my right, I saw another Marine aircraft near my wingtip. As I followed his instructions, my panic subsided and I piloted my ship down to an uneventful landing. I later went on to do eight take-offs and landings on an aircraft carrier to earn my Navy wings — but I never forgot that takeoff.

Somewhere along the way, I'd developed nerves of steel. One time, in my Cub, I was careless enough to run out of gas over the Everglades. Sid Lewis, an old friend sitting in the front seat, thought I was fooling around until we hit the ground. One and a half feet of water brought us to a sudden, violent stop, but I'd been able to slow our speed, turn into the wind and bring her in level. Fortunately for us, a passing airliner spotted the bright yellow plane in the sea of wheat-colored sawgrass below, and we didn't have to wait long for rescue.

The next day we returned with two airboats and pulled the barely damaged Cub about a mile to a dirt road. I filled her dry tanks and took off.

Afterward, I marveled at how calm I'd been. I couldn't remember one moment during the crash landing when I'd been scared. But I was always afraid in the nightmares.

Throughout the day the soft west wind strengthened, picking up steam until the wind gauge pegged twenty-six knots. With it came the worst waves I'd encountered so far.

I rode out the tempest below, sponge and bucket in hand, sopping up the water that trickled in around the closed hatch each time the twenty to twenty-five-foot waves crashed on the deck and buried the boat below.

At least it was a west wind that tortured me so. It made the beating a little easier to take. I was glad I'd given into hunger and eaten the day's food allotment early. The one can of Nutriment, small can of corned beef and twenty mixed nuts were long digested.

I wasn't prone to seasickness, but this ride would test a stomach of cast iron, so I was glad mine was empty. An empty stomach rode a storm like this much better than a full one. Maybe it would let up by nightfall.

If it didn't, I could forget about sleeping tonight. There was no way I could doze off with the toppling waves slamming me from one side of the boat to the other, icy water dripping in on my head.

There was one thing to be said for not sleeping. As long as I was awake, the dream couldn't return.

July 29th
Day 46

The emerging sun chased away my depression, with a lot of help from a wind that had pushed me more than ninety miles toward my destination in the past two days. I checked and rechecked my position, afraid to believe my luck had finally changed.

Today it was still howling from the west, but the seas had calmed enough to allow short periods of standing in the hatch. Under a rare blue sky, I hooked up the solar panels once again and watched the volts on the near-dead batteries start to climb.

A beautiful, spotted bird flew by. It was bigger than the other sea birds I'd seen, and much faster. The Northern Gannet craned its long, yellow neck to glance at me as it made a single pass and flew on.

Where was it headed? And where the heck had it come from? I was more than seven hundred miles away from Canada, more than eleven hundred from England, with nothing in between but an occasional iceberg. That sure was a long way to fly to catch dinner. There certainly wouldn't be any handouts from this hungry captain.

Just after noon, I had an airplane in the perfect position, about seven miles out on the same side as the aircraft VHF antenna.

With little more than ten volts in the battery system, I wasn't surprised when no one answered my call. Something still wasn't right with the solar battery charging system. While the volts were steadily going up, the amps were just as steadily draining away.

How could I let Johnnie worry for another month or more? I decided that I couldn't, if there was any way to help it. Adjusting the rudders and sails, I set a course for the well-traveled shipping lane, fifteen miles to the south along the 50 north latitude line. If I could find a ship, and manage to get its attention, I could ask the crew to call Johnnie. If it worked, it would be worth the extra miles.

The three sea bass, still under the boat, didn't seem to mind the change of direction. They headed south with me, apparently reluctant to abandon the shelter of *Father's Day's* concealing, dark shadow.

July 30th
Day 47
1,118 miles to go

The day started off with a cold bucket of seawater finding its way into the just-opened hatch. All day was spent mopping it up and drying out my bedding.

I was finally past the 35 degree west longitude line. The next goal was the 30 degree line, which marked the halfway point in the voyage.

My beautiful west wind switched to a southwest one, slowing the detour to the shipping lane to the south.

With clear skies and settling seas, I stood in the hatch and counted the passing aircraft. Seventeen before the day was through.

And not one answered my call.

July 31st
Day 48
1,072 miles to go

With the wind back out of the west at ten knots, I was feeling blessed. And confident enough to estimate a new arrival date.

I knew using the great mileage of the past few days as an average was being overly optimistic, but I based my calculations on it anyway. It made me feel better.

If the Wind Lords continued to favor me, I might make landfall by September 6th — one full month after I was expected. That was a long time for Johnnie and Dana to wait with their guts in a knot.

Tom McNally's son had died while he was at sea on his most recent east to west crossing.

A horrible thought hit me. What if that happens to me? I could arrive in England, call home and find out my only son has been dead for over a month. Or my wife.

What a curse these small boat crossings would carry then.

August 1
Day 49
1,029 miles to go

Rewiring the solar panel might help the dead batteries. Step by step I worked my way through the wiring system, grooming every connection, crawling over every inch.

Working in the cramped space of the boat took a lot of patience. I kept dropping the screws while trying to rearrange cables on a battery.

The ceaseless rocking of the waves didn't help, though I was so accustomed to it by now I accepted it totally, just as one accepts gravity in everyday life. After two dropped and lost screws, I remembered an old trick I learned while building a Pitts Special airplane in the garage.

Peeling off a tiny piece of masking tape, I taped the screw to the end of the screwdriver to get it started. Now I could work with one hand in the confined recesses of the radio rack.

In the late afternoon, a huge, gray dorsal fin caught my eye rotating about 100 yards away, just above the water. A whale. It had to be.

Judging by how long the gray hump remained visible above the waterline, it was a big one. Another fin broke the surface up ahead. Then another, this one between *Father's Day* and the first one.

It was a pod, traveling in my direction. Within seconds, the rubbery humps were everywhere.

The blasts from their blowholes always amazes me. Surfacing and diving, jetting a warm, fine mist three feet into the air, they rolled along on a course with the eastward-bound boat.

But they were coming too close! I wondered if they could see me.

Good Lord, *Father's Day* probably looked like a beachball to these barge-sized creatures. Visions of trained porpoises batting a ball high into the air with their tails put an abrupt halt to the pleasure I found in watching their graceful, awesome movements.

Whales have been known to ram boats before. No one really understands what triggers the violent reaction. Perhaps a young whale bumps the boat and the mother goes on the defensive.

Whatever it is, it doesn't take much of an attack on a five-foot four-inch boat by a thirty-foot long whale to end in capsize. Even an unintentional surfacing beneath the boat could be deadly.

I had to get rid of them. Twisting around in the hatch, I pulled the starter cord on the 4 h.p. engine, watching anxiously for the whales' reaction when its high pitched whine filled the air. As I prayed they would, the pod began to move off.

I was praying a lot these days. Always a believer, but never an overly religious man, I reflected on the change of attitude this voyage had brought over me.

How could anyone not believe out here? How could anyone spend day after day cowed by the immensity and power of it all, and not be convinced of a God in the heavens?

There are no atheists in the middle of the North Atlantic.

August 4th
Day 52
938 miles to go

Hallelujah! The half-way mark at last!

It took fifty-one days to get here, but we'd finally made it!

I noticed how I'd taken to referring to myself and the boat as "we," like the boat was another person, a partner in this wild adventure. As familiar as I was with her before, I now knew all of her quirks, strengths and weaknesses. I congratulated myself and my valiant boat companion. We'd come a long way together already.

Now we just had to survive the other half.

Standing in the hatch, I surveyed the flat horizon. Not a wisp of wind touched my face, now covered with a thick, bushy, silver beard. The three sea bass had deserted me. It was an eerie calm, languishing in 360 degree circles, wondering what was coming next.

Nothing is the same for long in the North Atlantic. I was only in the eastern half of the ocean by one and four-tenths miles. The slightest wind from the east would have me back over the line in no time. There was no telling what the Atlantic had in store for me.

"Please!" I begged the Creator. "I am ready to go home!"

Being back in the shipping lanes brought both comfort and worry. The more sea traffic encountered, the greater the chance of getting a message through to Johnnie.

It also made it easier to get help if I needed it. At sixty-one years of age, there's no telling what physical ailments could arise. One of my brothers had a pinched intestine and had to have emergency surgery at the same age.

But traveling the shipping lanes also increased the odds of getting run over. In this area of the ocean I had to be exceptionally careful. Beginning tonight, I would return to my old sleeping schedule, setting the alarm to go off every forty-five minutes so I could stick my sleepy head out the hatch and scan the horizon for ships.

I'd started sleeping longer between checks a week or so out of St. John's when it became apparent that ships would be few and far between in that sector of the ocean.

One night I neglected to set an alarm at all, a mistake I would remember for the rest of the voyage. That night I'd fallen into a deep, dreamless sleep, forgetting about the danger of being closed up too long inside the nearly airtight cabin.

Four hours later, I woke up gasping and choking, the trapped carbon dioxide emitted from my lungs silently poisoning me as I slept. I jerked open the hatch, wolfing down the flood of fresh air until the hyperventilating subsided.

Dana had been right. I could die in this sealed little box. After that night, three-hour sleep stretches were the maximum I'd risk.

In celebration of achieving the half-way point, I took the final swig of a bottle of rum. I'd brought two fifths along, taking a sip now and then to warm my chilled bones.

Most doctors dispute the warming effects of spirits on the body, but it sure made me feel better for ten or fifteen minutes, despite the surprisingly nasty taste of the expensive brand I'd selected.

Ripping a sheet out of the log book, I scribbled a note, stuffed it inside the bottle along with two $1 bills, and dropped it into the ocean. The two bucks should cover postage for whoever found the bottle.

The note said:

N50 Latitude, W30 Longitude
To whoever finds this bottle please write and tell me where you found it. Dropped in the middle of the Atlantic Ocean 4 August, 1993 by the smallest boat to cross the ocean — Father's Day, 5 - feet- 4-inches/1.625 meters.

Thank you,
Hugo Vihlen

August 6th
Day 54
881 miles to go

Today was a terribly frustrating day, knowing that wherever she was, Johnnie was worrying about me even more than usual. The only message she'd received, if she received it at all, was from the TWA crew over a month ago.

I'd told them I'd be in England by today. I hoped she wasn't waiting for me at the dock in Falmouth. She could have been on any one of the aircraft I'd seen in the past few days.

Her eyes would have never left the window, searching the

endless gray ripples below for a tiny speck of red.

With one gel cell battery unhooked, I was funneling all the solar power I could gather into the other. Maybe I would have enough charge in a week or two to get through to somebody.

Now at sea for more than seven and a half weeks, I was way overdue for a major storm. The hair-raising waves I'd ridden out on that windy day over a week ago would be nothing compared to the monsters a real storm would kick up.

Each day I wondered if today was the day.

Fishing was a much loved pastime in the Vihlen family, and I had planned to do a little angling way out here. I didn't have any way to cook my catch, and I wasn't desperate enough yet to eat it raw, but how many fishermen ever get the chance to fish in the middle of the North Atlantic?

But something had changed during the ten days the sea bass had hung out under my boat. As strange as it sounds, I'd actually grown sort of fond of them.

No longer were they just cold-blooded scales and fins. Their lives had gradually become precious in my eyes and a "live and let live" attitude had taken root. All I would do if I hooked one was release it anyway. And I might injure it in the process.

Hurting one of my new friends wasn't worth the small boast of saying I'd fished in the middle of the North Atlantic.

Something in the boat smelled like urine. It couldn't be my clothes because once a week or so — sooner if I got wet — I stripped down naked in the squat cabin, squirming around like a man escaping a straight jacket, and struggled into fresh clothes.

On calm days, I washed the dirty ones in the ocean, dragging them behind the boat to clean them. After a few miles, I'd wring them out and either wear them until they dried, or hang them up, hoping the dew and rain would rinse out some of the salt. On wash days, *Father's Day*'s sails and shiny stainless steel booms were aflutter with strings of drying socks, jeans, shirts and long johns.

The foul-smelling culprit turned out to be the sea anchor, unused for the past several weeks. I dragged it behind the boat to freshen it.

The pain in my back was tormenting. Some twenty years ago, I'd taken a bad fall while water skiing, compressing three vertebra in my spine. Between the old injury, arthritis that had crept in with the years and the uncomfortable sleeping accommodations onboard, I was suffering greatly.

Yesterday a school of dolphin collided with a large school of bait fish right in front of the boat. The ensuing feeding frenzy was spectacular.

Many people mistakenly refer to porpoises as dolphins, but a real dolphin is a fish, not a warm-blooded, tail-walking "Flipper." Tough fighters and excellent table fare, dolphins are prized by most fishermen. Big male bull dolphins can top sixty or seventy pounds, and sport a massive, heavy brow that gives them an impressive, powerful profile.

The school I encountered was made up of fish two to three feet long. With flashes of neon blue and yellow, they jumped clear out of the water in pursuit of their prey, churning up the ocean, creating an uproar with their splashes.

Today, it was porpoises who paid an unexpected visit. It was the second time I'd seen them on the voyage, and they enchanted me now more than ever.

At first I was afraid the gray dorsal fins were whales again, but as they came closer and slowed down next to me, they materialized into harmless, friendly porpoises. For a moment, they skimmed along the underside of *Father's Day*, as curious about us as I was about them.

Gone too quickly, they left a smile on my face. What is it about porpoises that humans identify with so? Maybe it's that frozen grin on their face. They always seem to be so darned happy.

I was getting hungry. Real hungry.

Sitting, standing, sleeping right on top of my supplies, day after day, was like being chained to the refrigerator, but forbidden to eat. It was going to take a lot of discipline to ration myself with the food.

A rumble echoed through my stomach.

CHAPTER TEN

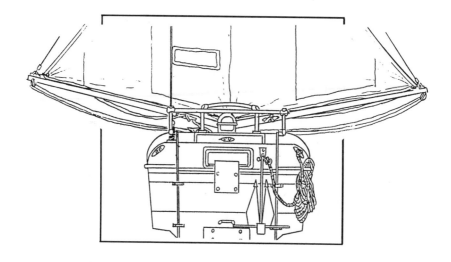

Character is what you are in the dark.
— Dwight L. Moody, Sermons

August 7
Day 55
853 miles to go

I WOKE UP thinking about death, just as I had every morning for the past few weeks. Ever since I'd gone on half rations.

Thinking about dying was nothing new. As a pilot I risked death every time I climbed into the cockpit. The military had told me that right up front. As might be expected, the airline executives weren't inclined toward such brutal honesty. After all, there were a hundred paying passengers riding behind me.

But this was different. In the air, the danger only lasts a few hours at a time. Out here it was hour after hour, day after day. A prolonged contemplation of my death.

There were so many ways it could come. A careless slip off the deck, my heavy water-logged clothes dragging me under the icy surface. The flip of a whale's tale. A powerful storm beating its way into the cabin.

Or simply, quietly starving to death.

Two weeks on half-rations had already dimmed my spirit. Yes, I was finally covering some distance, but I had a long, long way to go, and I'd learned how quickly the wind could turn on me.

There was still so much to do. So many places I wanted to go. So many things to see. The wonders of ancient Egypt. The dark wilds of Africa. So many things left undone. And so many things left unsaid. To my family. To my friends.

There was nothing to do but think out here. My mind found relief in its memories. Crisp January days in South Florida, the smell of fresh-baked bread in my mother's kitchen. I'd been ashamed of those homemade-bread sandwiches back then. Aside from Dorothy Engel, I was the only kid in school who didn't have thirty-five cents for the cafeteria.

Once in awhile my teacher, Mrs. Walker, would buy my sandwich, and I could stand in the lunch line with everybody else. It always embarrassed me. At least Dorothy's sandwiches were wrapped prettily.

From the distance of years, my impoverished childhood seemed more romantic. It was a different era back then, rugged and simple.

"I wonder how much a school lunch costs now," I mused.

Not that I would want to return to those days. Or want Dana to experience them. Things were hard back then. The good times were when daddy had enough money to throw lime down the outhouse to cut down on the smell.

Oh, but I would love some of Mom's bread now.

Today was dark with a light fog clinging to the water, the wind out of the west for the third straight day. The fog made it feel colder than the fifty or so degrees it really was. In the cabin, I slipped on a second layer of socks and tucked my feet back inside damp leather boat shoes.

The trickle of memories was a torrent now. Studying my shoes reminded me of Walt Cunningham.

Walt and I were roommates in Korea. We both continued the pursuit of adventure long after the war was over and both left our footprints in the annals of history — I on the ocean, my friend in a different frontier.

Walt went on to become an Apollo-Saturn 7 astronaut, one of

the three-man team, including Wally Schirra and Donn Eisele, who rode the first manned Apollo spacecraft into orbit. I went on to conquer the Atlantic. Twice, I hoped.

In Korea, we'd been instant friends, with our love of flying and solitary natures in common. Neither of us was given to talking too much. We took care of business and did our jobs. We weren't the kind to brag about our exploits.

I chuckled as I remembered one R&R in Hong Kong with Walt, the one my wet boat shoes reminded me of. We were young Marine Corps pilots, spit shined and dashing in our uniforms. And we were scouring the exotic city for excitement.

A Chinese shoeshine boy accosted us, insisting on shining our already spotless shoes. After declining the offer repeatedly, we tried to step around the pushy ragamuffin.

But as Walt strode past, the annoyed shoeshine boy took a swipe at Walt's brown leather shoes with a rag dripping with white polish.

Walt stood stock-still for a second, staring down at the milky stripe across his special-made, mirror-buffed aviator shoes while the ornery shoeshine boy high-tailed it down the street.

We took off after him, neither sure what we'd do when and if we caught him. He was just a kid, but a damned irritating one, and we couldn't let him get off scot-free.

At a dead run, we were weaving in and out of scurrying rickshaws and dodging pedestrians, the bobbing dark head of our shoeshine-boy quarry always a few steps ahead. After a mad dash across the market place, we finally cornered him.

Walt leaned on one knee, gasping for air, his hand twisted in the struggling boy's collar to hold him still. "Now," he managed to get out between labored breaths, "clean it off."

And the shoeshine boy did, though traces of the white polish remained, needling Walt for weeks to come, every time he looked down at his shoes. As out of breath as Walt, I laughed myself into near collapse.

It was obvious to all who knew him well that Walt had a special destiny. He was a unique, intelligent, strong-willed young man who would have chased that shoeshine boy all over Hong Kong and across the harbor into Kowloon if he had to. That's how determined Walt was about everything. Right was right and wrong was wrong. And wrong would be set right if he could do it.

After the service, we kept up with each other's accomplishments through news clippings and TV. After my landmark Atlantic crossing in *April Fool*, and before his ride on the rocket, a telegram arrived from Walt:

> *Hugo:*
> *Congratulations on crossing the Atlantic. I'm getting ready to cross it 163 times. Got any advice?*
> > *Walt*

My old friend had been chosen for the October 1968 Apollo-Saturn 7 space launch, the first to make it off the Cape Kennedy, Florida launch pad after astronauts Gus Grissom, Edward White and Roger Chaffee burned to death the year before. The late January flash fire on the ground aboard Apollo 1 was a national tragedy that left many Americans wondering if the race to the moon was worth the cost.

Walt's team fell heir to the job of picking up the shattered pieces of the NASA space program. One year after Walt's spectacular mission, Neil Armstrong's "one small step for man, one giant leap for mankind" restored the nation's pride, faith and passion for the space exploration program.

I fired off a return telegram to Walt. The message was simple:

> *Semper Fidelis.*
> *Hugo*

It was the United States Marine Corps motto, Latin for "Always Faithful." Walt would get the message; once a Marine, always a Marine.

I checked my watch for the umpteenth time today. Finally, it was 5 o'clock. Time to eat.

Tonight's MRE was spicy meatballs in tomato sauce, a feast to my knotted-up stomach. I was leaning in the hatch, taking my time with a can of fruit cocktail, when the silhouette of a ship took form out of the fog, about one mile away, at the outer reaches of my vision.

At first I wondered if I should even bother trying to call. None of my radios were functioning right.

But the thought didn't last long. This was only the third ship I'd seen since sailing out of St. John's nearly two months ago. I couldn't let it pass by without trying.

I dug out a handheld VHF transmitter Dana had insisted be brought for backup and peeled off its waterproof pouch. Its range wasn't very far, but nothing else was working.

"Eastbound freighter, this is the sailboat *Father's Day*. Do you hear me?"

"Roger, *Father's Day*, I hear you."

Someone was finally answering back! "Freighter, I need you to send a message for me. My radios are down, and I'm a month overdue. Please call my wife collect in Florida and give her my position. Tell her to stand by until she hears from me again."

As I rushed to give the freighter captain the telephone number, the signal started breaking up. In a panic I ducked into the cabin and flipped the switch on the regular ship-to-ship VHF, begging it to work for me now.

The captain's voice came in loud and clear. The solar panel rewiring job must have worked. "Go ahead *Father's Day*. Give me the number."

I quickly recited my home number. Over-excited, I messed up when the captain requested I spell my boat's name phonetically.

"Foxtrot, Alpha, Tango, Hotel, Echo, Yankee....."

What was I doing? I'd learned the phonetic system 39 years ago in the Marine Corps and used it every year thereafter with Delta. I knew it in my sleep.

"Correction, captain, that's Echo, Romeo, break, Delta, Alpha, Yankee." Even then I left out the "S" at the end of the first word. But at least I remembered my manners and thanked the captain profusely, asking once again for assurances he'd make the call.

"I'll call tomorrow," the captain promised.

As soon as I uttered the words "roger and out," I started worrying about what would happen if the captain called and no one was home. So I called the freighter again, and gave the captain my sister's telephone number as a back up.

I slumped exhausted in the cabin. I'd done it. I'd gotten through. But after all that, I'd neglected to ask the name of the ship. The captain sounded foreign, but his English was very good.

I thought aloud, "I hope he has a soft spot for homesick sailors."

After tomorrow, if the freighter captain was true to his word, Johnnie would know I was alive. It was time for a celebration.

Out here that's pretty basic. I ate three packages of almond M&M's in a row.

At midnight I awoke with a different sort of hunger. I'd been dreaming that my wife was curled up behind me as I slept on my side, our bodies fitting together like two nesting spoons. I could feel her warm breath on the nape of my neck, was agonizingly aware of her velvety thighs pressed against the back of my legs.

In my sleep, I turned and reached for her, felt her spine go supple beneath my caressing fingers. Her parted mouth turned up to mine, moist and sweet, and I could taste her need for me in the fire on her lips. I pulled her beneath my famished body, drowning in her softness, drunk on her scent.

The alarm clock ripped me sadistically from her arms. Raging like a penned-up bull, I yanked open the hatch and bolted through, wolfing down the cool night air.

An hour later, I was still there, watching dark, cavernous clouds scuttle across the gleaming, lunar marble. The wind was blowing a beautiful song, a soothing lullaby for the lonesome captain.

August 9th
Day 57
763 miles to go

Two days of Force 4 (11 to 16 mph.) winds from the west. I'm making great time; ninety miles since the wind picked up yesterday before dawn. This morning I woke up at 3:30 and stuck my head out the hatch.

I was supposed to be getting up every forty-five minutes to scan for ships. It took about that long for a ship that had just appeared on the horizon to run over me. But the schedule left me so exhausted that I'd gone back to three-hour stretches. I'd have to take my chances with the ships.

Sleep was more important. Not only for the sake of my body, it was a tool in the struggle to stay sane, a delicious release from the monotony of the long voyage. I was finding it harder and harder to get back to sleep after getting up in the night. With forty-five minute alarms I was just dozing off again when the blasted thing sounded.

The schedule had worked for me twenty-five years ago. But I'd done a lot more active sailing on *April Fool*. The weather to the south was much friendlier and I'd spent a lot of time in the hatch, tending the tiller. I was so exhausted at night, sleep had come easily, whenever and wherever I could get it.

Up here I spent day after day curled up in the cabin, hiding from the icy wind and waves, with little to expend my energy on except the infinite tossing from side-to-side and front-to-back.

I was older now too, and age is notorious for robbing its victims of the pleasure of sleep. The young can sleep anywhere, dropping off like someone pulled the plug. It's harder when a person gets older.

I was feeling every single one of my sixty-one years. And more.

The pre-dawn darkness was cold and wet, the wind whistling across my ears, the sails bulging to the east. Examining the rigging with a flashlight, I noticed the line holding the tip of the starboard sail to the boom track's sliding car had frayed through, leaving the end of the sail whipping uselessly in the wind.

I couldn't take a chance on waiting to fix it. I could feel the gale gathering force. The sea was relatively calm now, only six to eight feet, amazing in this wind, but I knew it wouldn't last. It was rough enough to make the repair work dangerous.

But it was even more dangerous to wait.

Inside the cabin, I cut a piece of parachute cord and melted the ends with a waterproof match. Up top, I reefed the flapping sail halfway and got a grip on the starboard track, pulling off the metal slide car that attaches the sail to the boom.

With one end of the parachute line in my mouth, I was busily tying the other end to the slide car when the Atlantic almost got me. With only one full sail to push against, the wind started to spin *Father's Day* around, trying to turn her backward with her bow into its howling face.

If the boat flipped around I was in deep trouble. When the wind got hold of the front of the sails, it would push the back of the boat down so far that the open hatch would be submerged.

In my panic to spread the crippled sail wide again, I dropped the slide car and the end of the cord that was clamped in my mouth. Reopening the sail worked and the bow came back around to the east, but I'd dropped the only slide car I had. It was probably a one-of-a-kind fishing lure by now.

I couldn't believe my luck when I found it lying at my feet inside the cabin. With my protruding body filling nearly every inch of the hatch, it was a feat I didn't think I could duplicate.

Lord, I didn't want to attempt the repair again. But I had no choice. The sail had to be fixed, sooner rather than later. I readied the engine, lowering it into the down position, and pumping the fuel line.

The engine might help straighten the boat out if it jibed again, a catastrophe on a night like tonight.

Visualizing that disaster made me work at top speed. I carefully positioned the port sail to counteract the effect of pulling in the other. With one eye on the outside compass as well as the waves, I made the repairs double quick and reset both sails.

Back in the cabin, I tried to get comfortable. The next four hundred miles would be the most treacherous weather-wise. The area was marked by a big red circle on the pilot chart. Notes off to the side indicated an average of three gales each month and waves more than twelve feet high, fifteen percent of the time. I fell asleep wondering how I would get through it.

August 11
Day 59
659 miles to go

Yesterday was one of the scary days. By one o'clock *Father's Day* was flying, sailing 3.2 knots per hour, an amazing speed in a boat of its design.

The gauge clocked the west wind at a little less than twenty knots. With waves fifteen to twenty feet, I would have guessed the wind speed was much higher.

Stir-crazy in the cabin, I tried to grab some fresh air in the hatch between the biggest of the toppling peaks, but gave up after misjudging twice left me wet and shivering. The ride in the cabin was like being locked in a thrashing washing machine.

The only thing I managed to eat all day was a few crackers spread with jelly.

Today was more of the same, only a little less intense.

I broke out the book I'd been saving for rough weather, none other than *The Saga of the Wayward Sailor* by Tristan Jones. The first few pages were filled with terrifying tales of the mast on Jones' sailboat being ripped from the hull and his engine being knocked loose from its heavy steel base. I decided I didn't need to read about nightmares like that, especially in a wind like this one.

I switched to the *First Aid Afloat* book, but its vivid descriptions of appendicitis attacks and compound fractures frightened me even more. It, too, was discarded.

I lay staring at the ceiling. The dread of being cooped up with nothing to do ran a close second to the fear I found in the books.

During the midnight check I noticed the light of a ship three or four miles off the starboard side. There was no need to try to call. I didn't have anything new to report to Johnnie. The only thing I could ask for was a storm forecast.

And that I really didn't want to know.

August 12th
Day 60
612 miles to go

The day started off badly. I made my morning cup of cold cocoa with seawater by mistake. Chocolate-flavored salt is no prize. I squirmed my way through the hatch and spat it over the side.

Brushing my teeth with seawater was bad enough. Twice a

day, I carefully scheduled the ministration to coincide with an empty stomach. Sometimes the saltwater made me gag and I couldn't afford to lose the precious food in my belly. My body needed every single calorie of it.

I must have grabbed the wrong water jug. The used ones had been refilled with seawater for ballast. I'd tried to mark them, but the waterproof marker hadn't worked very well. I rifled around until I found a new one, and put a big, black X on the seawater jugs. I didn't intend to make that mistake again.

A lone water spout erupted from the surface about a hundred yards away. For half a minute the whale hung near the top, its thirty-foot body hidden just under the surface. Then it tucked its head, sending its entire tail out of the water, and headed straight down.

I never saw it again. The whale could have gone a thousand feet down after a squid or something. It was a magnificent, fearsome sight.

I turned to check on my other companion. A different, unmistakable dorsal fin had been stalking me for the past three days.

Sure enough, there it was, a ten to twelve-foot shark, just twenty yards off the stern.

I wondered what the shark was waiting for.

For me, maybe?

August 13th
Day 61
576 miles to go

Friday the 13th — always a lucky day for me. Maybe because I was born on a Friday the 13th.

I spotted a three-masted sailboat just to the north, about five miles out. Desperate for the sound of another human voice, I called to it over the ship-to-ship radio, but didn't receive an answer. Could be it wasn't my lucky day after all.

Yesterday I crossed the twenty west longitude line. It was time for another food inventory.

Scouring the compartments, I counted my treasure.

35 MREs
23 cans Nutriment
19 cans fruit cocktail
6 2-oz. bags dried fruit
19 bags M&Ms, almond, 1 and 1/2-oz. each
4 bags M&Ms, plain, 1 and 1/2-oz. each
1/4 gal. M&Ms plain
7 health bars
3 rolls toilet paper
9 gallons water

Ten cans of Nutriment had expired freshness dates stamped on the bottom. No wonder I threw up the other day, right after drinking one. Wine might get better with age, but Nutriment sure doesn't. I'd have to save the out-of-date ones until absolutely necessary. If I reserved them 'till the last, maybe I wouldn't need them. And if I did, and they made me really sick, medical attention would be easier to get when I was closer to shore.

I should have checked the dates. The cans were purchased before my first attempt, over a year ago now. I didn't even think about that when we stowed them in the garage all that time.

They still might have been all right. It was air conditioned in the garage. But Hurricane Andrew knocked out electricity for more than seven weeks last August and temperatures soared even in the coolest parts of the house.

It's strange how that hurricane just wouldn't go away. It was still affecting me — even way out here.

August 14th
Day 62
528 miles to go

The inside compass was practically useless. I wasn't sure if it was the fault of all the radios and wiring inside the radio rack below it or the cheap price we paid for it. Whatever it was, the compass wasn't reading right.

We'd mounted a second, sturdier one outside the cabin, right in front of the hatch opening. On most days I didn't mind leaving the cabin to check the boat's heading. I spent as much time in the hatch as I could anyway. But it was a pain in the butt during rough weather or cold nights when I just wanted to make a quick check and get back to sleep. The more awake I came during the checks, the harder it was to return to dreamland.

Sighting that ship yesterday made me re-think my sleeping schedule. England was little more than five hundred miles away. The closer I got to it, the more ships I would encounter. Three hours of sleep, uninterrupted by alarms, was too much on this leg of the voyage. As much as I needed it, I could no longer afford it.

I compromised with myself at an hour and a half.

The approach charts to Falmouth were vacuum-bagged away, like a tightly wrapped Christmas present I was forbidden to touch until the proper moment arrived.

Today was close enough. I hungrily pulled them out, and spent most of the day poring over them, searching out and marking beacons, distances, shipping lanes and the like.

Any time I'd put them away, I'd think of something else to check and drag them out again.

I studied a ten by twenty-mile stretch of island-sized rocks with particular attention. The Isles of Scilly — beautiful to the people who call the larger ones home — but to a well-read seaman, the name alone is enough to impale the bravest of hearts with fear.

Standing sentry at the western edge of the mouth of the English Channel, the Isles of Scilly have taken a terrible toll in human lives. More than eight hundred ships have gone down on or near the isles — a testament to the accuracy of their evil reputation.

One episode alone, involving four ships from a naval fleet of twenty one, claimed 1,607. It was upon those very rocks that the largest sailboat ever built was dashed into flotsam. The *France II*, measuring three hundred sixty-eight feet in length, collided with the deadly isles in 1922. Even her steel hull couldn't save her. Being the biggest in the world hadn't made much difference in the end.

I could only hope things would go better when the world's

smallest transoceanic sailboat tried to snake past the infamous isles.

A closer inspection of the smaller-scale charts revealed some of the most heavily traveled shipping lanes in the world going in opposite directions on both sides of the Isles of Scilly. The ship traffic in those lanes, especially if the legendary English fog rolled in, was a major concern. Wouldn't it be something if I made it across nearly two thousand miles of ocean — only to be run down within sight of my destination?

The closest I'd be able to cut it was about six miles to the inside of the shipping lanes, bringing me that much closer to the merciless rocks. If the current was too strong, the ocean too angry, or the wind shifted even slightly, they'd be waiting.

But the rocks, listed on the large-scale ocean chart as "Bishop Rocks" represented my finish line. There was no way to stay completely away from them.

My flare gun would be critical. Those big ships would never see me in the thinnest of fogs. *Father's Day* was too small to be picked up on their radar. And radio success would obviously be sporadic at best.

The 25mm aluminum flare gun was so corroded its breech would hardly open. I searched the boat for something to use as a lubricant, turning up a bottle of suntan lotion I'd naively thought might be needed out here. A generous application, with pliers adding some persuasion, freed the stubborn breech.

"Well, Johnnie, I missed your birthday," I talked out loud as I worked. "Looks like I'm missing our anniversary, too." Today was our thirty ninth.

I couldn't believe nearly forty years had gone by since that quick, secretive ceremony in the Marine base chapel. That moment was a shadowy memory now. Forty years was a long, long time. Oh, we'd had our share of problems. A man and a woman don't spend a lifetime together without those.

"Wherever you are, honey, forgive me for all the trouble," I said. Maybe the wind would carry my whispered words to her distant ears.

CHAPTER ELEVEN

Isn't God upon the ocean
Just the same as land?
— James T. Fields,
Ballad of the Tempest

August 15th
Day 63
509 miles to go

THE SEA ANCHOR went out in the night.

It was about 11 p.m. when the east wind came calling. I was sleeping, but the wind shift woke me up. A sailor never really sleeps out here. Oh, he might have his eyes closed. He might even be snoring. But his senses are still tuned in.

In the blackness, I reefed in the two sails and dropped the sea anchor overboard. There was no light from the heavens to light my way tonight. A thick layer of clouds, clamped tight over the ocean, blocked out the moon and stars.

I was surprised and disappointed that I hadn't once seen the aurora borealis, or northern lights, on this voyage. The strange phenomenon was almost commonplace at this latitude. I'd seen it many times from the air; eerie fingers of light that seemed to emanate from the earth. It reminded me of pictures in a child's Bible, illustrations that depict God's voice as branching sun rays breaking through a hole in the clouds. Only the aurora borealis shines up from below.

But clear skies had been the exception on this trip. Last week, the Perseid meteor belt ruptured the earth's atmosphere in a glorious blaze of flames nearly one hundred miles overhead. Dana had told me to watch for it, thinking I would have a front-row seat in the raven-black nights of the mid-Atlantic. Overcast skies curtained the entertainment. It was supposed to be the best meteor show of the twentieth century, but if Dana hadn't told me about it, I wouldn't have had a clue it was happening.

Today's dawn GPS shot put us nineteen miles ahead of yesterday's. But with last night's wind change, I could expect tomorrow morning's reading to be dismal.

I was climbing through the hatch, fighting off the blues, when I saw a gray ship, about two hundred yards off the starboard side. I was surprised I hadn't noticed the ship approaching. Topside just fifteen minutes ago, I'd been trying to contact a passing airplane — unsuccessfully. I was amazed I hadn't seen the ship then.

More than a week had passed since I'd sent the last message to Johnnie. And I couldn't be sure she'd even gotten it. I might as well try again.

Elbow deep in the aft bilge compartment, I hooked both gel cell batteries together. A few amps of power had been collected from the miserly northern sun. Time to see if it was enough.

I gave the ship a call. A voice answered back in perfect English.

Fantastic! Not only was I transmitting, I wasn't wasting my meager battery power on someone who couldn't understand me!

"This is the *Sir Frederick Williams*," the ship's second mate replied after I identified myself and my boat. "We're out of Rotterdam, in the Netherlands."

I asked my usual. "Can you make a collect call for me?"

"Stand by," the second mate answered. "I'll have to ask the captain about that."

The ship's captain came on, his accent a heavy Dutch. "We're on satellite," the captain explained, "so we can't make your call now. But we'll be in port in two days. We'll do it then."

He handed me back to the second mate for the necessary information transfer. The message was simple: "50 north, 18 west. I'm ok, the boat's ok. ETA September 3rd."

My next question concerned the weather. "What can I expect in the next few days?"

The second mate relayed the latest report. "Winds to change from east to north to west. Gale Force Nine disturbance at 46 north 25 west."

Gale Force Nine! That was winds of forty-one to forty-seven knots, more than enough trouble for any sailor unlucky enough to be ensnared.

I did some fast calculating on my soggy plotting chart after signing off. The storm was one hundred eighty miles to the south of *Father's Day*. I breathed a sigh of relief. It would never touch us way up here.

I felt good now. Even if I was still riding the sea anchor.

August 16th
Day 64
511 miles to go

I was amazed that thirty hours of east wind and waves had only stolen two miles from beneath the boat. Amazed and unbelieving. Using the sea anchor made a difference, but not that much of one. The morning reading made me suspicious of my GPS.

With the sails still reefed and the sea anchor stretched taut, it was as good a time as any for a bath. I'd been sixty-four days without one, and I was smelling pretty rank, even to myself. I studied the water with apprehension. The past few days had been the warmest yet, with daytime temperatures a comparatively sweltering sixty to sixty-five degrees Fahrenheit.

But the water would be colder. Much colder. Probably fifty-eight degrees at the most. My testicles climbed for my belly at the thought.

I scratched my head, my hair matted and oily. The ragged, gray beard was in disgraceful shape. And a brown crud was making itself at home on my skin, even under the thick long johns I hardly ever removed. At first I thought it was liver spots. God, I'd aged so much out here. But the crud scraped off easily under a little pressure from a grimy fingernail.

Dirty as I was, it was still hard to believe I'd been so long without a bath or shower. At home, I couldn't imagine ending the day without one. Guess it helps that it's so cold up here. Too cold to sweat.

I scrutinized my fingernails. Definitely disgusting. Where had all the dirt under them come from? You wouldn't think there'd be any dirt in the middle of the Atlantic Ocean. Yet the trade winds route had been a gritty trip, too. Sand from Africa's Sahara Desert had followed me way out to sea, settling on everything and coating the water's surface until the ocean eventually saturated and sunk it.

I had plenty of fresh clothes on board. Too many actually. Extra changes of clothing, vacuum-bagged to stay dry, were stuffed inside a constantly dank, nylon duffel bag stowed at the front of the cabin. Some were for my triumphant arrival in England, though now I wished we hadn't wasted the space on them. I really only needed two or three changes of clothing on the boat. And at this point, I couldn't care less about my impression on England.

I found only one use for the surplus wardrobe. The plastic packages made great cushions when Mother Ocean took to squalling. Wedged between and around items in the cabin, they spared me a lot of bruises when supplies wouldn't stay put.

I continued my contemplation of the frigid ocean. The trailing shark had given up a day or two ago. With no dorsal fins to discourage me, there was no use postponing it. It was 2 p.m. — the warmest it was going to get all day.

My first bath in sixty-four days. I hoped it didn't give me a heart attack.

Today, the Atlantic was as flat as a Midwestern prairie. With the sails down and sea anchor out, I was confident it was safe to jump in without the harness and lifeline.

Dana would have pitched a fit had he known. He'd been adamant about my wearing it. Hooked to a harness around my chest, the six-foot lifeline attached to a stainless steel ring embedded in an inside cabin wall. That way I could hook it up in bad weather before I even opened the cabin hatch.

The arrangement also allowed the hatch to be closed quickly, without the delay of having to detach the lifeline before I ducked inside. True to the promise to my son, I wore the safety harness and lifeline each time I stood in the hatch in rough weather or leaned across the boat to work on sails or engine. If I lost my balance, or a big wave knocked me over the side, there was no one to stop the boat and pull me back aboard. Forgetting to put it on at the wrong time could easily be the last mistake I ever made.

But today was so calm neither I nor the boat was going anywhere. I peered over the side, into the glimmering, cobalt-blue ocean. It was so beautiful when the sun was out. The murky, somber water was transformed by the yellow rays into a liquid, opalescent jewel, suffused with a fire that seemed to burn from within. It was deep here; well over 16,000 feet to the ocean floor.

It was a weird feeling to know there'd be almost three miles of water beneath my dangling legs. Oh well, what was the difference? A couple of feet or a couple of miles? Once it's over your head, it's all the same.

I chuckled when I recalled one of Tom McNally's favorite sayings: "No matter where I am on the ocean, I'm never more than a few miles from land." Yeah, straight down!

Peeling off garment layers before my resolve melted away, I poised, naked and shivering, on the side of the boat. One reluctant toe at a time, I slipped into the icy water.

Yikes! The shock bolted up my body. Teeth chattering a tempo, I treaded water and scrubbed soap over my pale, skinny body. Lord, I barely recognized myself naked. I must have lost twenty pounds. Spurred on by the bitter cold water, and the insecure feeling of being out of the boat in mid-ocean, I washed my hair and was done in a flash.

Climbing back in wasn't easy. I could imagine what it would be like weighted down with wet clothes. Glad I'd remembered to close the hatch, I managed to pull myself up by the handrail, my weight tipping the boat perilously to one side.

Once on deck, I sacrificed a pint of my fresh water treasure, pouring the silky liquid over a goosebump-rippled body. A few passes with a rough towel and I hustled into clean clothes.

It felt wonderful to be bathed again. The cold water was refreshing and invigorating. And it made me very hungry.

Waiting for meal time was the hard part. I'd fallen into the habit of checking and rechecking my watch. Sometimes I didn't even notice what it read. I just kept flipping up my wrist — a hundred times a day — and unconsciously looking at it.

The watch was a special one. I'd worn it for dependability as well as good luck. It was a Rolex Oyster Perpetual, given to me by Irving Getz of Mayor's Jewelry in Miami before I embarked on *April Fool.* I'd needed an accurate watch then. Navigating with the sextant required one.

But with the advent of the GPS technology, that need was passé. The GPS holds so much information, it can not only give a position report day or night, under clouds or in fog, but can display the time of sunrises and sunsets for any day the operator asks.

Not given to wearing fancy jewelry, I had passed the Rolex on to my son, who'd worn it proudly for the past twenty years. But I'd reclaimed it from Dana's wrist for this trip. Its solid weight and handsome, familiar face were somehow reassuring. I was becoming an expert at guessing how much time had passed since the last time I allowed myself a glimpse of its luminous, black dial. I played little games with my patience, with my hunger. When meal time finally rolled around, I'd stall.

"Just a few more minutes," I'd tell myself. "Just five more minutes. You can wait that long."

And when those five sixty-second ticks were gone, I'd barter with my stomach for five more. If I stretched it out as long as I could, maybe I wouldn't be so anxious for the next meal.

August 18th
Day 66
464 miles to go

In the middle of the North Atlantic, every night is kind of spooky, but last night something really spooky happened. It was 2 a.m. when the alarm buzzed. Groggily, I climbed through the cabin hatch into the cold, glancing the narrow beam of the minimag flashlight off the deck compass.

All was well. It read 120 degrees. The same course I'd been on for the past few hours. Anxious to get back to sleep before I came fully awake, I slammed the hatch and slithered back into my sleeping bag.

Wait a minute. Something wasn't right.

Did that say 120 or 210?

Naah! It had to be 120. 210 was practically in the opposite direction!

I snuggled deeper into my cozy bedding. Forget it. Everything was fine. Of course it said 120. The silent argument went on. 120 or 210? I had to check it again.

Throwing the cover reluctantly back, I snatched up my flashlight and dragged through the hatch again.

What? 210? I was going in the wrong damned direction! In the stupor of sleep, I'd almost sailed the night backwards! Would I have been mad in the morning!

There was no telling how many miles I'd have lost. I was incredulous I hadn't noticed the boat turning around! Exhaustion was starting to take its toll.

Adjusting the sails and rudder brought the bow back easily to the east. I returned to my cocoon, but couldn't sleep. Lying on my back, legs folded, I stared up through the clear cabin hatch, seeing nothing.

I'd heard of men at sea having hallucinations. Isolation and fatigue played tricks on a solo sailor.

Bob Manry in his thirteen-and-a-half-foot *Tinkerbelle* reported seeing an imaginary island he couldn't seem to steer clear of. Manry was convinced two murderers were waiting for him on shore. Their harsh voices, discussing his demise, were carried to him across the water. "One shot between the eyes is all it'll take," one ape-like man said to the other.

Struggling fiercely against the wind and his own boat, which seemed determined to deliver him to their hands, Manry finally managed to sail around the illusory island, only to hear one of the plotting voices coming from inside *Tinkerbelle's* cabin.

A desperate fear seized him when he thought he recognized his son's small voice too, coming from the dim below. How on earth had Douglas gotten on board the boat? Manry didn't know, but one of the killers must have him in the cabin!

He had to save his son!

With no weapon on board, a sneak attack was the only tactical plan he could think of. It was dark now. If he could blind the killer with his spotlight, maybe he could wrestle the gun away. Manry rushed the cabin hatch, spotlight clenched in his hand.

Flick! No one was inside.

Plenty of sailors talked of seeing ships that weren't there. Hallucinations involving phantom crewmembers were fairly common, too.

It never happened to me on the long *April Fool* haul, but I'd read about imaginary shipmates who took turns standing watch while the weary captain slept, gave advice when it was needed and, perhaps the most critical, kept lonely sailors company.

Some apparitional companions appeared uninvited. Others were purposely summoned to save the sanity of a solitary sailor.

Gerry Spiess, another North Atlantic record holder, created a companion to combat the overpowering loneliness of a 1981 five-month Pacific Ocean voyage in his ten-foot *Yankee Girl*. Spiess said the friendly shipmate disappeared the moment he arrived at the docks in Sydney, Australia, but even years later he couldn't talk about the experience without emotion choking his voice.

But other sailors told of a kind of out-of-body experience. Too tired to care anymore, they'd fall into a dead sleep, only to feel someone shaking them, refusing to go away until they got up and checked conditions. Annoyed and angry, they'd comply with the insistent demand to come awake. And discover a very real freighter bearing down on them or find razor-sharp rocks in their path.

It must be the psyche. Standing apart and keeping watch while the rest of the done-in body sleeps. Was that what warned me? Or was it a guardian angel?

Sleeping too soundly is dangerous on the ocean.

Fellow sailor Wayne Dickinson was jarred awake by the appalling sensation of his eight-foot-eleven-inch *God's Tear* grinding itself to bits on the rocks of Ireland's western coast.

It was 1983, and Dickinson was headed for the same destination as I am now. One hundred and forty-two days later, Dickinson found his boat impaled on the boulder-strewn Irish cliffs, frustration and fear escalating as he tried to abandon the disintegrating craft. Nearly five months on board had atrophied his muscles. Dickinson was reduced to crawling to safety, and almost died of hypothermia before a lighthouse keeper found him.

I lay wide-eyed until dawn brushed the hatch with gentle gray.

The morning GPS check marked another milestone. Fewer than five hundred miles to go.

The next goal was the 15 degrees west longitude line. I'd adjusted my sights long ago, learning it was better to break the voyage up into smaller, incremental milestones. Looking at the big picture was too overwhelming.

Confidence in the accuracy of the GPS was reaffirmed yesterday. The *Fullness*, a freighter from Montreal, Canada steamed into view just about dinner time.

I jumped to spread the sails. The ship was just a dot off the stern, at least fifteen miles away. They'd never see me with reefed sails.

I was pleased when my transmission was answered. With nothing new to report to Johnnie, I simply asked for a position report.

The accommodating *Fullness* headed straight over. The ocean-going freighter cruised past, the teeming white water off her bow taller than my *Father's Day*. Directly off the starboard side, no more than forty yards between us, the *Fullness* crew radioed their position reading to me.

What a relief! It corresponded exactly to my GPS readout. High up on the deck, the crew lined the rails, waving and taking pictures of the strange, bearded man and his pocket-sized boat.

By 9:30, I was ravenously hungry. I couldn't wait one minute longer for my morning Nutriment. Pulling out a can, I said a quick prayer for chocolate.

The milkshake-style protein drinks came in three flavors: chocolate, vanilla and strawberry, and the boat was stocked with an equal assortment of all. The cans had been painted with enamel to keep them from rusting. Unfortunately, the well-meaning perpetrators had neglected to mark the flavor on them. The luck of the draw turned up strawberry for the past five days.

Come on baby! Let it be chocolate!

Ah-h-h-h. Chocolate.

Life's small pleasures are important in times like these.

Popping up through the hatch, my breath lodged sharply in my throat. What the hell was that?

A humongous, ghostly white ship loomed just a few miles away. I rubbed my eyes, but the Goliath remained! Was I finally hallucinating? I rubbed again.

The ship was still there, a towering spear of shimmering pearl on the slate colored mid-morning horizon. It seemed way too big to be real!

On the radio, I called out. The ship responded with concrete authenticity. Hallucinations don't answer back on the radio. At least I'd never heard of it happening.

A second later, I had my explanation. It was the world-famous *Queen Elizabeth II,* a legendary passenger liner out of Southampton, England, just a little past my intended harbor in Falmouth. No wonder the ship looked so massive! At nine hundred sixty-three feet, the *QE II* was one of the largest ships afloat. I could see dots of tiny, human figures at the gleaming, white rails. *Father's Day* must look the size of an inner tube from up there!

What did the captain of that grand queen of passenger ships think, ensconced in his lofty command tower as he steamed past the bedraggled captain of the world's smallest ocean-crossing vessel? Did he admire my audacity? Envy my freedom? Or merely pity the effort?

I made my request, and the *QE II* radio operator put a call through to Johnnie, right then and there. They tried to patch us together, but the connection wouldn't work properly. Johnnie could hear me, but I couldn't hear her. It didn't really matter though. The radio operator simply relayed her answers back to me.

I heard him telling her she had a call from the yacht *Father's Day.* I was sure that elicited a snicker! My tiny boat had been called many things, but never a yacht! Ah, those proper Englishmen!

We were able to pass several messages back and forth. Johnnie wanted to know how much weight I'd lost and should she bring smaller clothes to England for me? I wanted to know if the roof still leaked from the hurricane and other odds and ends about business I'd left unfinished. To my wife, I was inquiring about ancient history — things long taken care of in my absence. But to me, time had stood still more than two and a half months ago when I pulled out of the driveway. It seemed the roof was dripping only yesterday.

Then the *QE II*, headed for port, was out of range. The transmission dried up to a buzz of static. But it had been a wonderful few moments. To know Johnnie was right there, listening to my voice. What was she doing now, after it was all over? Probably still holding the phone in her hand, eyes fixed on the ceiling. I wished I could be that phone, and feel the comforting cradle of her gentle hands.

August 19th
Day 67
451 miles to go

Downright placid all day yesterday, the Atlantic rebelled just after dark. All night long, the wind squealed from the southwest, driving the careening *Father's Day* ahead of it — the exact opposite of the prediction of the *Sir Frederick William* crew.

After a near sleepless night, I chanced a moment in the hatch. The turbulent seascape was as impressive as it was spine-chilling. There was little or no wave pattern up here, unlike the predictable waves that ply the trade winds route. Just when it seemed like they were all heading in one direction, a colossus would come along and take a swipe at the boat from the left; in the next instant from the right.

The theory is that one in 300,000 waves may exceed the average size of the others by a factor of four. There was at least one every day that tried to swamp me. That must be the one in 300,000.

Right after that one, another titan usually came along to deliver one last swift kick to the vitals.

Another whale stopped by for a look-see during yesterday's calm. I heard the blow hole right behind the stern and saw a 25-foot shadow glide to a halt beneath the boat.

The whale didn't appear to be heading anywhere, but sooner or later the huge mammal would need air, and if it came straight up for it, a capsize was in the making.

I made a beeline for my safety harness.

August 20th
Day 68
417 miles to go

The guardian angel was back again.

Last night's east wind had sent me through the hatch to make the proper sail adjustments and toss the sea anchor over the side. Almost comatose, I performed the tasks on auto-pilot, scurrying back to my warm bed with a firm slam of the hatch door.

This morning, when I reeled in the sea anchor line, the nylon bag on the far end was hanging by one thin string. The rope had frayed to a single, tenuous strand. If the sea anchor had been lost, my life could have been lost as well. With *Father's Day* at the absolute mercy of the slightest adverse wind, I'd never have made it to England.

What if I'd waited to check the anchor? A few minutes more? An hour? Who knew how much longer I had before I'd have pulled in an empty line. To whoever or whatever made me check it right then, I offered a softly-spoken word of thanks.

Apparently, I was being allowed to continue. I'd better get busy rigging and improving that sea anchor. If I could find a way to close off some of the holes in its open nylon weave, it would offer more resistance to the drift of the boat, holding more of its own when the wind opposed the captain's desires.

I remembered my days back in Pensacola, as a trainee in the naval aviation program, and a solution to the sea anchor problem germinated. For one survival exercise, we had to swim a mile in our swim trunks, followed by a mile in full clothing. We were taught how to make a flotation device from our pants.

Wiggling out of them was the hardest part, but once accomplished, you tied knots in the ends of the legs, grasped the waist with two hands held high and wide and swung the pants over your head. If you dunked the waist end under the surface fast enough, air was trapped inside. Then you could crawl between the legs and float for awhile, until the pants slowly deflated.

I tied knots in the salt-stiffened legs of a pair of Levi's, threaded a rope through the waistband and secured the jeans inside the sea anchor. Voila!

The heavy denim did the trick. With the increased drag created by the blue jeans, the sea anchor was working much better. Geez. What an endorsement for Levi's!

Imagining the commercial, I entertained myself aloud.

"Going the wrong direction in errant seas? Our *Father's Day* Levi's can get you back on the path of your dreams."

Speaking of endorsements, I'd give one any day for the game little Evinrude mounted on the stern.

The tiny outboard was taking a tremendous beating. For the past couple of weeks I'd been cranking her up for twenty or thirty seconds a day, just to make certain she was still running. The manufacturer never intended that engine to be used in conditions like these.

Knowing it would be repeatedly submerged under heavy seas during the voyage, Dana and I cut a hole in the top of the plastic motor case and built a PVC snorkel facing forward for the engine to breathe. Then the normal breathing hole at the bottom of the case was plugged along with just about every other gap in the casing. Tiny holes were left for water to drain out should waves breach the snorkel.

The four-horsepower engine had been swamped so many times already it was incredible it still ran. She began the trip with a special cover over the top for protection but that went with the first good wave. Another pounding storm broke the rear latch on the casing. Five-hundred pound test parachute cord, wrapped around the engine, now held the casing in place.

She'd sounded kind of sickly during yesterday's test, so with today's light winds and waves, I got busy doing maintenance. Changing the spark plugs didn't make her run any smoother, though.

The engine would be crucial when I reached Bishop Rocks. It would be impossible to maneuver clear of ships and shoreline without it. I'd have to find a way to keep her drier. Maybe a little more wind pressure on the sails and a little more ballast in the bow.

I coaxed the Evinrude like a pleading lover. "Come on sweetie," I urged. "Just hang in there a little bit more, baby. I promise I'll take better care of you."

"Besides, we're almost there," I fibbed again.

CHAPTER TWELVE

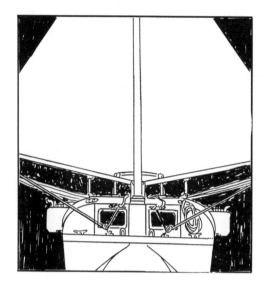

Little is the luck I've had
And oh, tis comfort small
To think that many another lad
Has had no luck at all.
                    — A.E. Housman,
                            Last Poems

August 23rd
Day 71
414 miles to go

THREE DAYS LATER with only three miles more under the keel, I searched the boat for another good luck charm. I was desperate.

Deep inside the very bottom of the compartment nearest my right ear, my probing fingertips brushed a scrap of soft leather.

Ah ha. There it was. The penny necklace. It would do nicely. Given to me by a gentleman I'd met at the dock in St. John's, the leather thong was hung with an unusual American penny — one of only four in the world, according to the giver, David Osborne.

It was stamped with the erroneous date of "194". Osborne

handed the piece to me a few days before my departure. I'd promised to send it back to him after the voyage.

Riding across the North Atlantic on a world-record boat might make the special penny even more valuable, if only to another sailor.

Two freighters came by yesterday, one going east, the other going west. Neither replied to my VHF calls.

August 28th
Day 76
401 miles to go

Hunger gnawed at my rib cage, each curved bone easy to trace when I slipped a thin finger under my long johns. Thirty pounds must have evaporated from my frame since I sailed out of St. John's in mid-June. I'd resorted to punching extra holes in my belt — the only way to cinch it tight enough to keep my pants up.

My bony knees and tailbone, their protective cushions of fat burned away, hurt the most. At night, one of the vacuum packs of clothes cradled between my legs eased the misery of my sharp knee bones rubbing together. I protected my tailbone as best I could when cabin-bound, and spent as much time as possible standing in the hatch — as many as fourteen hours a day if the weather permitted.

Mouth salivating in anticipation, I pulled out today's MRE. It was high noon, and the morning protein shake, consumed over two hours ago, hadn't done much to ease my empty belly. The MREs, made famous by Operation Desert Storm in Iraq and Kuwait, weren't too bad — considering they were military-issue food rations. When I was really hungry, which was all the time now, they were downright delicious.

I scattered the MRE's contents over the already cluttered floor cushion. It was amazing how much food and other items were packed inside the wafer-thin tan cartons, bagged inside a heavy, brown, waterproof outer pouch.

Each day I opened one MRE and doled out its contents over the day. The main entree — today it was tuna with noodles — was saved for the evening meal.

Accompanying the tuna with noodles was a 3.2 oz. chocolate

nut cake, eight plain crackers, a pouch of cheese spread, two flavored powders for improving the taste of water, a bullet-sized bottle of Tabasco sauce, a couple of caramel candies, two gum chiclets, instant coffee, sugar, creamer, salt, wet-nap, a few wraps of toilet paper, a plastic spoon and a book of matches. Other MREs offered variations on the menu, but the theme was basically the same.

I avoided using the powdered-drink flavors. It made the water taste too good, and I drank too much of it.

The cold weather latitudes were good for one thing. Not perspiring greatly reduced my body's need for water. A little more than seven gallons remained of the twenty-five I'd carried. It was enough to reach England if I kept moving. Or at least until a ship with supplies could be intercepted. Only a fool would count on either one out here, though. Anything could happen next. Or nothing at all. I had to play it safe when it came to my supplies.

The MRE's crackers and snacks held me over between evening meals. A twelve-ounce Nutriment drink along with an occasional health bar, handful of M&Ms or a bag of dried fruit, filled out the day's calories.

But I was running low on the Nutriment too. Most of the remaining cans were the out-of-date ones I was saving for desperate times. Lately I'd been cutting down to only one every other day, trying to make the good ones last as long as possible. My stomach squirmed at the memory of the last expired one I drank.

Military food had come a long way since the C-rations soldiers in the field survived on in my day. Not only does it taste better now, but a tailor-made chemical heating pouch can be used to warm up MRE entrees. No bigger than an ultra-thin slice of bread, the space-age heaters, encased in a plastic sleeve the length of a forearm, are activated with water. A heat-producing reaction takes place when the water is absorbed by a packet of chemicals in the bottom of the sleeve. An MRE entree pouch is placed inside the sleeve with the heater, both stuffed back inside the cardboard carton and set at an incline for ten to fifteen minutes until the contents are warm.

Most often, I was too hungry to take the time to use the heaters, or being tossed around so much it was ridiculous to even consider. I'd already gotten used to cold coffee and cold food anyway. But on days when the ocean lay flat or my mood was particularly sour, a warm meal gave a lift to my flagging spirit.

It also perked up the flavor of the less-appetizing entrees, like last night's hamburger or the hot dog of the night before. They were awful, like cardboard imitations of the real thing. I guess some flavors just don't hold up to preservation. But by heating up some tasteless beans, mixing in the crumbled-up hamburger and doctoring it all up with a dash of Tabasco and a soup bouillon cube, I had a gourmet dinner.

Meal cleared away, teeth brushed and flossed, I perched in the hatch, reluctant to face the closing night. Accustomed to the endless pitching, it was weird when the ocean was calm, like tonight. The onyx water was so boundless and untroubled; the smoke-gray overcast extinguishing what was left of the faint-hearted, falling sun. With no waves to chop up the view, I could see for miles in every direction. Nothing moved, except the lethargic, gentle swelling of the sea.

It made me feel so small, way out here with no one around for miles and miles and miles. The only sound was the rustling of the rigging as a sporadic west wind teased the sails.

So quiet. So frightening.

The crescendo of silence rained upon my ears.

August 30th
Day 78
354 miles to go

I jerked awake to find five fishing trawlers scattered across the slowly brightening eastern horizon.

Thank God! Surely I could communicate with one of them! Yesterday I'd seen two others, and made contact with both, but no one on board spoke English. Annoyed at my inability to converse with the French fishermen, I'd slammed down the mike in frustration.

I was due in Falmouth in four days. It was obvious a week ago that I wasn't going to make it on time. My anxious family might be boarding a plane for England right now!

I dove below. Several different radio channels brought no response. *Father's Day* was too tiny to be seen by even the closest of the huge fishing boats; we were nothing but a crumb on the water, more than half a mile away. I spread my bright sails, hoping to catch their attention. I needed to get a message to Johnnie. And I needed supplies. I could stretch out my food for weeks if I had to, and there was always the reverse osmosis kit when the water ran out.

But I couldn't hope to navigate the English Channel without fuel for my engine. Only two gallons still sloshed in the tank lashed to the deck.

And if the fishermen offered food, I'd be obliged. A hungry man at the whim of the winds doesn't turn down a chance to fill his cupboard.

I had to be careful though. Even in two to three-foot seas like today's, getting close to one of those gigantic hulls would be dangerous. *Father's Day* would bounce off their steel sides like a tennis ball. Protecting the boat's vulnerable booms and mast would be the tricky part.

An hour passed, with no one on board the still-distant trawlers taking notice of the little red boat. A twin-engine airplane buzzed by, circling and low. A fish-spotting plane, working with the fleet!

I tried to raise the pilot on the marine-VHF. No answer, so I took a stab at channel six, the same channel on which I'd contacted yesterday's trawlers. Those had been French. These probably were, too. The pilot might be talking to the boat captains on six.

"Aircraft, this is the sailboat *Father's Day* below. Do you read me?" Three times I repeated the call into the mike.

The third try was the charm. "Yes, *Father's Day*. This is 463X!!xx....," but the numbers never penetrated my brain. Yes! I had contact! In English!

"I'm about a mile to the west of you. Do you see me?" I asked. The plane began an instant turn back toward me.

Our conversation continued when it was directly overhead.

My first priority was Johnnie.

"I need you to do me a favor," I began, and spun out the tale as rapidly as I could. The pilot assured me he'd call Johnnie with a position report as soon as the plane returned to Brest, its home base in France.

I had learned my lesson about sending home arrival dates. It was just too hard to second guess the wind. My family would know by my position that I still had a long way to go.

"*Father's Day,*" the pilot broke the short silence that followed my request. "Be advised, the *Centaure* is coming over."

Here was my chance for supplies. I waited impatiently for the lanky gray trawler, the pride of the Brest fishing fleet, to plow her way across the mile or so that separated us.

When she settled to a halt one hundred fifty feet away, I looked up into the incredulous faces of dozens of French fishermen leaning over the top rails of the work deck.

I smiled and waved to them all as a small RIB made its way down the ship's rusting side, two crewman carefully balanced on board.

A bottle of wine was clutched in their hands. They pulled alongside with shouts of greeting in English and offers for whatever supplies I might need. An invitation to come on board the *Centaure* for a hot shower and meal was issued.

I drew back at the suggestion, though tempted by the offer. Visions of a ballroom-length dining table, wafting with the tantalizing smells of cluttered dishes sent a spasm through my stomach. And what I would give for heavenly hot, fresh water to scrub my filthy hair and warm my stiff body to the core.

But I was reluctant to leave my boat. No real reason why, it just made me feel uneasy.

Maybe it was the memory of climbing off *April Fool* twenty-five years ago to visit with my wife on the *Sea Wolfe II*. I never made it back on board my tiny boat. And it vexed me for all the years that followed.

Or maybe I'd just become so accustomed to my reclusive life on *Father's Day* that I shrank from the prospect of a swarm of people. These two crewmen on the RIB were the closest I'd come to human contact in seventy-eight days. And while their visit was certainly welcome, it was somehow unnerving, too.

I shook my head, politely declining the hospitality. But the supplies — those I'd gladly take. Six gallons of gas, a big plastic bag of canned food, four loaves of bread, a hunk of Swiss cheese the size of my head and some smaller, softer cheeses were shuttled over from the *Centaure*.

In return, I sent the French captain my small, spare Swiss Army knife and my log book with a request for him to sign it.

When the exchange was done, I sat scrunched up in the miniature cabin, contentedly munching three cheese sandwiches in a row, washing them down with red wine.

Shoving the food in my mouth with one hand, I picked up the log book and turned to the captain's entry:

> *With courage, with bravery, you have left your friends*
> *and written your name on the pages of oceanic history.*
> *Lt. Commander Vaisseau*
> *RHM Centaure*

The plane must have spotted fish somewhere else, because the trawlers were moving off. I leaned in the hatch and watched them fade to a blur on the pleated horizon.

A sinking feeling accompanied the realization that had I gone on board, I could have used the *Centaure*'s radio to call Johnnie myself. I could have spoken right to her! Explained it all and heard her replies! What an idiot I was not to think of it!

It was too late now. The trawlers were gone.

Loneliness moved in to take their place.

August 31st
Day 79
355 miles to go

A humming noise penetrated my sleep. Fumbling for the minimag, I tried to focus on my watch. The LCD display on my battery-driven alarm, velcroed to the padded cabin wall, had long since faded away. I just kept punching the reset button and so far it continued to sound on time. It was just after midnight. Not time for the alarm yet. Something else had awakened me.

Peering out the hatch, I discovered a small, red light, then a green one, just a short distance away in the ebony darkness. It was a two-toned running light, the kind found on the bow of a ship. And if both colors were visible, I had to be staring right down its nose.

The ship was headed straight for me.

Flicking on my own running light, mounted high atop the mast, I reached for the tiller. But despite my efforts to move out of its path, the ship seemed determined to run me down, the wings of roiling, white water at her bow intent on a closing collision course.

My adjusted eyes could now pick out her form. It looked like another trawler. Feverish calls on the radio brought no response. I threw out the sea anchor in an attempt to slow my speed, trying to let the trawler pass in front of me.

But she slowed up, too.

Snatching a flashlight off its velcro patch on the cabin ceiling, I shined it on the sails, hoping to be seen in time to avoid a collision. But the ship kept coming, and I knew I was in a deadly situation.

Cabin lights blinked on and off, sporadically piercing the blackness that cloaked the big ship's upper deck. The pursuing shadow continued to close in.

What the hell was its captain doing? He must see *Father's Day* by now! Was he trying to teach me a lesson, irritated because my running lights hadn't been on?

I knew it was dangerous not to keep them lit at night. The tiny red and green lights were visible for miles on the open water. They were vital in avoiding nighttime collisions.

But they were also a constant drain on my persistently weak batteries, and I'd elected to take the risk of turning them off. I was three hundred fifty miles from the coast, for God's sake! I wasn't expecting a whole lot of traffic!

I was grateful when the churning engines eased into neutral, and the trawler slid to a halt just twenty feet away, *Father's Day* rocking in its ever-expanding wake.

A barrage of expletives split the night, followed by one clear command in English.

"You come with me!" the voice barked.

I assumed it belonged to the captain. I could make out the trawler's name, painted in chipped black letters on the gray hull: *Matanza*.

"What?" I shouted back. "No!" Who did this guy think he was? I wasn't going anywhere with him!

The voice kept repeating, "Come with me! You come with me!"

"NO! NO! NO!" I hollered in return.

Running silhouettes of crewmen appeared on the deck and began tossing lines, trying to entangle them in the rigging of the *Father's Day*. Like slithering snakes, the ropes reached out to snag my boat. Why were they doing this? They had no right to take me anywhere!

Springing into action, I scrambled around the boat, throwing off the lines as soon as they landed, screaming "America to England! America to England," until my voice rasped hoarse in my throat.

Our vessels were now less than a car length apart.

I winced fearfully upward at the fishing boat's trolling rig, a hefty steel bar jutting out over her side. It didn't look high enough to clear the seventeen feet of mast and antenna on *Father's Day*, not if the waves hit wrong.

But the captain would not give up. A piercing whistle rent the night. He was trying to get someone's attention on the radio. Whoever he finally reached must have told him to leave the tiny sailboat alone, because suddenly he yelled, "America?"

"YES!" I shot back with exasperation.

With that, the captain turned his back, dropped his engines in gear and drove away without a backwards glance.

What the hell was that all about?

Had the *Matanza* captain thought I needed rescuing? Maybe he thought I was washed out to sea. He sure was hell-bent on dragging me in! If his crewmen had been successful in roping *Father's Day* and pulling her up against that battering hull, damage to my little boat would have been inevitable. And most likely irreversible in the pitching, black seas.

Sleep was sketchy after that.

Right after dawn, I spotted another ship, this one far astern, heading west.

A second chance to call Johnnie. The ache for my wife turned into a raw wound. I had to talk to her. Hearing her voice would be worth leaving the boat for.

But it was more than just a hankering for the sound of her. I'd sent a message via the fleet plane yesterday, but, as always, I couldn't be sure anyone at home received it.

It was aggravating having to depend upon the good will of

strangers to carry out favors like that. Asking someone who doesn't know or care about you to take the time to make an international call to your family — even if it is collect — was an imposition that would be easy to neglect to do. A stranger would have no idea how important it was.

Fortune was with me. The ship turned in my direction.

I headed for the mike. And got an answer.

It was a Spanish naval ship, the *Chilreu*, and after a few moments of initial confusion, I secured an invitation to come aboard.

As the *Chilreu* motored over, I excitedly prepared for the visit, smoothing my scraggly hair, locating my reading glasses and log book and a list of questions I wanted to ask Johnnie. I didn't want to forget anything in the few precious moments we would have.

A RIB was launched to bring me over. I readied *Father's Day* for my absence while I waited, dropping the sea anchor overboard, aligning the rudders and reefing the sails. It was calm today. My boat would be fine. The RIB's crewman tossed me a line, and with one last glance at my boat, I climbed into the small inflatable for the short trip to the *Chilreu*.

Pity the first man who greeted me on the naval ship. Grungy and unwashed as I was, I threw my arms around the officer and gave him a bear hug, a gesture completely out of character for someone as normally reserved as I. I tried to clamp a lid on my overwrought emotions, restricting myself to a handshake with the rest of the receiving line, an effort I suspected they all appreciated. I didn't want these people to think I'd gone mad at sea!

They all knew who I was and what I was doing out here, courtesy of yesterday's fishermen. The *Chilreu's* radio room had eavesdropped on the fleet's chatter about their encounter with an absurdly small boat in the middle of nowhere. They'd been keeping an eye out for me all morning.

I was seated at a table and served several cups of hot coffee, a real treat after the cold stuff I'd been consuming. It felt strange to be sitting there, almost like a dream or hallucination. People were talking, asking me questions.

My voice sounded alien, engaged in polite response. I had

used my own voice so little for so long. I fidgeted for the sound of Johnnie's. I looked at my watch, still set on Eastern Standard Time. I'd left it that way on purpose, even though it was now three or four hours earlier than the actual time in this part of the globe.

A small thing, but it made me feel closer to my family. I could look at its face and guess what everyone was doing at home.

It was 4:30 a.m. in South Florida. Johnnie would be sound asleep. But I couldn't wait any longer. Besides, what better time to be sure she was home?

On the bridge, I watched nervously as the radio operator dialed a series of numbers and handed me a phone.

My legs felt like over-cooked spaghetti.

It was her; her voice settling around my shoulders like a warm blanket. She was half-asleep and incredulous it was really me.

The words rushed out in a stream of jumbled tears.

"It's me, honey. It's really me."

"What's wrong, Hugo?" Johnnie asked worriedly. She'd never heard me so distraught. "Are you okay? Is the boat okay?"

"Yes, yes, hon. We're both all right. I'm just so glad to hear your voice. I miss you so much."

It was our first real conversation since the day I left shore, and the questions and answers flew rapid-fire. True to his word, the pilot of yesterday's plane had called her. She'd been grateful for the information and had made him promise to check on *Father's Day* regularly.

We talked about the family, an arrival date, unfinished business and travel arrangements.

The minutes zipping by, we were both in mid-sentence when the phone connection broke. With me hanging over his shoulder, the radio operator re-punched the sequence of numbers, and this time my daughter-in-law, Nancy, answered the phone.

"Who is this?" I asked anxious and bewildered. I was expecting to find my wife on the other end.

"Who?" I asked, still confused after she identified herself. "Nancy who?"

"Your daughter-in-law!" Nancy answered, perplexed at my

apparent loss of memory. "You know, Dana's wife? Remember Dana? Your son?"

"Oh, yeah! Nancy! Hello!" I managed to stammer. What was wrong with me? How could I have not known Nancy? I must really be out of it!

Nancy quickly passed the receiver on to Johnnie. We tried to talk some more, but I kept breaking down.

Rivulets of tears, hastily wiped away in impatience, trickled down my wind-reddened face.

Why was I crying so much? It wasn't like me to be so emotional. Her voice was the key. Months of pent-up fear and frustration, loneliness and exhaustion, erupted from their tightly held chains.

And now I was so happy. So very happy. Everything was fine back home and Johnnie still loved me. I'd thought so much about the possibility of losing her during this trip. With few options to choose from, she'd eventually thrown her lot in with Dana when he'd decided to get behind this latest adventure. But underneath her calm exterior, I knew she was seething. When I risked my life like this, I was risking hers as well. I was secretly afraid she'd get tired of it one day.

I told her how much I loved her and hung up the phone.

More coffee was offered along with a seat on the deck. Spanish crewmen and officers alike gathered around, prodding me into a narration of my voyage.

The second officer spoke excellent English and translated for those who didn't. Surrounded by the perfectly creased naval uniforms, I was painfully aware of my beggarly appearance. I asked if I might be allowed to wash my hair.

Once escorted to a cabin with a shower, I dropped my filthy clothes in a heap around my ankles. Stepping into the narrow shower stall, I turned the water as hot as it would go and braced myself for sheer rapture, the heat penetrating to the marrow of my bones. Soaping myself into a giant bubble, I rubbed off layers of dead, caking skin and stubborn grime, scrubbing my nails deep into my scalp. Reluctant to leave the delicious wet heat, I finally emerged in a cloud of steam and reached for a towel.

Turning to the mirror, I stood stock still, towel halted in midair, and stared — shocked by the gaunt old man who stared back.

Who the hell was that? I looked awful. Slowly, I lifted one hand and caressed the thick white beard. My hipbones and ribs were barely covered by pale, hanging skin pocked with festering saltwater sores. The weathered face added years to my appearance. Lord, what a price this world record demanded. That old guy in the mirror couldn't possibly be me.

No clean clothes had been offered, and I hadn't thought to bring any over with me. I redressed in my dirty ones, loathing their stiff, grimy feel on my freshly scoured skin.

Lunch was served in the officers' mess. Seven Spanish officers accompanied me to a table heavy with soup, baked chicken, French fries, red wine, fresh-baked bread, desert and coffee. After months of cold food eaten on the floor from a pouch, the meal was manna from heaven. Talk around the table was a lively concoction of English and Spanish, the gracious men intrigued by my quest. We stayed long at the table, enjoying after dinner drinks, talking of the sea, of boats and the weather — every sailor's immediate concern.

With my belly full to bursting, I posed for pictures with various crewmen and collected my parting gifts: three gallons of water, two dozen oranges and a dozen bottles of Aguila Spanish beer. There were many hands to shake. A photo of the *Chilreu*, signed by the captain and crew was added to the trove of gifts.

> *For Hugo S. Vihlen with our admiration and*
> *respect as a memory of his short but intimate*
> *and historic stay on board the Spanish patrol*
> *boat "Chilreu"*
>> *On board at sea,*
>> *Aug. 31st, 1993*
>> *L.C. Commander*
>> *Santiago Boliber Pineiro*

Captain Pineiro himself accompanied me back across in the RIB. He wanted a closer look at the world's smallest ocean-going boat, bobbing along empty for nearly four hours now.

When I was deposited back on board, the RIB made big

circles around *Father's Day* while Pineiro took pictures of the little sailboat, its small stature dramatized even more by the tall ship patiently waiting just a stone's throw away.

With a wave from its crew, the RIB moved off toward the *Chilreu*, me shouting "Gracias!" in its wake. I'd thanked them several times while on board the big ship, struggling to express what their simple kindness meant to a man in my position. But they'd shrugged off my gratitude with flashing smiles.

Aw heck, I'd never been too good with words anyway. I could only hope they understood what they'd done for me today.

I felt like a human being again.

They'd brought me back from the outer threshold of despair, back to the land of the living.

CHAPTER THIRTEEN

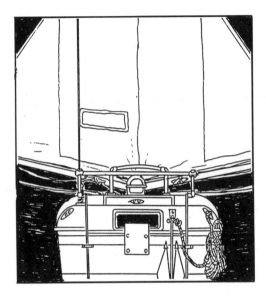

The wonder is always new that any sane man can be a sailor.
— Ralph Waldo Emerson, 1802-1883

September 1st
Day 80
369 miles to go

TODAY I HAD what was undoubtedly a once-in-a-lifetime experience.

The plane from the French fishing fleet, the same one whose crew called Johnnie and hooked me up with the *Centaure*, returned. Just as they had promised my wife they would.

That woman of mine had a way with people. Johnnie could get just about anybody to promise her almost anything, and the amazing part was they usually delivered. There was something about her that most people just didn't want to disappoint.

The plane's crew had been looking for *Father's Day* for more than two hours. Running low on fuel, they were just about to give up and turn back when I saw their aircraft.

"Where are you?" the co-pilot asked when I raised them on the radio.

"Turn to your right. I'm right below you," I bellowed into the mike. It was easier for me to see them than the other way around.

The plane banked to the right, dropping into a low circling pattern, zeroing in on me, standing in the hatch, both arms waving wildly. The co-pilot's voice drew me back to the radio."Would you mind being interviewed for French television?" came the request.

"What? Out here?" Surely I'd misunderstood.

"We have a television reporter and film crew on board," the co-pilot explained. "Will you talk to them?"

"Well, sure" I wasn't really ready for this. What on earth would I say?

A young woman came on the radio and machine-gunned a series of questions. What was my goal? Why was I out here? My brain switched into automatic and spit out an abridged version of the story. Then she asked if there was anything I'd like to say to the people of France. My mind drew a complete blank.

Say? To the entire nation of France? Well, heck, I really hadn't given it a whole lot of thought, especially since I was planning to come ashore in England. Ummmm....let's see.

"Tell them that next summer I would like to bring my wife and ride my motorcycle through their country. I've flown in many times but haven't really seen it all."

Where the heck had that come from? They were probably expecting something a bit more profound than that lame message. Forget it. It was the best I could do on such short notice.

The plane made several more passes for the TV camera, and then disappeared into the distance. It was hard to imagine that my bearded, scruffy image, so starkly alone in this alien world of water, would be beamed into the living rooms of millions of French households tonight.

September 2nd
Day 81
377 miles to go

The panicked scrabble of tiny toenails made me nearly jump out of my skin when I slid open the hatch this morning.

Creeping up through the opening like a soldier from a foxhole, one inch of head at a time, sleep-swollen eyes cleared the rim and did a quick scan of the deck.

Nothing out of the ordinary here, except what looked like bird droppings scattered across one of the solar panels. Standing tall in the hatch, I spied the source of the leavings. About twenty yards out, a beautiful, gray pigeon was circling, eyeballing *Father's Day* with longing.

Judging by the size of the pile of droppings, the bird had been on board most of the night. I was surprised I hadn't detected its presence in the dark during my routine position checks. Each time I came up from below in the night, it must have lit out with the first scrape of the sliding hatch, landing again only after I went back below.

The bird, tightening its circles around the boat, looked like it wanted to land again right now, despite my obviously disturbing presence. Motionless, I waited, afraid to twitch a muscle lest it discourage the bird's building bravery. So close now I could hear the whoosh of beating wings, it dropped toward the boat's deck, legs outstretched, feet extended forward and reaching for the solar panel, less than an arm's length from where I leaned frozen in the hatch.

But the Atlantic had picked up a little momentum since last night, and the bird, clawing for a foothold on the rocking, slick-surfaced solar panel, slid off its intended landing pad. Its frantically flapping wings bit into the whistling wind just in time to escape the tentacles of the reaching waves.

It continued its circuit, interrupted by more failed attempts to set down. Over and over, the pigeon dipped clawing to the boat, only to slide helplessly down and over the side. The bird must be exhausted to be so intent on landing on *Father's Day*.

I had to do something to help it.

Pulling a sweatshirt from below, I flung it across the droppings, using the arms to tie it in place. The thick cloth might give the bird something to grab hold of.

Desperation overrode caution, and the pigeon wasted no time trying its luck on the newly outfitted solar panel. Sure enough, the sweatshirt did the trick. Claws stretched wide, wings still thrashing, the bird landed on the deck with a depleted thump.

"Hey, pretty girl," I murmured softly. Was it a girl? Who could tell? "What are you doing out here in the middle of nowhere?"

Her head snapped toward the sound of my voice, metallic orange eyes inspected me from rumpled hair, down to where the hatch cut off the view of my lower body. Satisfied such a wrinkled creature could not possibly be a threat, she lowered her guard and sank down, drawing skinny red-hued legs into the cushiony down of her breast. But not before I saw the two tiny bands that jiggled around her ankles.

She must be a homing pigeon, the racing kind so popular now. She had to be from somewhere in Europe. She was just too far from anywhere else. The same nasty east wind that had pilfered twenty-two miles from me in the past forty-eight hours must have blown her off course and out to sea.

This bird must have been tired indeed to seek my company, though I supposed I was a damned sight better than her other choice. A little bird like her wouldn't last long trying to rest on this ocean. Her lightly-oiled feathers would soon become saturated, dragging her under to drown. That's if she lasted that long. Most likely she'd first become appetizer a la mode for some cruising, finned predator.

I'd read somewhere that these highly bred racing birds were sometimes worth a fortune. I remembered hearing of one selling for $200,000! Studied by some of the best scientists in the world, their mysterious powers of navigation remain a secret. Inside that pea-sized brain exists a navigation system that rivals just about anything found in today's multi-million dollar high-tech aircraft.

These feathered thoroughbreds can routinely fly six hundred miles in a single day, somehow finding the way to their home loft over territory they've never seen before. All kinds of experiments had been performed to determine just how they orient themselves. Blindfolds were tried, along with tiny backpacks crammed with various instruments and devices intended to ruin readings of barometric pressure and magnetic and electrical fields. But nothing worked. Even homing pigeons released in places where the earth's fields are known to play havoc with the most sophisticated navigational instruments managed to find their way home.

The unique homing talent of these pigeons has been put to work over the centuries. Five hundred years before the birth of Christ, Cyrus the Great of Persia was using pigeons like this one to communicate with the far-flung fringes of his empire. Homing pigeons helped Caesar conquer Gaul.

The ancients weren't the only ones to recognize their usefulness in warfare. Legendary birds like Cher Ami and G.I. Joe were credited with saving entire battalions of soldiers in both world wars. The messages they carried, sometimes through a hail of enemy fire, spared the lives of thousands of Allied soldiers. The Swiss Army still keeps its own army of homing pigeons, thirty thousand strong, against the possibility of an outbreak of war.

It was an honor to provide a much-needed rest stop for a creature of such noble heritage. I hoped she'd stay awhile. I could use a little companionship. The other birds, the fish, the porpoises, even the whales and sharks had been wonderful to see.

But this pigeon was more from my world, familiar with the ways of civilized humans. She reminded me of the pigeons I'd once kept myself. I never did much in the way of racing them, just enjoyed having them around. Until a neighbor's dog developed a taste for killing them. I remembered my growing rage as each day's grisly discovery fueled my own taste for blood. Part of me wanted to shoot the dog on sight, the other part was relieved I never got the chance. The sneaky mutt continued his deadly raids until nothing remained of the flock.

But I found comfort in the other winged critters that visited our nine-acre spread back in South Florida. Our driveway was usually scattered with birdseed for the wild white wing and ring neck doves, blue jays, woodpeckers and tame peacocks that roamed the property. The memory of a peacock's haunting boom, echoing across the rooftops, shattering the balmy peace of a silky tropical sunset, produced a sharp stab of homesickness. That's a sound I'll only hear at home.

No longer the least concerned with my presence, the visiting pigeon lurched to her feet and began pacing the rolling deck. I sat rooted to my spot, half expecting her to fall overboard again. But somehow she managed to keep a grip on the slippery deck, her thorny claws clacking on the Airex hull.

Cautiously, I reached out a tentative hand. The bird came within inches of my fingertips, then scurried away. I withdrew and waited. When she came around again, I sprang.

Expecting a struggle when my fist closed around the spongy feathers, I was surprised when the pigeon went limp in my grasp. With both hands, I wiggled her into the right position, careful not to damage her satiny wings, and gently tugged one leg after the other from the ball of black-tipped feathers.

The right leg bore a green band with the inscription GB-93 R00 805. The GB must stand for Great Britain. On the left leg was a white band with the number 5985 written on it. That must be her entry number for the race she'd been flying when the wind drove her to me.

With the pigeon cradled gently in one hand, I searched out my ship log and scribbled down the numbers inscribed on the bands. When I finally got home myself, I'd trace the numbers and find out who she belonged to. Whoever her owner was, they'd probably get a kick out of knowing where she spent at least one night of her wayward journey.

Back up on deck, I set her free atop the solar panel and was pleased when she merely ruffled and settled down to preening her already immaculate mantle of iridescent feathers.

Great! She was going to stay! Maybe even until I sighted land. Wow! Company on board at last.

Only another solo sailor could appreciate the meaning of such a small thing. Tom McNally used to bring along a pet snail for company on his voyages.

Ernie Shackleton was the name of McNally's thumb-sized shipmate, so christened for E.L. Shackleton, the famed British explorer. E.L. Shackleton's most extraordinary adventure came in 1914, when he led twenty-eight men on an expedition to the South Polar continent. The goal was to cross the continent from sea to sea, but the encroaching Antarctic ice closed in on their ship, the *Endurance*. Imprisoned for ten months on the drifting ice pack, the crew lived on board until the tremendous pressure of the ice trap shattered the ship's hull.

For five bitter months, the crew survived on the slowly melting pack, until unpredictable fissures began ripping through the ice beneath their feet. Forced to take their chances with the horrific conditions at sea, Shackleton and his men loaded up three lifeboats and steered a course for the nearest firm land — barren, uninhabited Elephant Island, sixty miles to the northeast.

One week later they landed on its rocky, icebound shore, frostbitten and battered, only marginally better off than they had been on the ice floes. It was April and the Antarctic winter was moving in fast. There was no hope for rescue from the outside. Certain death awaited if they couldn't save themselves.

Shackleton and five other volunteers set out on the impossible task. The six men, vowing to return with help, set sail in the largest lifeboat for the only possible goal, a whaling station on South Georgia Island, eight hundred miles away.

The appalling, seventeen-day journey was a monument to human will and courage. Two of the crew were near death when they finally came ashore on a boulder-strewn beach, on the opposite side of the island from the whaling station. Shackleton and two others set out on foot over the glacier-encrusted mountain range that saddles the backbone of South Georgia. For thirty-six hours the three men, tied together with rope, struggled up and down snow-covered peaks, driven by desperation, afraid to stop for sleep lest they freeze. At one point, in the dark of night, their fading endurance on its last legs, they stood on the summit of a mile-long glacier.

Shackleton convinced the other two to sit close behind him, legs and arms around the man to the front. Rocketing down the face of the glacier, the three-man toboggan slid the mile in a couple of minutes, dropping more than two thousand feet in altitude. With no sled beneath them, and no idea what lay ahead in the darkness, I could appreciate their wild ride to the bottom. It must have been one hell of a scary trip. When they finally came to a stop at the end of the slope, the seats of their trousers were smoking.

At last they reached the warmth, food and safety of the station, and sent a borrowed whaler to pick up the three men left behind in a cave near the beach. It would take the rest of the winter and four attempts to rescue the crew shipwrecked on Elephant Island. But Shackleton never lost hope, ultimately saving each and every man from their nearly two year ordeal in the sinister clutches of hostile Antarctica.

Yes, McNally had given Ernie the snail quite a moniker to live up to. But, as might be expected when you ride with the daredevil McNally, Ernie had had his share of adventures as well. Most people wouldn't consider a snail much of a companion, but every speck of life was a comfort in the deep isolation of mid-ocean. I could understand McNally's attachment to Ernie.

Once, earlier in the voyage, I thought I caught a glimpse of a cockroach between the floor cushions of *Father's Day*. Excited at the prospect of sharing my ordeal with something — anything — I yanked back the cushions to find the black splotch was only a fallen dried date. I was amazed by the depth of my disappointment. Back home I'd have squashed the bug under the heel of my shoe. Out here, I was ready to take it to my bosom.

McNally's Ernie traveled in a matchbox when on board *Vera Hugh*. I first met the globe-trotting escargot when I bumped into McNally in St. John's.

Living on a budget so tight it creaked, the Englishman, to avoid dockage fees, had tied his *Vera Hugh* to the houseboat of his friend, Frank Pilgrim. Pilgrim was a former Canadian and Commonwealth light heavyweight boxing champion, once rated number one in the world behind the legendary Archie Moore. But boxing doesn't provide much of a pension for its heroes, so after his retirement in 1963, Pilgrim, still a grizzly of a man, took to fishing in the summer and lumberjacking in the winter.

To save money, Pilgrim docked his dilapidated *Kittiwake* in the only spot along the St. John's waterfront that no one else wanted, near the pipe that carried the raw sewage effluent of the town out to sea. Needless to say, the water around *Kittiwake* wasn't too pleasant.

But McNally wasn't too picky himself, and when he and Pilgrim became friends, McNally was happy enough to take the former champion up on his offer to tie *Vera Hugh* alongside *Kittiwake*.

On one morning, while McNally was puttering around *Vera Hugh*, preparing for an upcoming launch, a local reporter stopped by to see what he was up to. Ernie was out of his matchbox, taking one of his frequent strolls along the boat. Engrossed in conversation with the female reporter, McNally let his usually watchful eye drop, and Ernie slithered off his customary path on the edge of the deck into the dangerous territory of the underside.

By the time the ever-social Englishman remembered his little friend, Ernie had dropped with a plop into the rancid water below.

"Oh my God! Where's Ernie?" McNally was frantic, searching up and down every inch of the deck. "Where is he? I've got to find him!"

"Who?" the reporter asked. "Who's Ernie?"

"My snail! Oh, no! I can't believe this! I've lost him!"

"Snail? You're missing a snail?" She looked at McNally like his head had suddenly spun full circle.

"There he is!" he screamed, pointing at clump of brown floating just beneath the surface of the darker water. "He's overboard!" Without a moment's hesitation, McNally leaped off the edge of his boat into the freezing, sewage-laden harbor.

Hey, this was the same guy who just told her he couldn't swim worth a damn! And even a good swimmer would have to be crazy to jump into that disgusting water.

Nabbing the gunk-encrusted Ernie, fortunately still semi-afloat, McNally treaded water clumsily, a broad smile lighting his face.

"I got him! I got him!" he hollered. "Frank! Help me! Take Ernie! Grab him!" He held out a dripping hand to Frank, who stood watching from the dock.

"Hell, no!" Frank laughed. "I'm not touching either one of you! You stink!" He held out an oar for his shivering friend to grab on to.

A good hosing down and a bit of warming up restored both to their former selves, but the reporter had long since beat a hasty retreat.

Alas, in the end, poor Ernie met an untimely fate. He had the misfortune of being accidentally bailed overboard when *Vera Hugh* was rammed by a ferry off the coast of Portugal. McNally mourned his loss for weeks.

I was startled out of my reverie by the sound of flapping wings. The pigeon had taken off! Was she gone so soon? But one circle of the boat brought her back to rest on the solar panel, where she seemed to settle in. Fantastic. Looked like she was calling the place home.

She was probably hungry. And thirsty too. Down below, I pulled a slice of the Frenchmen's bread out of its wrapper and grabbed my water jug. Topside, I crumbled up the bread and placed it gently before her on the damp sweatshirt. But she showed no interest in my offering, so I tried the water. Spilling more than I could afford to, I filled the jug's cap with the vital clear liquid, and nudged it beneath her beak.

Nothing. No reaction at all. Oh, well, maybe she was too tuckered out. She'd probably be more accepting when she was rested.

By now the sun had climbed a little higher. Maybe I should try to take a picture of her. Ducking below again, I located my camera and slid back up through the hatch.

She was gone.

I combed the sky until I found her. But this time her graceful wings were beating their way east. This time she never looked back. And I couldn't stop watching until she vanished into the climbing sun.

I dragged my eyes off the spot where she disappeared, down to the pile of droppings decorating both my sweatshirt and the solar panel. Feeling like I'd been left at the altar, I brushed off the mess and stared after the long-gone pigeon.

She'd probably be home before nightfall, even in this rotten wind.

I hoped she'd make it. My heart felt so empty.

September 3rd
Day 82
381 miles to go

Helpless in the face of an ever-steady, southeast wind, *Father's Day* drifted northwest, its despondent captain teetering on the razor edge of his patience. I'll never get there like this! Hell, everybody — including my own mother — had been right all along.

I remembered the day I picked her up and drove her to our house to see *Father's Day*. My dad had died a few years back, at age ninety-three, the same age Mom is now. Dad had been so proud after my first voyage, and over the years, he'd grown into a treasured and irreplaceable friend. I still miss him.

But now, I was excited about showing my mother the just-built boat. It was a thing of great accomplishment to me, a miracle of creation, and I couldn't wait to see her face when she saw it.

Even in old age, my mother's mind was sharp as a bayonet, and the points she drove home were sometimes as painful.

Leaning on her cane in the cluttered garage, Mom's pale hazel eyes beheld our handiwork, standing shiny and resplendent on its altar in the center. With one swift fell of the blade, she delivered her opinion: "Is that all you have to do with your spare time?"

I could feel my face redden; my tongue stumble for recovery. She certainly had a way of putting me in my place. No one else affected me like that. All the years and all the accomplishments had done little to reduce her power over me. It didn't matter that I was a full-grown man now, confident, successful, mature. In the face of her disapproval, I felt like a naughty schoolboy caught playing in the groves when I should have been doing my chores. Well, she'd never been one to mince words. I should have predicted her reaction. To someone like Sadie, whose life had been dominated by the need to survive more than the pursuit of dreams, all of this stuff was a tremendous waste of time.

God knows she was right about that part anyway. I was wasting an awful lot of time right now.

Just before sunset, I picked up my log and searched out a pencil. Its lead point snapped with the first press on the damp paper and I once again sharpened the fragile tip with a small knife. The pencils had been nothing but a pain in the butt. I wasn't but a few weeks out when the three I'd brought became so waterlogged the wood swelled and all the leads fell out. I'd had to super-glue a couple of inches of lead back inside the wood casing in order to keep my daily journal. But at least I'd been able to do something to fix them. The ink pens had seized up almost immediately.

Tonight's entry: "Losing ground every day. Averaged 2.28 miles per day for past two weeks. Something has to change. I'm already in serious trouble."

September 7th
Day 86
415 miles to go

Change it did. But only for the worse. I was going backwards and fast.

For the past two days the waves were so wicked, I'd only managed to get one health food bar into my stomach. And I hadn't been able to use the bathroom either.

Urinating was tricky enough, lying on my side in the see-sawing boat, but I'd gotten the hang of it, using an empty water jug with the cap quickly replaced. A man's anatomy is a definite advantage when it comes to situations like this.

But even if I could manage a bowel movement in the pitching cabin, I couldn't open the hatch to dump my latrine. It was difficult enough in much calmer waters, since both me and the cut-off jug I used for the need wouldn't fit through the narrow hatch at the same time. It was a delicate maneuver in the best of conditions, timing the waves, opening the hatch, slithering through with the open jug held high overhead for a quick flip over the side.

I'd never manage it on a day like today. I'd end up either with the crap all over me, swamping the cabin, or both. The alternative of leaving it inside the cabin with me was just too unpleasant. Conditions in here were already bad enough!

My stomach was starting to knot painfully. Unable to decide if it was hunger or constipation, I moaned as another wave crashed over the stern and several cups of water rained down from the forward edge of the closed hatch above my head.

Damn it to hell! We should have found a way to seal that thing better! If I'd known it would be this rough this often, I'd have spared no expense making the boat more watertight.

As it was, I'd found another use for the soiled sweatshirt I'd offered the pigeon. Tying it to the boom gallows outside, I'd stuffed the excess into the pocket where the sliding hatch door recessed when open. It didn't stop the gap completely, especially in seas like this, but it did deflect the splash of the more timid swells.

That last wave carried a warning: There would be no food or bathroom use today either.

Several hours later, when it seemed the biggest of the waves were coming a little further apart, I darted through the hatch, desperate for a few moments in the fresh air.

But the instant my head cleared the opening I saw a leviathan bearing down. In my haste to get back inside, I banged my head on the exposed edge of the hatch door, slicing a quarter-sized gash in my forehead. The door slid shut just as the twenty-five foot wall of water slapped the boat with the force of a speeding train.

Like a child rooting for comfort, I curled up in a ball and closed my eyes tight, cradling my bleeding head on the life jacket, shielding my bruised body with my own aching arms.

This pitiless headwind had beat me one hundred and one miles to the north of Falmouth's latitude. I'd have my work cut out for me when it finally wore itself out.

**September 10th
Day 89
336 miles to go**

Thirty-six cheese sandwiches and eleven days later, I was finally back where I was when the *Centaure* handed over the huge hunk of Swiss and loaves of bread.

Knowing the fresh food would spoil quickly in the damp cabin, I'd devoured it ravenously, sparing my meager supplies further strain. But now the Frenchmen's gift was nearly gone, and while I'd replaced a few pounds on my emaciated frame, I'd really only gained a few miles. Basically, I was right back where I was before, when dwindling supplies had me relegated to half-rations.

It was hard to believe it only took eighty-five days to sail 4,480 miles in *April Fool*. I had no idea the modest little boat was such a speed demon.

In eighty-eight days at sea this time, I'd only covered one thousand five hundred thirty-seven miles. Of course, that was measuring my progress in a straight line.

In reality, I'd voyaged many more miles than that.

Unfortunately, too much of it was in the undesired direction.

September 11th
Day 90
315 miles to go

Blessed peace finally settled over the North Atlantic and I cranked the motor, intent on improving my mileage today. Six hours and fifteen minutes later, gas tank number one went dry.

The GPS told me I'd averaged the blazing speed of one mile an hour. What a waste of my precious fuel. There were six gallons of gas left in the other tank.

I couldn't risk using it, even if it had been worth it.

I'd need every ounce of that fuel when it came down to the end.

CHAPTER FOURTEEN

I don't know who named them "swells."
They should be called "awfuls."
— Hugo Vihlen, 1993

September 13th
Day 92
293 miles to go

A MARE'S TAIL ARCHED across the morning sky. The high, wispy stretch of clouds, shaped like the outflung tail of a high-stepping horse, meant only one thing to a sailor.

Trouble ahead.

There was nothing to do but sail on into the darkening stew to the east. Oddly enough, the west wind I'd waited so long for was suddenly now the enemy, muscling me into the heart of the maelstrom that lay ahead.

By late afternoon, the sea was rocking hard, the escalating gusts plowing the nose of *Father's Day* deeper and deeper into the multiplying swells.

I needed the mileage badly, but billowing even a little canvas would be too much in this blow. I'd better take the sails down now, before it got too bad to open the hatch.

I struggled up through the tight opening and glanced around.

Ho-lee-y smokes! Eyes round with fear, I measured the white-capped mountains that leaped and dipped on all sides. This was going to get a lot worse before it got better.

Straight off the bow, the writhing black ocean merged with an angry sky that seemed to have fallen from its customary place in the heavens.

"Ok, baby, here we go," I spoke aloud to my tiny ship. "This looks like the one we've been expecting."

I was leaning forward, twisting the bottom of the mast to wind in the remainder of the sails, when a stealthy wave sloshed over the stern, hitting me in the back with an icy slap. Even with my body filling most of the hatch opening, a good half gallon of ocean made its way past and into the cabin. Tonight was already going to be bad enough. A wet cabin would make it even more miserable.

A next wave was bigger, clawing for me as I hurried to secure the sails. Breaking over the boat with a cascade of liquid thunder, I was suddenly chest deep in ocean, as everything from the deck downward disappeared beneath the frothy, gushing surface.

For the next few minutes, I wasn't at all certain I would make it out alive, as a regiment of avalanching waves mounted a unified assault on the open-hatched *Father's Day*, each trying to shove the boat deeper and deeper under the sea.

Images of the boat spiraling downward, with me still standing in the hatch, scared the hell out of me. It would be too late to close myself up in the cabin then. If I tried to pull myself inside, the ocean, unhampered by my body mass in the hatch, would follow me inward with such power, there'd be no way to get the hatch closed before the tiny cabin was full.

As it was, if we'd made the hatch even an inch or two bigger, I'd be dying right now. Seawater gushed past my waist, down my legs and into the cabin with every toppling wave. It was already ankle deep. The boat wouldn't stay afloat very long like this.

At last, the sails were tied closed and *Father's Day* inched above the surface for a brief respite between waves.

I seized the opportunity to scramble below as a thirty-foot wall of water, the first in a long line of many, bore down on the minuscule boat.

The hatch banged shut just as the tidal wave smacked into the hull. Bam! My rag-doll body slammed into the far wall of the cabin, my already sore shoulder screaming in agony, the boat knocked limply on its side.

The valiant little ship righted itself with a jerk, only to be cold-cocked again and again. Outside the half-inch thick hull, the demonic wind howled, its mounting fury mirrored by the lathering seas.

Like a yo-yo on a string, I rode the stomach-twisting swells from trough to crest, trough to crest, trough to crest, until a swooping villainous wave even bigger than the rest would slam down and devour the tiny boat, mauling it in a merciless barrage. Each time a big one hit, icy fingers of water rained down inside the cabin around the inadequately sealed hatch.

"Lord, I know you've been good to me," I prayed as night crept in and I fought back the terror of confronting the storm in the pitching blackness. "Just get us through this one. Just get us through the night. Please don't forget me out here!"

All alone, in the dark, I tightened my seat belt and wedged whatever padding I could find around my body, keeping my busy sponge and small bucket close at hand. I couldn't even try to mop up the cabin in this mess, but at least I could sponge away some of the water that kept dribbling in on my head.

There was no other way to sit or lie; no place to move to that would allow me to get out from under that blasted leaking hatch. The cabin was too narrow to angle my body from side to side, even if I was willing to give up the security of the seat belt. And I'd bash myself to death on the radio rack if I turned the other way, with my head toward the bow and my legs under the hatch.

Every few minutes, another frigid cup or so of water hit my head and drooled down my face, into the neck of my polar jacket. I was glad that the temperature had turned progressively warmer as I beat my way east. Days in the 60s were commonplace now, and I'd been taking off the jacket more often up top during the day and slept without it at night.

I even did most of my after-hours compass checks in shirtsleeves now. As long as I hurried, it wasn't too bad, and when the hatch remained closed, my own body heat warmed the tight cabin to a fairly toasty temperature. The impact of my radiating body heat was apparent by the condensation that had to be continually wiped from the windows and by how much colder it felt inside the storage hatches of the hull. It was probably ten degrees colder in there, with only the thin outer hull for insulation against the North Atlantic.

But tonight I wore the polar jacket for padding as well as warmth in the face of the rapidly dropping storm temperatures. It was a good thing we'd cushioned the cabin interior with foam padding. Even with the seat belt pulled tight across my lap, I couldn't seem to keep my head out of the low flung ceiling.

The night wore on. Around 2 a.m., I gave up on the sponge and bucket routine. The water I'd painstakingly sponged up and squeezed into the bucket just sloshed back out over the rim anyway.

It no longer mattered. Everything, including me, was already drenched anyway. My back was racked with pain. Sitting in the scrunched-up position hour after hour was excruciating. I couldn't even feel my legs anymore. I had to change positions. The boat hadn't keeled over in a while. Maybe I could risk lying down.

Unfastening the seat belt, I scooted my numb butt forward until I was flat on my back, electric needles shooting through my now curled up legs as the blood began to flow once again. The surge of relief in my back was complete joy. I found if I tilted my head to either side just right, I could manage to avoid most of the shower around the forward edge of the overhead hatch.

And by planting my body as firmly as I could between the duffel bag, life vest and extra clothing, I was able to stay in one place. Well, most of the time anyway. The really big waves still managed to swat me around.

Nestling my chin deeper inside the damp lining of the jacket, I tried to convince myself it was ok to relax. But a man caught in a minefield has a hard time letting down his guard. Two peeled-open eyes stared relentlessly at the hatch above, mesmerized by the green shards of glowing phosphorescence dancing across the lexan with each breaking wave.

The neon specks reminded me of fireflies, flitting across a freshly mowed field, pungent with the smell of green growing things and the cooling earth at the close of a long, hot summer day.

God, I was homesick.

September 17th
Day 96
263 miles to go

Grateful I could still summon it, I retreated into the zombie state. The calm that followed the storm grated on my threadbare nerves worse than the gale itself.

The three days since it had let up brought a soft, chaotic wind that blew from all directions. With a ten-mile per day average for the past two weeks, there was no more counting of how many days to go, no more dreaming of the moment it was all over. My goal was just to get through each day. Progress was now gauged in sunrises and sunsets.

British Airways Flight 249 from London's Heathrow Airport flashed in the sun between gray tufts of clouds. Just this morning two distant freighters, one of each side of me, had neglected to answer my radio calls. Despite the morning's failures, I picked up the mike, and felt my cold heart warming at the sound of the co-pilot's voice.

Flight 249 was heading to Caracas, Venezuela, but its crew promised to call my family when they returned to England, two days from now. The co-pilot also insisted the toll was on him, despite my request that the call be collect.

As the sun sought its bed, I lay below doing the same, cursing the bad luck that had plagued me on this voyage. Unreliable radios, fickle winds, it seemed nearly everything plotted against me from the very start.

Feeling sorry for myself, I drifted into a restless sleep, with no inkling of just how blessed I'd been.

Unknown to me, Hurricane Floyd had just ripped a calamitous path up the English Channel. Several lives and numerous boats were lost up and down the English and French coasts. If I'd gotten the steady west wind I'd so fervently wished for, I'd have sailed right into the middle of hell.

Back home in South Florida, Johnnie was gently setting the phone back on its cradle, the conversation she'd just had with the British Coast Guard running in a loop through her head.

"As you may know, Mrs. Vihlen, Hurricane Floyd just came up the English Channel," the call began.

Oh my God, Johnnie recoiled on the other end. Was Hugo caught in the hurricane? Was her husband dead? Was this the call she'd been dreading?

"Yes, Captain, I know," she answered softly. She and Dana had been excruciatingly aware of every twist and turn of Floyd's wandering, lethal path.

"Have you heard from your husband lately?"

The question consoled her a little. They wouldn't be asking her, if they'd found anything, like Hugo's floating body or the shredded wreckage of *Father's Day*.

"It's been several weeks," Johnnie said slowly, remembering every word of the last message, the second one that came via the crew of the French marine aircraft. She recited the last known coordinates of her husband.

"We-e-ll, we're sure he's all right," the officer tried to comfort her quickly. "I wouldn't worry too much, Mrs. Vihlen."

If you were so sure of that you wouldn't be calling me, she reflected in the uncomfortable silence that followed.

"Let us know if you hear anything. Good day now." He hurried off the phone with a rapid click.

"Oh Hugo, why did you have to do this again?" Johnnie moaned the question aloud to the vacant room. "Why did you have to put us through this again? Isn't once enough for anybody?"

She wandered around the house, winding up in Hugo's alcove, the small hallway where the mementos of his first voyage were displayed.

There, in a heavy frame, hung the treasured letter from President Johnson. Half a dozen or so black and white photos were scattered around it, scenes of Hugo and *April Fool*, shots of him and her together after the trip, his arms wrapped around her in a warm, smothering bear hug.

To the left was the yellowed proclamation from the city, proclaiming a Hugo Vihlen Day in his hometown. A variety of certificates and notes of congratulations filled out the walls.

Everyone was so proud of him. They all thought what he did was so wonderful, so amazing, so admirable. It really was an incredible accomplishment. She had to admit it.

So why was she so mad at him?

September 19th
Day 98
215 miles to go

Twenty-two knot winds drove me toward Falmouth, as well as for cover below. Ten to fifteen-foot waves smothered *Father's Day* in a blustery blanket of froth and kept me entombed in the cabin, hustling with the bucket and sponge.

Suddenly, I noticed a change in the motion. Looking up through the hatch, I saw the red-and-orange sail cloth billowing over the lexan, toward the back of the boat.

That should never be! Something was terribly wrong!

Fumbling into the safety harness, I was through the hatch, assessing my precarious situation.

I'd been cruising with my half-opened sails in a tacking position, trying to gain maximum mileage to the east in the southwest wind. That meant tying the port boom in tight toward the rear, and the other boom forward toward the bow.

The wide V configuration had worked pretty well throughout the morning, but the amplifying waves of early afternoon must have pushed the nose of the boat around just enough for the wind to catch the other side of the sails and complete the job.

Now the bow was pointing back toward home, the flat-faced stern refusing to cut through the water as the relentless wind continued to steamroll us eastward.

The well-ballasted keel would probably keep us from tumbling head over heel, but the hatch was only an inch above the heaving waterline. Releasing the nearby port boom didn't help much, so I groped for the engine.

A while back, however, I'd stretched one of my T-shirts over the little outboard to protect its underside from the beating waves. Now the tight-fitting cotton wouldn't give me access to the starter cord. Cursing and twisting the shirt, I maneuvered the neck hole into the right position and reached inside for the cord.

The engine responded on the second yank, and I kicked it into gear to bring the bow back around. With the port boom still loosened, the boat wouldn't keep the heading, so I had to cut the engine long enough to re-tie the sail further forward.

The moment the little propeller stopped spinning, the bow was swept to the west again and waves scaled the stern. Racing through the motions, I tugged on the last knot and cranked the Evinrude once again. This time, the boat came around and held steady.

When it was over, all I could do was lie below, trying to slow my panting breath and pounding heart. I'd almost lost it that time. No wonder my silver hair was turning a ghostly white.

September 20th
Day 99
187 miles to go

With fewer than two hundred miles to go, it was time to set my watch to Britain's time zone. I had waited for this moment since the day I sailed out of St. John's.

Pulling out the tiny stainless steel knob, I gleefully turned the hands four hours ahead. It was time to let go of my psychological hold on home. I could afford to think in terms of my destination now.

I could also allow myself to fish out the charts and resume my studies. Ah ha. I was well past the Great Sole Bank, where the ocean floor rises from two thousand three hundred twenty-six fathoms to eight hundred forty-six. That explained the huge waves I'd been encountering.

Judging by today's GPS reading, I was now on the east side of the bank. The depth would decrease to about seven or eight fathoms over the next fifty miles or so, where it would remain for most of the duration of the voyage. The ocean here was ink black, even in the cloudless high noon sky.

It must have a muddy bottom. In South Florida, the water is a beautiful blue, no matter how deep, thanks to its sandy, white floor. And the warm southern ocean teems with sea life, especially when compared to up here. But wide-spread commercial fishing, pollution and habitat destruction had taken their toll, even in Florida's waters.

I'd noticed the changes long ago. There was a time when it was fairly easy to catch trophy-sized fish, even without a boat. Fishing from shore and bridges produced a nice-sized string of keepers. But now it usually took a lot of luck and plenty of hard offshore angling to make the effort pay off.

The bountiful waters of my youth had provided critical, affordable nourishment for the growing Vihlen children. My father and a close family friend, Mr. Jensen, used to have an all-business approach when it came to fishing to feed their hungry clans.

The two men built a small boat that had a wire basket hanging out over the bow. Near dusk, they'd head offshore, build a fire in the basket and wait for the light to attract the bugs, which in turn drew in the small fish, whose presence lured the bigger fish. When the water under the bow boiled with circling fish, they'd light the fuse on a quarter stick of dynamite and toss the charge into the fray.

Ka-boom! Dead and stunned fish would float to the surface and into their waiting nets. It wasn't a method I would approve of today. The fish were in enough trouble already, and dynamiting is illegal as well as destructive.

But I certainly didn't fault my dad for doing it. Times were tougher back then, and those fish went a long way toward sustaining the two families.

A deep satisfaction had come with the conservation projects I'd had a hand in. My Fish and Game Unlimited set an annual fundraising goal of $30,000 to aid the dwindling fish populations of our home waters.

One of our pet projects had been the creating of artificial reefs. Old freighters, no longer seaworthy, were sunk in a long staggered line, just outside the natural string of coral reefs. The huge ship hulls offered protection and additional habitat for all types of sea creatures. It was a legacy that would survive long after my demise.

The Air Force Reserves were called in to sink the old freighters. The eco-mission provided valuable target practice for training pilots.

One day in particular stood out in my mind. I was standing on a boat, watching the awesome F-4's zoom in from nowhere and disappear to the same, the scream from their engines exploding in my ears long after they were already gone. Dropping from the clouds, they dove on the rusting hull of a doomed freighter, bombs dropping like wicked confetti, the target ship sinking lower and lower with every exploding charge that found its mark.

In one of those jets was Dana, behind the stick of that glorious machine. I felt a stirring of envy. It must be something to sit at the controls and ride a supersonic rocket like that.

The fighter jets I'd flown in Korea were state-of-the art at the time. But compared to the incredible power, grace and feather touch control built into today's flying machines, the F3D was an albatross. Still, I'd gotten a good taste of the feeling, ripping through the sky with your stomach in your shoes and a fingernail hold on your fear. I remembered being constantly astounded that I was even allowed to touch such an expensive invention, much less that anyone would pay me for playing with it.

I was fortunate. Only a few ever know what it feels like. But my son knew. And I was happy for him.

It was one of my proudest days.

September 23rd
Day 102
122 miles to go

First thing on the morning list of chores, I dug the yellow quarantine flag from the bowels of a compartment, stretched it across my chest to smooth out the wrinkles and ran it to the top of the mast. The "Q" flag was required to alert Falmouth port authorities that I intended to come ashore and would be in need of a vessel health inspection.

The inspection was a routine part of international voyages,

and passing it was required before permission to enter the country would be granted. But it wasn't the inspection I was concerned about.

I had another reason to be unsure of the reception I'd receive in Falmouth. The voyage had taken so long that my passport was now expired. The date stamped inside had come and gone a week ago.

What if the port authorities denied me entry? It would almost be funny, in a demented sort of way. To survive all this, and be denied my victorious landfall by a lapsed passport. I could only hope the British officials would be reasonable.

By mid-morning, the outbound *Queen Elizabeth II* was in my line of sight once again, right behind a freighter I'd been unsuccessfully trying to contact. I immediately gave up on the freighter and focused my attention on raising the *QE II*. Its crew had been happy to help me before. I might even be able to get another call patched directly to Johnnie via that soaring, white ship's far-reaching electronics.

When the *QE II's* crew answered my radio call, it was like a visit with dear, old friends.

Delighted I didn't have to repeat my whole story again, my request for a call home was immediately processed. But before the international telephone patch could go through, the west bound passenger ship was moving out of range and my radio connection with her crew began breaking up.

"Forget the patch," I told them in a rush. "Just please make the call for me and tell her where I am. And can you please relay your latest weather report?"

It was more important that I get an accurate weather forecast while I still had the chance than to talk to my family in person. The next few days' winds would be everything when it came to the fate of my landfall.

Just a week ago I'd been way too far north of Falmouth, and had begun resigning myself to a beaching on the surf-pummeled rocks of Ireland's western shore. But a few days of the right wind had carried me back to the southeast; Falmouth had resumed its place as the target.

Today's north-bound wind had me a little worried though. *Father's Day* was still more than forty miles north of its intended latitude.

If this kept up, I'd better get my thoughts back on Ireland.

My buddy on the *QE II* told me to expect winds to shift from northwest to west to southwest. In other words, expect a kettle full of confusion and not a whole lot of cooperation.

Late in the day, I was able to catch the attention of another French trawler, whose crew sent over three loaves of bread, three big candy bars, sardines, butter, strawberry jam, salami and bananas.

I sat down to a feast, using a hastily wiped-off knife to spread the thick, chunky jam across slice after slice of soft, fresh bread. Smacking my lips with pleasure, I licked the sticky, red residue off my fingers and popped half a banana in my mouth. The fresh, ripe fruit was sheer bliss to my taste buds.

"Vive la France," I toasted with gratitude, the limp banana peel saluted in the direction of France.

That night, under September's full moon, I stood in the hatch, excitement making sleep elusive. Three months ago I'd have bet the house I wouldn't be out here under this fat moon tonight. This voyage was supposed to be over long ago. I'd figured on being home in my easy chair by now.

Well, only a few more days and this would all be history, something that would fade into memory — mine as well as everyone else's.

Sadness tinged the elation at nearing the journey's end. I was sixty-one years old now. Too old to believe I'd ever find myself out here again. Most men my age were at home tickling their grandchildren.

I had no idea what made me so different from them, no idea why my restless soul refused to be satisfied with the quiet comforts of home. Even now, still more than a hundred miles out to sea, I could feel the wanderlust bubble deep inside.

I just wasn't meant for the rocking chair.

I remembered, as a child, listening with rapt attention to family tales about my great-grandmother in Sweden. Her husband Carl, my great-grandfather, and their son Claus, who would eventually come to America, were both tapped by the King of Sweden for royal duty to the crown. Carl, a music teacher for more than fifty years, often soothed his royal highness with pleasant melodies, while Claus's green thumb was put to good use in the King's gardens.

But it was Great-Grandma Fredrika who always fascinated me. She was a midwife of some renown in Stockholm. During the latter half of the eighteenth century, Fredrika delivered more than three hundred babies, more than one on a sled at night, in the middle of the forest.

When she died, the community took up a collection and erected a special tombstone in her honor. She must have been fearless, a strong, brave woman. Her genes lived in my flesh, her courage in my spirit.

Maybe it all came down to heredity. The blood of adventurers and pioneers flowed through my heart. But why was everyone else in the family still at home?

Overhead, in the crisp, clear Atlantic night, the galaxies hung like wisps of stardust in the endless sky, almost within reach of my outstretched finger tips.

A part of me would mourn the journey's end.

September 24th
Day 103
120 miles to Falmouth
61 miles to Bishop Rock

Talk about coincidences. The famed Royal Navy Ship *HMS Endurance* came by at about dusk. True, the original *Endurance* had been crushed in the pack ice during Shackelton's 1914 ill-fated Antarctic expedition, but the British navy had simply built a new, updated version and christened it with the same legendary name. Each time one *Endurance* reached the age of retirement, a new one was commissioned to carry on the proud tradition.

This latest namesake was commanded by Captain D. A. Phillips. After radio contact was established, Phillips promptly dispatched an inflatable, bearing six gallons of gas, several magazines, a newspaper and a six-pack of cold beer. I popped the tab on one malted brew immediately, hoping to enjoy its bitter taste before the coldness wore away. A shiver galloped up my spine at the impact on my stomach.

The radio conversation with Phillips resumed, while his crew placed a call to Johnnie. The captain relayed the results. She'd received yesterday's message from the *QE II* and was heading out the door for the airport. Johnnie would be at the Falmouth dock, waiting for me to arrive.

That night I burned one of the tiny flashlights until its light glowed faint, poring over the British magazines and newspaper, my famished brain hungrily consuming the fresh information. I'd practically memorized all of my books on the long-ago second and third readings. This was like massaging an aching vacuum in my head.

When the light was finally extinguished, I settled contentedly on my side and let my thoughts roam. Sleep drugged my body.

September 25th
Day 104
98 miles to Falmouth
38 miles to Bishop Rock

In the thick, deep black of night, I spotted the flashing light of Bishop Rock, its pulsing white beam calling to me like a beacon from the great beyond. Minutes ticked by, as I stood in the hatch, transfixed by the light and what it meant to my world.

That beam was civilization. It was steady, dry ground, a warm bed, a hot meal, a long bath, a loving wife. It meant I'd scraped by once again, life would continue, and I'd probably die of old age at home, instead of out here alone in the cold Atlantic.

My luck had held. It was nearly over.

Over.

The word sounded hollow in my head. None of those things waiting on shore felt real. They seemed like a dream, like something I'd seen in a movie or lived in some long-forgotten life.

This was real, this water, these waves, this clean night wind rustling past my ears and sweeping through my mind. How would it feel to be with people again? To hold a quiet conversation or eat a meal with manners? To live indoors and forget to watch the sunset? To answer all their questions and wonder about their thoughts?

I suddenly felt uneasy at the prospect. There would be such

chaos on shore. So loud, so busy, so many people, all coming and going and talking to me at once. I wanted to share all of this with them, tell each and every one what an incredible adventure it had been.

But I'd never be able to make them feel it. It was something you had to live for yourself, every single hour of it, just like I had done. No amount of talking would ever make them truly understand it. There'd be no one I could fully share this thing with.

I felt utterly, and completely alone at the realization — in a much different way from my physical aloneness out here. I'd survived an ordeal, and it had changed me. I could feel it on my face.

Would it make me a stranger among my own kind?

I'd have to find McNally. McNally was the only one who could really appreciate what I'd been through.

I'd feel at home with McNally. It was probably the only place I would.

CHAPTER FIFTEEN

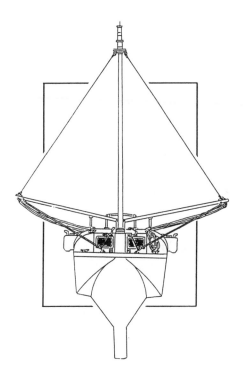

The world is a better place to live in because it contains people who will give up ease and security to do what they themselves believe worth doing. They do the useless, brave, noble, the divinely foolish and the very wisest things that are done by man. And what they prove is that man is no mere creature of his habits, no mere automaton in his routine, but that in the dust of which he is made, there is also fire, lighted now and then by great winds from the sky.
— *Epitaph to **Amelia Earhart***

September 26th, 1993
Day 105

THE WORLD RECORD was mine with the morning position fix off Bishop Rocks. The famed landmark itself lay hidden in the distance to the left, as my aim at the center of the broad channel carried me well south of England's southernmost peninsula.

It took three and a half months of what most people could consider hell to get here. I didn't even know if the world record I was breaking was my own or if McNally and *Vera Hugh* had been successful in beating that one during the long summer I'd spent at sea.

It didn't really matter. The record was mine for sure now. All mine.

Despite the hardships, despite my age, despite what everyone said. My shoulders felt lighter, chin a little higher. By God, I'd done it again. And it was over!

Well, almost over.

There was still the English Channel to contend with, and a northeast wind that was leaning toward France.

By 10 a.m., the sails were reefed as I tried in vain to hold my position, the wind escalating to a force four blow. This was the reason I'd headed for the middle of the seventy-five mile wide channel, instead of directly for Falmouth.

Compared to the wide-open sea, seventy-five miles was a stroll. A day or two of the wrong wind would easily eat that up. Sailing too close to either side could be a ruinous mistake if that adverse wind came along. The rocks on shore would be much less forgiving of meandering than the spacious sea had been, especially the forbidding Isles of Scilly.

My family would be in Falmouth by now. I knew my son well. If *Father's Day* didn't show up there soon, Dana would charter a boat and come looking for me. Finding me in these big swells would be a grueling, if not impossible, task.

Three times already this morning, I tried to contact as many passing freighters, hoping to get a message relayed to Falmouth. The effort produced nothing but a foul mood. No one on board the big ships heard my calls.

By noon I was ready to pack it in. With the record now under wraps, I could come up with little convincing argument for prolonging this part of the journey. It could take days or even weeks for a wind that would enable me to reach Falmouth on my own.

And even though I had yet to sight land on either side, I knew today's prevailing winds were moving me toward France.

Ｔrue, with the record bagged at Bishop Rocks, it made little difference where I landed now, though remaining in one piece was a definite priority. Local charts revealed mile after mile of brutal, rock-littered shoreline on both sides of the channel.

But even if I was lucky enough to wash up on a smooth spot, I didn't relish the thought of coming ashore in the midst of strangers who weren't expecting me. If this wind continued, I'd be separated from the familiar arms of my family by the breadth of the English Channel.

Very clearly, it was time to get to Falmouth. And the only way to get there appeared to be a commercial tow.

The British Coast Guard, that's who I needed. They could dispatch a tow boat to fetch me.

But they didn't answer my radio calls either.

Ｐreoccupied at the radio rack, I stayed below too long — an oversight that nearly ended the voyage in violent disaster.

By the time I admitted defeat at the radio and shimmied up through the hatch, my heart stumbled in mid-beat. I'd neglected to keep an eye on the third freighter, and it was bearing down on me like a train off a mountainside, no more than a football field away.

Obviously, my tiny boat was invisible to whoever was at its high-reaching helm.

Electric bolts of panic shot along my nerves as I snatched at the engine's starter cord.

"Come on sweetheart," I begged when she coughed and hesitated on the first pull. My pleading switched to cursing when the second yank fared no better.

The engine sputtered to life on the third try. The encroaching whirlpool of white water accompanying the advancing bow slipped behind as I motored safely out of the way.

The freighter barreled past without a backward glance.

Shakey and breathless, I cut the motor and tried to calm down.

"Good God, man!" I admonished myself for the carelessness that could have cost me whatever years I still had coming to me. "You almost blew it! Don't get stupid now! You've got to keep your guard up! You've come too far to screw it up now!"

My words were snatched away by the ferocious wind.

Resolved to be more careful, I kept a wary eye out.

Late in the afternoon, another fishing trawler appeared from the east. As it steadily consumed the distance between us, I waited with the engine humming, a white T-shirt clutched in my fist, determined to be noticed this time. I had flares, but I didn't want to use them unless I absolutely had to. A fiery orange flare arcing across the sky meant 'emergency,' a condition that simply didn't apply here.

True, some might consider being virtually adrift in a five-foot-four-inch boat as qualifying nicely for just such a description, but I'd just come nearly two thousand miles that way, so I couldn't justify calling it one now.

After all, I wasn't in any immediate danger of starving or sinking. My supplies, while not exactly a bumper crop, were adequate, thanks to the generous ships I'd encountered on this last leg. And my boat was a warrior. She'd been battered and bullied, her sparkle of newness long since worn away, but she still rode tight and true.

We'd been so right when it came to her construction. She'd kept me alive during the long, rough voyage, climbing back to her keel after blows that would have split many a bigger boat and sent its captain to his doom in the deep abyss.

Yes, the wrong wind could have us back out to sea, shamelessly begging for mercy, but I didn't want anyone to get the notion that I had to be helped ashore at the last minute. I'd seen on *April Fool* just how widely perceptions could differ. Next thing you know, someone's claiming to have "rescued" you at sea.

Even if it took a few more days and I missed a few more ships, the flares just weren't worth the message they'd convey.

The trawler loomed increasingly larger, until it was near enough for me to detect the sound of her bow wave.

When I figured her to be about a hundred yards away, I waved the white shirt in a few wide swoops over my head, plunged below and tried to raise the trawler.

When no response came, I resumed my shirt-waving position in the hatch. But the ship never hesitated or altered its head-on course. Nerves wire taut, I stood my ground in the risky game of nautical chicken. Prudence had come and gone by the time I kicked the idling engine in gear and scooted out of its path.

Desolate, I watched as the sixty-five or so feet of its red and black hull slipped by with no indication that anyone on board had seen me. I felt like an amoeba treading among elephants, too minuscule to catch anyone's attention no matter how much of a fuss I kicked up.

Turning away, a ragged sigh rattling in my chest, I stopped short, twisting my head back toward the outbound ship. Something was happening. The trawler's bow was swinging to the north and I could just make out tiny figures running about the deck, pulling in the fishing gear. The big net was winched up the side, reclaimed from the ocean with a cascade of dripping seawater.

The ship continued its about face and once again, the bow came around to bear on *Father's Day*. Only this time she slowed as she approached, coasting to a stop beside me in the still rolling swells.

I signaled with my arms held high, one thumb up on one hand and all five digits extended on the other. I heard one of the men on deck yell "Channel Six!" to the helmsman.

I don't think I've ever heard anything as sublimely beautiful as the brassy British accent that erupted from the radio.

"This is the *S.D.J. PZ 47* from Penzance, England," the voice announced with a lilt of amusement. "Capt. P. J. Downine in command. And who might you be, little friend?"

"This is Hugo Vihlen and the *Father's Day* from the United States. We're headed for Falmouth on a world-record voyage and are in need of assistance. My radios are malfunctioning. Please contact the British Coast Guard and request a commercial tow for me."

But the captain tossed out an offer too good to refuse. "There's no need for a tow, *Father's Day*. We'll pick you up in the morning on our way back to port."

Yahoo! I'd struck the Mother Lode! The only thing left to do was haggle over the price of my delivery. After settling on a bill of four hundred pounds, the trawler moved on to attend to the day's work at sea and I lolled inside the cabin, imagining every detail of the moment of my arrival.

It would all be finished tomorrow. How could it be that it was almost over? I'd been doing this for so long, I wasn't sure how I'd do at not doing it anymore. Functioning on automatic, I'd purposely dulled senses and emotions, needs and desires just enough to insulate my sanity and survive.

But now the end was so very close. I stood tall on my tiptoes in the hatch and inspected the horizon on both sides. Still no land to be seen, but if I inhaled deeply and filled my nostrils with the salty air, I could almost swear I could taste it. Yes, something different was definitely in the air. Land. It had to be land. Excitement bubbled in my blood, chasing away the last cobwebs of my voyage-induced aloofness.

Tonight would be my last one on board. By tomorrow night, I'd be stretched out in a warm, soft bed with real sheets and a real pillow and a very real Johnnie beside me.

Civilization would take some getting used to again, but I knew it would come.

I must look awful, though. The donated food had replaced a few pounds on my bony frame, but I was still at least thirty pounds lighter than I was when I left home. At least Johnnie had been schooled to expect it. She'd learned her lessons during the *April Fool* voyage, too. She probably was expecting me to look like a walking corpse.

Almost done. Almost there. Almost home. Unbelievable.

I was surprised when the trawler returned only two hours later. It took a few moments in the falling dusk before I convinced myself it was even the same one. Waiting in the hatch, watching her approach, I wondered what could have brought her back so soon. Pulling alongside, the crew was relieved to see me.

"Where ya been, Yank?" a fisherman yelled down over the side and across the gap to me. "We've been looking all over this ocean! We almost didn't find you!"

The sound of my name over the radio summoned me below.

"You're drifting too far toward France," came Downine's explanation for the early rendezvous. "When you weren't where we left you, we decided to come find you. No telling where you'll be by morning with this wind and current. If you hope to make Falmouth anytime soon, we'd better take you on now."

Well, sure, why not, if that's what the captain thought was

best. Cranking up the motor, I crossed the fifty feet of choppy water between us as a tall steel derrick swung out over the side.

Positioning my boat beneath its extended arms, I grabbed the dangling cables with a swipe, hooking them securely to the lift rings embedded in the hull of *Father's Day*. Every swell of the ocean drew the little red boat closer to the trawler's solid, pitching side. With one eye on the cold steel, I prepared my boat for the impending contact, pulling both booms in tight, tying them protectively within the relative safety zone of the hull.

Something was flicked over the trawler's top rail. A Jacob's ladder made of rope, unwinding as it fell. The end hit the water with a splash. While the ocean maneuvered me ever closer, I pulled my legs free of the hatch and knelt shakily on the deck, holding on to the mast for balance. When the ladder was within arm's length, I reached out and grabbed it.

Both feet found a wooden rung, but my fists still refused to ease their white-knuckled grip on the ropes. Dangling just above the waterline, I kept my eyes firmly fixed upward on the faces peering down over the rail. Beneath me, the substantially lightened *Father's Day* careened into the trawler with a bang. The dreaded sound went through me like a bullet, spurring my weakened body into action.

I had to get my butt up this ladder and out of harm's way before they could see to getting *Father's Day* on board. Wham! The two boats collided again with a nauseating thud.

Taking a deep breath, I forced my right hand to move upward. God, I was weak. My body felt like it weighed a thousand pounds, my legs rubbery from too many days without walking. My eyes, two leery pools of blue in a face as pale as drifted snow, followed the ladder all the way up the trawler's side. Though it was only a dozen feet or so, it looked like it stretched on forever.

One hand over the other, one rung at a time, I scaled the swaying ladder upward. Each passing wave caused the ship to roll from side to side, swinging me like a spider from a thread of web.

Strong hands reached over the side and pulled me the last few rungs. Landing on the deck with a wobble, I flashed a weak grin at the men who surrounded me.

The captain stepped forward and stuck out his hand. "Pleased to meet you, Vihlen. Welcome aboard."

"Yes, yes, pull her up," was all I could manage between labored breaths.

The captain gave the signal, and the winch groaned into motion. Turning my back on the greeting party, I leaned out over the side, anxious to catch a glimpse of red below.

She looked ok, as far as I could tell from up here. The cables whined as they hefted the little boat's full weight and she began her ascent. But as soon as she had shaken off the restraining hand of the ocean, the boat began to swing like a pendulum in ever-widening arcs, every wave exaggerating the motion further.

I held my breath, unable to do anything to stop the inevitable. Slam-m-m! *Father's Day* crashed into the side of the rolling trawler. I squeezed my eyes shut, fists pressed to my face. This was torture! It felt like I was taking the beating myself. It didn't matter that the adventure was nearly over and I'd probably never sail her again. I'd protected her so long. I simply couldn't stop now. Especially now. Not after all she'd been to me on this voyage.

The next blow snapped off the navigation light at the top of the mast. Feeling like I'd been personally sucker-punched, my anxiety raged, barely under wraps, until the crane finally hoisted the tiny sailboat above the bulwark wall and swung her over the deck. I headed for the spot where the crane operator aimed his load, one of the few clear spaces to be found on the crowded work deck. It felt strange to walk after being confined for so long. My uncoordinated gait, as ungainly as a toddler, made running impossible. But my straining hands were still the first ones to touch *Father's Day* as she was lowered onto the stern, sea water weeping from her keel.

The boat had to be settled to the deck at an angle on her side, the deep keel making it impossible to set her upright without a special frame. Hovering like a worried mother, my relief was immense when the damage appeared minor.

Now there was time to be civil. Reaching for the captain's hand, I pumped it vigorously. "Thank you captain. Thank you for everything."

But Downine wasn't listening. The captain, examining *Father's Day* with a critical eye, brushed aside my show of gratitude absentmindedly. "Mr. Vihlen, I hate to tell you this, but we can't fish with your boat on board," Downine said. "I'm afraid it's in the way of our gear. You'll have to compensate us for a day of lost fishing."

My brain was sluggish. "I see," I answered slowly. "Well, how much will that be?"

"Twenty-five hundred pounds," Downine replied.

I gasped, choking on the quoted price. "But Captain, that's almost $3,000 dollars in American money! That's outrageous for a tow to shore!!"

"I'm sorry," the captain shook his head firmly. "But we can't fish with that boat sitting there so you'll have to pay for it if you want to go to Falmouth." He punctuated the sentence with a jab of his finger at my chest.

"No way, Downine," I shot back stubbornly. "That's downright robbery. You can put me back in the water right now if you expect that kind of money."

It was a good thing *Father's Day* hadn't been seriously damaged in the loading. It looked like I might need her again right now.

"Well, that's a fine thing, Vihlen!" the captain shouted back. "That's just what we'll do!" Downine stalked off angrily, cursing the ungrateful American.

I slumped down on a nearby crate, drained and uncertain. Maybe I should just go ahead and pay the exorbitant fee. After all, they did come to look for me and if taking me to shore was really costing them a day's fishing, maybe it was a reasonable price.

But that wasn't the point. What stuck in my craw was the fact that I would have turned down the offer immediately if Downine's original bill had been even half of what he wanted now. I simply would have bided my time and waited for another opportunity for a tow.

Maybe I just wasn't desperate enough yet.

I shook off all doubts. I'd stick to my guns. I wasn't going to end this thing on a note I'd regret, being taken advantage of by someone who smelled a quick buck.

Downine was striding toward me. I rose, both palms upheld

in protest. But the captain took the wind from my sails.

"Forget it, Vihlen," the Englishman said resignedly. "We'll take you in anyway."

I grinned. Now it was my turn: "You know I can't pay you until we get to shore, don't you?"

"Yeah, yeah, whatever you say." The captain walked away with a capitulating wave of his hand.

I was offered what hospitality there was, a meal and a small cabin to call my own for the night. With twelve hours between us and Falmouth, it would be morning before the trawler arrived.

One radio call to the Coast Guard turned up the name and phone number of the hotel where my family could be found. My son had been in touch with the Coast Guard since the moment he arrived in Falmouth.

The helmsman patched me through to the bed and breakfast, where I left the following message with the proprietor: "Will be one mile offshore at 9 a.m. tomorrow."

"Sign it from Hugo," I instructed the man lastly, as if my family wouldn't know exactly who the message was from.

I was coming the last mile on my own. I'd already arranged for Downine's men to put my boat back in the water just out from Falmouth. I'd sacrificed too much to deny myself a single detail of the triumphant arrival.

That night I slept fitfully, unaccustomed to my surroundings and the drone of the diesel engines, excited about what I knew the dawn would bring. At midnight, I gave up trying and made my way topside to pace the deck. No one was about. I preferred it that way.

There was still no sign of land, no lights from on shore; just the sparkle of the stars and the soft glow of a cookie-cutter moon. I worked my way forward, around the boxes and piles, and found refuge in the deep shadow cast by the resting *Father's Day*.

Sinking to the deck, I leaned my back against her bulk and admired the galaxies overhead one more time.

The stars just don't glitter like this when you're standing on dry land. A trace of sadness tinged the observation. Turning my head, I rubbed my cheek on the cool, smooth, miraculous Airex of her hull.

"You must be so tired, my girl." I patted her like a rider strokes a gallant steed when the race is won. "You did so good. So very, very good."

I wished I'd realized last night that it would be my last one on board. I'd have done something special, something symbolic to commemorate it. I had no inkling of what it would have been.

It wasn't as if I had a long list of exciting things to choose from. But I'd have noted it somehow, so that in years to come I could have closed my eyes, turned inward and mustered the feeling of my last night at sea on what was most likely the greatest adventure of my life.

A hot blush of nostalgia washed over me, forcing me impatiently to my feet. What was wrong with me? This trip had been a living hell! Why on earth was I missing it already?

Tilted as *Father's Day* was on her side, it was an easy reach up to open the hatch. The scent of the cabin rushed out to greet me, the smell more familiar now than the aromas of my own home. It was a mix of canvas and musty dampness, human occupation and not enough baths.

But it wasn't offensive. At least not to me. It was a scent I would forever recognize, one that would never wear off; a scent I'd notice in years to come, every time I opened the hatch to show the boat to a curious visitor.

It was hard to believe I'd spent three and a half months of my life inside that little box of a cabin. At least 30 days had been spent sealed entirely inside — held hostage by seas fourteen to more than twenty feet.

With my feet planted firmly on the trawler's rambling deck, the sailboat looked ridiculously small.

Running my hand down her side, I trailed my way back to the stern, where I resumed my study of the heavens, one shoulder propped against the hull.

The wind was fresh and cool back here, untainted by the foul-smelling diesel engines. I wished I could slow everything down just a little, grab on to this moment and wring every drop from it. Tonight the voyage, the world record, the triumph was exclusively mine. Tomorrow, I would have to share it all with the world.

The wee hours came and went before I was willing to forsake my last night at sea to seek my berth again.

Up at the first sign of sunrise, I paced the deck, ready for the sight of land. There it was. A dark blur on the horizon. I stared at it transfixed. It was really land. It had been so long since I'd seen it. But there it was.

I'd come all the way across an ocean. And here I was on the other side. I was slightly amazed at that accomplishment alone, even though I'd crossed the Atlantic before, way back in *April Fool*, and hundreds of times in the air. I was a much better navigator than I was a sailor. Finding my way from point A to point B wasn't the triumph here. It was doing it at a crawl, one wave at a time, all alone in the smallest boat ever to do so. Truth was, I didn't consider myself much of a sailor at all.

The voyage wasn't intended to be a sailing feat, though it certainly was that in its own right. But it wasn't a love of sailing that lured me out here. Yes, I'd enjoyed it a lot when I was younger, but in the era that followed *April Fool*, years flew by between sailing trips with friends. And in all that time, I hadn't ventured out a single time alone.

No, my Atlantic voyages had little to do with a desire to set a sailing record. But they had everything to do with the dream of a world record. I supposed it really wouldn't have mattered if I'd chosen a pogo stick or the world's smallest boat, as long as it had a shred of dignity, and I stood a chance of winning.

"I must be a hopelessly competitive man," I reflected as the stripe of land gradually grew solid and began to take on three dimensional proportions. "It's a wonder anyone can stand me at all."

By 9 a.m., we were a mile off the coast of Falmouth, and I was once again dangling from the end of the ladder, one foot on the bottom rung, the other on the wobbling deck of *Father's Day*.

Downine had turned out to be quite a decent guy after all. Not wishing to steal another man's thunder, the captain didn't even argue when I asked him to set *Father's Day* back in the water so I could come ashore unassisted.

Trusting me to pay him later as I said I would, the captain shook my hand, wished me luck and ordered his men to comply with my request.

Back in my familiar position in the hatch, I was just pushing away from the trawler's side when I heard a commotion behind me. It was a boat, a thirty-foot open fishing boat packed with people, and they were all waving and yelling at me.

Maybe, just maybe, it carried the faces I was longing to see. I examined every form at the rails, discarding and eliminating those that couldn't possibly belong to anyone in my family.

There she was. It was Johnnie. And there were Dana and Nancy beside her. I could see my son's broad grin from here, his waving arms high over his head.

A rapid tug fired the motor and I closed the gap between us, my eyes transfixed by their profiles. Cutting the engine, I coasted to a stop with the gentle bumping of hulls.

Cameras were flashing and hands were reaching across the rails. Everybody seemed to be talking at once, a verbal barrage that made me recoil. I reached out to Johnnie, but the tepid morning swells instantly widened the space between the boats, and my arms came back empty.

I tried to speak, to respond to the questions and shouts of greeting, but my voice choked and died in my throat, and my vision clouded with tears.

Embarrassed at my unexpected display of emotion, I clamped both hands over my face and collapsed downward into the cabin. Several moments passed before I trusted myself to emerge again, this time with a two-fisted grip on my emotions. Johnnie was still waiting anxiously at the rail, and hers was the first face I saw when I surfaced through the hatch. Grabbing a tossed rope, pulling my boat closer. I reached for her like a lifeline. She leaned down to meet me and I buried my face in the soft crook of her shoulder.

"We made it! I told you we'd make it! I told you. I told you," was all I could say, as she cradled my head on her chest and smoothed my tangled hair. "I'm sorry I couldn't call you. I'm so sorry." I was blubbering out of control.

"It's okay, Hugo. It's okay." Johnnie comforted me like a wounded child. "Don't worry about it. It's all over now. You're alive. That's all that matters. Thank God you're alive."

From deep in the rear of the pack, Dana hung back, brows lowered in concern as he watched his dad's confused attempts to respond to a crossfire of questions from the reporters: What had he eaten? What took him so long? What about the storms? The loneliness? The waves?

He heard Hugo stutter and stumble over his words, each answer splintered by tearful sobs.

What had happened to his father out there? Dana looked closely: He looked and sounded so different from the eternally strong, imperviously confident man the son had always known. There was something foreign in his eyes, something new in his mannerisms. He looked almost fragile, like a man who'd been to the precipice of endurance and had seen what lies just over its edge. The blue eyes, always so piercingly steady, now blinked rapidly. His shoulders, perpetually Marine ramrod, were now hunched forward in a profile Dana didn't even recognize. That wasn't the same guy who sailed out of St. John's.

Dana took a halting step forward, then hesitated as his trembling father wrestled his way out of the hatch, climbed up and over the rail and stumbled onto the press boat. A thrust of helping hands reached to steady him as Hugo straightened his back, a wince of pain flicking across his face. Watery eyes lifted and connected with Dana's worried ones.

A spark flickered and warmed the blue. Hugo's hand curled into a triumphant fist that rose high and proud in a jab of victory.

"Manifestly unsafe my ass!" he roared at his son. Dana saw the familiar fire ignite the weary face.

Ah, there was his old man. That was a face he knew. His dad would be all right. But it was obvious he'd taken a brutal beating. Both body and psyche bore the evidence. It must have been even worse out there than they imagined.

Dana couldn't help marveling. Even with all the meticulous planning, they'd understood the odds from the onset. Standing on that windswept bluff in St. John's, watching until his dad was nothing but a memory on the horizon, he'd known full well that this might be the last the world would ever hear of Hugo Vihlen.

But, somehow he did it. Here was his dad, on the other side

of the ocean, just as he said he would be. Somehow, he withstood it.

A slow smile spread across both of their faces and Dana's strong hand closed tightly around his dad's. Hugo had returned with his life and with a new world record.

Equally important, he had returned with honor.

There is no thrill in easy sailing when the skies are clear and blue,
there's no joy in merely doing things which everyone can do.
But there is some satisfaction that is mightily sweet to take
when you reach a destination that you never thought you'd make.
                                                    —Spirella

EPILOGUE

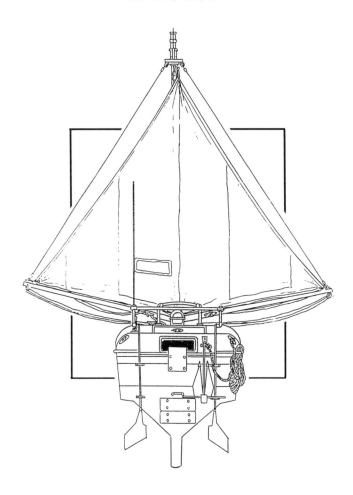

THE NEXT FEW DAYS streamed by in a headlong rush of activity. I regained my physical strength rapidly, though it would be several weeks before my shoulders and upper back lost their stoop, acquired in the cramped dimensions of the tiny cabin. Energy returned with each calorie consumed, though my first day on land was fueled primarily by high-octane adrenalin.

Looking back on it now, it was a wonder I didn't simply collapse. I was drunk with exhaustion, inebriated with anxiety, my stomach a contortion of nerves. Food was the last thing on my mind.

Someone in the small gathering on shore shoved a Falmouth Pasty in my hand, a burger-sized pie concocted of beef and potatoes in a golden brown crust, a dish for which Falmouth is apparently well known. Not wanting to seem unappreciative, I gave it my all, managing to persuade a few bites past my dry, sticky throat.

Judging by the scrambling going on, it appeared I'd caught just about everyone unprepared. Coming the last leg by trawler had surprised them. The big ship covered the miles much faster than *Father's Day*, and I'd made it to shore much sooner than anyone had calculated.

The famous Royal Cornwall Yacht Club, where the press boat unloaded its burden, was closed as it usually is on Mondays, its sea-loving members oblivious to the opportunities missed on their own front lawn that very day.

A neighbor and member of the club, Pam Richardson, embarrassed at the lack of organized pageantry, ran to fetch the requisite champagne from her own kitchen cupboards. She returned moments later, flushed and out of breath, a couple of glasses in one hand and a dusty bottle in the other.

"I've been saving this champagne for thirty years," the woman said as the cork popped with a volcano of foam. "I think this occasion will do."

Obsessed by the fantasy of a steamy hot shower, and weak from the ordeal, I was content with the comparatively quiet reception.

When the champagne ran dry, I extracted myself from the reporters and well-wishers and let Johnnie assist me to the front seat of a rented car, her arm under mine, giving support. Whisked to a small inn, I indulged my uppermost desire — a shower — until my fingertips bunched into little mountains of water-logged wrinkles, my skin and scalp tingling from vigorous scrubbing.

Johnnie had seen to my wardrobe. Newly purchased clothes, several sizes smaller than my norm, were donned and found wearable, if still a bit on the baggy side. Most everyone was determined to feed me, no doubt inspired by my sapling thin body. I was taken downstairs by the family for a hearty lunch of fish and chips, but afterward, I barely remembered what I ate.

Funny, I'd thought about food almost ceaselessly on the ocean. Now that it was available in an endless supply, I was too wound up to enjoy it. The same held true when Tom McNally joined us for dinner that evening, though my lack of interest in that meal was most likely the result of my delight in a visit with my cherished friend.

My success had ripped McNally's short-lived world record into tatters. The half-an-inch size difference between our two boats was as good as half a foot or half a mile. But McNally didn't begrudge me the victory. Both of us had realized long ago our rivalry on the ocean didn't extend to dry land. We enjoyed each other's company too much to allow that. But God only knew what would happen should we ever meet at sea.

That night I slept like a dead man, falling into a deep, dreamless stupor the moment my body dropped on the downy mattress. I awoke before sunrise, and lay in the half-light of dawn, content for the moment just to lie still in a room that did the same, listening to the soft, steady breathing of my slumbering wife beside me. Slipping out of bed, I padded across the cold floor in my bare feet, searching for my clothes. By the time everyone else was stirring and stretching, I'd already explored the neighborhood, returning with an armload of newspapers, each packing a tale of yesterday's arrival of an odd little boat from America.

The following days were consumed by receptions and ceremonies, official luncheons and dinners, as the British scurried to compensate for my unexpected time of arrival. I answered questions and shook hands with an attentive smile, the preordained responses rolling off my tongue with ever-increasing lubrication.

But underneath it all I felt like a refugee, painfully out of place amid the clink of cut crystal, the clatter of fine china and the warm glow of candlelit rooms. I'd been immersed in survival for too long.

Falmouth port authorities proved to be sympathetic. Caught up in the excitement of the journey's end, I had forgotten all about my expired passport. Several days after my arrival, port officials, alerted to my presence by an avalanche of local news coverage, dropped by to bestow a temporary extension on my passport.

Arrangements were made to ship *Father's Day* home. Three days later, I found myself crossing the North Atlantic again, only this time I was in a window seat of a Delta L-1011, with Johnnie next to me, contentedly thumbing through a magazine. Dana and Nancy were in the row behind.

On the other side of the thick, double-paned window, the mud-colored ocean swept into the distance as far as my eyes could take me. The sea was so very different from up here, a vast, corrugated reflecting disk, as impressive in its perfection as it is in its proportions.

The phone was ringing when the front door swung open and I thankfully crossed the threshold into my house. It was a trend that would continue for months as guest shots on national television and numerous magazine and news articles informed the world I'd made it home alive.

My mid-journey message in a bottle, tossed over the side more than nine hundred miles from anywhere, has yet to surface, but my short-lived companion, the beautiful, exhausted racing pigeon was easy to trace. Running her band numbers through the computer of the sport's British Racing Association revealed she belonged to Dennis Hearnshaw of Rochdale, Lancashire. Hearnshaw had last seen her in June, 1992, when she failed to find the home loft after a race from Weymouth.

To have her appear more than a year later, in the middle of the Atlantic, had Hearnshaw perplexed. He supposed another pigeon flyer had taken her in after the Weymouth competition. The numbers on the second band led to a race flown from France. She must have been flying in it when she went off course, eventually landing on *Father's Day*.

Where she was headed from there is anyone's guess, but if it was to Hearnshaw's loft, she never made it.

I was pleased to learn that every message I'd relayed home from sea had made its way to my family. Each pilot, each captain had kept his word and seen to my requests. It was a small payback indeed, but in return, I called the ones I knew how to reach, thanked them exuberantly and promised to send a copy of my forthcoming book on the voyage.

The good-luck penny with the misprinted date was returned

to David Osborne. I can only hope he cherishes it as I did on *Father's Day*.

By Christmas, I'd shaved off the itchy beard, shed the nervous tics and replaced most of the thirty-four pounds I'd lost. A lot of folks preferred the beard and were openly disappointed when it was gone. Maybe they thought a sea captain should have one.

But I'd endured it longer than I wanted to, remembering with disdain the uncomfortable fake one I'd had to wear for publicity photos after being in too much of a rush to shave off my *April Fool* whiskers. Then, a number of photographers and TV show hosts had insisted I be bearded, just as I'd been on the day of my arrival, when my image had been flashed around the world.

With a characteristic lack of patience in relaxing, I soon found myself on the road again, crisscrossing the nation with *Father's Day* in tow. Only this time I wasn't hiding from anyone. In demand at an apparently never-ending stream of boat shows, I and *Father's Day* enjoyed an enthusiastic tide of interested and impressed fans.

Without fail, the inquisitive walk around the tiny boat and circle back to where I sit, shaking their heads in disbelief.

"You crossed the Atlantic in this?" always comes first.

"Why?" inevitably follows my nod of confirmation.

For that there's no glib answer, at least not for me. It's an unanswerable enigma for a man who hopes to die peacefully in bed but is fully prepared to do otherwise.

Why look beyond the everyday? Or ponder the mysteries of the universe? Why hope for the future, even when it extends beyond our own lifespan? Why even get out of bed?

So much more than the sum of flesh and bones, the quest for the next challenge runs like sinew through the fabric of the human soul.

Those like me hunger openly for the test. It's an appetite the years and the victories simply don't appease for long. Casting an eye down the road toward age seventy, I'm busy planning another assault on my second world record. Much to the vexation of Johnnie, a Naval architect is hard at work, designing a three-foot-eight-inch aluminum boat for my third voyage, this one a re-tracing of my original Trade Winds route, set for the year 2002. My goal is to bring the East to West record back to the U.S.A.

But how much smaller can I expect a viable boat to be? One day, inescapably, I'll reach the boundary between small enough and too small.

As might be expected, I harbor faith.

To those who ask, I simply reply with a grin: "Don't be surprised if one day, I come ashore with a handkerchief held over my head and toothpicks strapped to my feet."

ACKNOWLEDGEMENTS

Thanks to the following for their invaluable help on this book: Johnnie, my wife of forty-plus years, and Dana, my son. Also, special thanks to U.S. Navy Commander (retired) Tony R. DeMarco for his editing skills and advice.

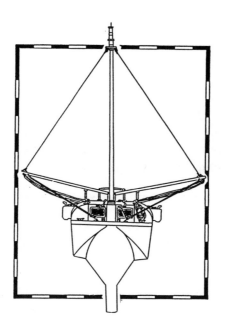

APPENDICES

TRIBUTE

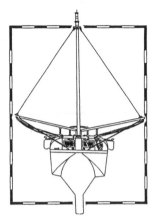

There are others who dared to cross big oceans alone in small boats and lived to tell the tale. Here are some of the most notable voyages sailed in craft smaller than twenty feet in length.

North Atlantic - East to West

Dr. Alain Bombard

Bombard's voyage was unique. The French doctor of medicine is the only known person to deliberately set sail on the ocean without food and fresh water. Bombard was twenty-seven years old when he went to sea in search of something more important than world records, though he managed to set one in the process.

His 1952 journey in the fifteen-foot *L'Heretique* from the Canary Islands to the West Indies proved that humans could survive at sea with nothing more than could be gleaned from the ocean.

For sixty-five days, Bombard sailed his short-masted, collapsible rubber dinghy, surviving on raw fish, plankton and small amounts of seawater. He arrived in Barbados fifty-five pounds lighter, but very much alive.

His voyage has been an inspiration of survival to other sailors who suddenly found themselves shipwrecked or adrift at sea unprepared.

Jean Lacombe

This French photographer boarded the eighteen-foot *Hippocampe* on April 19, 1955 and set sail from the Mediterranean seaport of Toulon in his homeland. Lacombe followed the trade winds route to the south with ports of call in Barcelona, Magazan, Las Palmas, Puerto Rico and Atlantic City.

Ninety-three days out of France, July 20, 1955, he came ashore in New York. His longest stretch of solitude was the sixty-eight days from Las Palmas in the Canary Islands to Puerto Rico.

The adventurous Lacombe would later finish dead last in the first single-handed race from east to west across the Atlantic, held in 1960. His *Cape Horn*, slightly larger than the *Hippocampe* at twenty-one feet overall, took sixty-nine days to sail from Plymouth, England across the finish line just offshore of New York. The winner of that race, in a thirty-nine-foot boat, claimed victory in only forty days.

Dr. Hannes Lindemann

Lindemann's milestones at sea came in the mid-1950s. A German working in Liberia for an American rubber company, Dr. Lindemann is notable in this chapter for crossing the North Atlantic twice in what amounted to modified dugout canoes.

Lindemann's second craft, the seventeen-foot-one-inch, fifty-nine pound *Liberia III*, was smaller than her predecessor, the *Liberia II*. Both were fitted with closed decking, sails and outstretched corkwood stabilizers. Lindemann shipped *Liberia III* to Las Palmas, Canary Islands, where he set sail on October 20, 1956. Seventy-six days later, December 31st, he arrived in the Leeward Islands' St. Martin. It was a rough trip for Lindemann. He lost fifty pounds on the voyage.

Hugo Vihlen

1968, six-foot *April Fool*.

Tom McNally

Englishman Tom McNally seized Hugo's world record for the

smallest boat crossing in either direction with a voyage of eighty-nine days in 1993. The gentleman from Liverpool sailed his five-feet-four-and-a-half-inch *Vera Hugh Pride of Merseyside* from Sagres, Portugal to Fort Lauderdale, Florida, for his eighth transatlantic crossing.

Along the way he was rammed by a ferry, ran out of food and had to survive on raw fish. McNally arrived at a stopover in Puerto Rico with kidney failure from drinking salt-tainted water. It was in that port that he received the news that his son had committed suicide.

McNally sailed on, despite a broken heart, only to have Hugo retake the record on September 26, 1993.

North Atlantic - West to East

Alfred Johnson

The first person to cross the Atlantic alone was Alfred Johnson, a young Newfoundland Grand Banks fisherman. His twenty-foot dory *Centennial* was a gaff-rigged cutter with a small bowsprit. She was decked over except for a small cockpit, which Johnson could cover with canvas. He sailed from Gloucester, New Brunswick, on June 15, 1876.

Before an approaching gale, he removed his mast and lashed it on deck. A huge waved turned the little boat upside down, with Johnson hanging on the bottom for twenty minutes because the iron ballast had fallen to the now-submerged top of the boat. He finally managed to right the boat and bail her out, and with all his food, clothing and bedding saturated, he continued on to Albertcastle, England. The voyage took sixty-four days. After a two-day rest, he continued on to Liverpool.

Josiah W. Lawlor

In 1881, Lawlor had heard about William Andrews' forthcoming attempt to cross the Atlantic and proposed a race between the two boats. The two boats were 15 feet in length. However, Lawlor's boat, *Sea Serpent* was designed by his father, a naval architect. The race began June 21, 1891, from Boston to any port in England.

Enroute, Andrews' *Mermaid* capsized twice; he was finally

rescued in an exhausted condition 600 miles from the European coastline.

Lawlor sailed *Sea Serpent* as fast as she would go. For a safer passage, the boat had two air-tight compartments as well as a six-foot long, twenty inch cockpit that Lawlor could cover. During a gale, his boat capsized while he was wearing three layers of clothing with hip boots, which filled with water. He was washed overboard but saved by his safety line. Twenty miles from Lizard Point, England, his boat flipped over once more.

During his voyage a shark kept rubbing up against his boat, so Lawlor took a patent yacht salute, which made a noise like a cannon, wrapped it in newspaper, lit the fuse and threw it overboard. The shark went for it just as the salute exploded.

Lawlor arrived safely at Coverack, England, on August 5, forty-five days out of Boston.

Andrews challenged Lawlor to another race the next year and both men built new boats. Lawlor named his *Christopher Columbus*, with dimensions of fourteen feet six inch in length and carrying three hundred fifty pounds of ballast on her keel. During his race to Palos, Spain, Lawlor disappeared at sea.

Paul Muller

A penniless German with no sailing experience, Paul Muller left Hamburg, Germany, in July 1928 in an eighteen-foot converted fishing boat *Aga*, begging his way along. After running aground for five days at the mouth of the Elbe River, in north Germany, he continued on to cities in France, Spain, Portugal and Morocco before sailing to Cape Jube, Africa, and then on to the Canary Islands.

He averaged only twenty-four miles a day because his boat had a badly fouled bottom and he could not afford bottom paint.

Nine weeks later, suffering from exhaustion and starvation, Muller landed on one of the Bahama Islands, then went on to Cuba and arrived June 1, 1929, in Miami, Florida. He put to sea again for New York, but fell asleep and ran aground in Fernandia, Florida, damaging his boat considerably.

After making repairs, he sailed again but ran into bad

weather and beached *Aga* near Charleston, South Carolina, where he set his boat on fire.

Twenty years later, he set sail in a sixteen-foot boat named *Berlin* from Germany to South America with his eighteen-year-old daughter. During the voyage, Muller died somewhere on the northwest coast of Africa. His daughter made it to safety after walking barefoot to the nearest village.

William Albert Andrews

Surviving six extended voyages in tiny boats, William Albert Andrews held the record for seventy-three years for sailing the smallest boat to cross the Atlantic.

A native of Beverly, Massachusetts, he spent sixty-two days in his first failed solo attempt in 1888 to cross the Atlantic in a twelve-foot, nine-inch boat *Dark Secret*. In 1891 he raced Lawlor and failed in his fifteen foot *Mermaid*, which capsized seven times.

Racing Lawlor again, he set sail July 20, 1892, from Atlantic City, New Jersey, in his new fourteen-foot, six-inch *Sapolio*. Stopping in the Azores, he landed September 20 at Burgau, Portugal. On August 24, 1898, he made another attempt to sail alone from the United States to Europe in the thirteen-foot *Phantom Ship*. After twenty seven days at sea, with a leaking boat and spoiled food, he asked to be picked up by a passing ship.

Rebuilding that boat, but to the shorter length of twelve feet and renaming her *Doree*, he sailed again June 17, 1899. Andrews lost track of four days of time and was hallucinating when he was picked up three weeks later by a passing ship.

His seventh and final voyage was in the twenty-foot dory *Flying Dutchman*. With his new wife on board, he set sail in 1901 from Atlantic City for Spain. About one week into the voyage, the newlyweds were sighted and spoke with a passing steamer. They were never heard from again.

Ludwig Eisenbraun

Details of German-American Ludwig Eisenbraun's 1903 transatlantic trip are scarce. It is known that Eisenbraun left Halifax, Nova Scotia on August 28, 1903, in the nineteen-foot sloop

Columbia II. He arrived in Gibraltar on Nov. 20, 1903, eighty-four days later, after sailing some 2,700 miles. Ports of call included Funchal in the Madeira Islands. From Gibraltar, he proceeded to Marseilles, France.

Robert Manry

Newspaperman Bob Manry's thirteen-foot-six-inch *Tinkerbelle* carried him 3,200 miles from Falmouth, Massachusetts to Falmouth, England in seventy-eight days, successfully breaking William Andrews' two-man seventy-three-year-old transatlantic record by one full foot.

An exhausted Manry hallucinated several times on the voyage, imagining phantom stowaways, jagged rocks and stalking murderers. He wound up overboard more than once.

Fifty thousand people turned out to greet the copy editor from Cleveland's *Plain Dealer* upon his triumphant arrival in England on August 17, 1965.

Tinkerbelle is now on permanent display at The Western Reserve Historical Society in Cleveland, Ohio.

Bill Verity

American Bill Verity was following a three hundred-year-old family tradition when he chose to venture upon the world's oceans. The Verity family had been building boats and sailing the oceans since 1644. Surveyor, author, pilot, adventurer, Verity was a decorated veteran of World War II Pacific naval battles.

He sailed across the Atlantic six times (three times solo), and the Pacific twice (once solo). His record came in 1966, when he sailed the twelve-foot *Nonoalca* for sixty five days from Port Everglades (Fort Lauderdale), Florida to the port of Tralee in Fenit, Ireland, a voyage of 4,550 nautical miles.

Gerry Spiess

Spiess sailed the North Atlantic from June 1 to July 24, 1979, making great time in his ten-foot *Yankee Girl*. Blessed by agreeable winds, he covered 3,800 miles between Norfolk, Virginia and Falmouth, England in fifty-four days.

Prepared for a maximum of one hundred days on board, Spiess auctioned off the excess supplies upon arrival and donated the proceeds to charity. Two years later, he took *Yankee Girl* across the Pacific. Spiess said debilitating loneliness was his greatest challenge on the voyage.

Wayne Dickenson

A computer technician from Melborne, Florida, thirty-nine-year-old Wayne Dickenson crossed the Atlantic in the eight-foot-eleven-inch *God's Tear*. Nearly five months after the October 30, 1983, launch from Hull, Massachusetts, *God's Tear* slammed into the rocks off Ireland's western shore, shipwrecking its weak, exhausted captain.

Unable to walk after one hundred forty-two days on board, Dickenson was fortunate enough to be rescued by an Irish lighthouse keeper, who spared him probable death on the bitter, wind-blasted cliffs of Arenmore Island.

More than three hundred miles off course, (he thought he was in Scotland), the physically drained Dickenson said he was sleeping when the wreck occurred. *God's Tear* and nearly everything it contained was ground to splinters by the pounding surf.

Tom McClean

This Irishman set sail across the "big pond" on June 9, 1983 in the seven-foot-eleven-inch *Giltspur*. Like several other transatlantic sailors, St. John's, Newfoundland was his launch site of choice. McClean landed in Oporto, Portugal on August 10th, sixty-two days later.

He had already completed one successful Atlantic crossing, just the year before. But several weeks afterward, his triumph was shattered by Bill Dunlap in the nine-foot-one-inch *Winds Will*. It was up to McClean to return with a shaved down version of *Giltspur*, temporarily reclaiming the small boat record for west to east Atlantic crossings.

A former member of Britain's crack Special Air Services Unit, today McClean runs an adventure training school in Scotland with the help of his wife, Jill, and two sons.

Sailing wasn't McClean's only claim to nautical fame. In

1969, he rowed a repeatedly capsized twenty-foot dory for seventy days from St. John's, Newfoundland to Blacksod, Ireland.

Hugo Vihlen

1993, five-foot-four-inch *Father's Day.*

Pacific Ocean

Kenichi Horie

Kenichi Horie became Hugo's inspiration when he sailed the Pacific Ocean from Japan to the U.S. in 1961. Forbidden to sail by the government of his homeland, Horie, aged twenty-three, covered 5,000 miles of open ocean alone, sailing from Osaka to San Francisco in the nineteen-foot *Mermaid.*

Ninety-four days later he sighted the Golden Gate Bridge and came ashore with $5 in his pocket.

Horie, an instant celebrity in America, donated the *Mermaid* to San Francisco's Maritime Museum.

Time on the voyage was whiled away with Horie mentally designing the perfect small boat. Twenty-seven years later, at age fifty, he finally went to sea in her, the nine-foot-six-inch *Mermaid*, named for his original record setting sailboat.

It was 1989 by the time Horie retraced his earlier route, only now he traveled in the opposite direction — from east to west. For one hundred thirty-seven days he sailed from San Francisco to Osaka, traversing some 7,400 miles. He arrived in Osaka on September 30, recapturing the small boat record for the Pacific from Gerry Spiess.

Gerry Spiess

Spiess sailed the veteran ten-foot *Yankee Girl* from Long Beach, California, to Sydney, Australia, in 1981. It took Spiess five months to sail the 7,800 miles of the voyage, an adventure that would carry him one-third of the way around the world.

One amazing aspect of this particular Pacific voyage is the accuracy with which Spiess was able to predict his ultimate landfall.

Launching on June 1st, he vowed to arrive by November 1st, hoping to demonstrate that the *Yankee Girl* was the master of her own destiny, and not at the total whim of the winds as was assumed. Pulling into Sydney on October 31st, one day ahead of schedule, he proved to the skeptics that the *Yankee Girl* design was good enough to take him where he wanted, when he wanted.

High waves kept Spiess closed up inside with the cabin hatch tightly shut for a good portion of the voyage. Heat plagued the captain as the warm Pacific waters reached a sizzling eighty-six degrees and the cabin was transformed into a sweat box. Despite five ports of call for supplies, Spiess reported the prolonged deep solitude of the voyage nearly defeated him psychologically.

Around the World

Serge Testa

Australian Serge Testa circumnavigated the globe in the homemade *Acrohc Australis*, an eleven-foot-ten-inch "yacht" crafted of marine-grade aluminum.

"The idea was that I would be able to travel the world without carrying luggage or having to look for accommodation...," Testa writes in his account of the 500-day solo adventure. Equipped with a four-horsepower engine for maneuverability, Testa launched from the Brisbane River in his homeland on June 11th, 1984.

In May of 1987, after exotic ports-of-call, encounters with whales, fierce storms and a near-fatal fire at sea, Testa sailed into Moreton Bay, just outside the Brisbane, successfully completing the loop and establishing a world record for the smallest boat to circle the earth.

INVENTORY
Items on board *Father's Day*

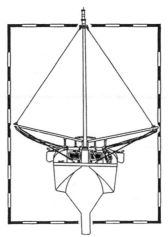

Food and water inventory
25 gallons water
85 Meals Ready to Eat (MREs)
75 cans Nutriment
10 cans Franco American spaghetti
75 cans Fruit Cocktail
6 cans Corned Beef
2 gallons M & M's candies
1 gallon dried fruit
1 gallon (22) Health Bars
2 small bottles rum
1 pint bottle rum (a gift in St. John's)

General location of items on board
Top side compartments hold lighter items.
Bilge and bottom side compartments hold heavier items.
Port top compartments have emergency items.
Starboard top compartments have clothes, daily use items
Weight will be moved lower as room becomes available. Empty
   jugs will be used for added buoyancy, one will become a toilet.

Bilge, Forward
12 x 1-gallon heavy-duty plastic jugs of water
10 x 12-pound ballast weights

Bilge, Aft

2 x 100-amp hour 12 volt batteries

1 x Survivor-35, a water maker

1 x Repair kit for Survivor-35

1 x Backup sail, with jury rig attach points installed

1 x Ship's repair kit, in Tupperware containing: super glue, duct tape, Leather Man tool, short handle hammer, manual drill with bits, vise grip small & large, 2 wrenches, channel-lock pliers, hacksaw with blades, 10-inch flat file, 4 screwdrivers, 2 c-clamps, small sharpening stone, homemade jumper cables to parallel batteries, numerous nuts and bolts, sandpaper, stainless steel wire brush, 6 hose clamps, sparkplug wrench, eyeglass repair kit, 1 x lift harness, stainless steel cables (In case the boat had to be lifted aboard at sea.)

Port, Top Aft Compartment

1 x Manual bilge pump, secured in place. Handle is put into place from outside

3 x Hand-held smoke signals, Pains-Wessex

3 x Hand-held flares, Pains-Wessex, U.S. Coast Guard (USCG)required

8 x 25mm. meteor flares

2 x 25mm. parachute flares

1 x Signal mirror

5 x Epoxy repair kits

1 x Air Horn, USCG required

1 x Spare SSB antenna cable

1 x Small Tupperware containing: Emergency handwarmers (in case of hypothermia), 1 x roll duct tape, 1 x roll stainless steel safety wire, 1 x bag of spare nuts and bolts, 1 x fishing Yo-Yo with 100 lb. line, lures and hooks, 75 feet of parachute cord, plastic tie wraps.

Port, Top Forward Compartment

1 x GPS unit (Vacuum-bagged Magellan Nav 5000)

2 x Emergency fishing rigs

5 x Charts English Channel (Vacuum bagged)

7 x Charts Bristol Bay approach (Vacuum bagged)

2 x Sony 8mm. film packs, plus one in video camera

2 x Battery packs for Sony video camera

1 x 12 volt recharger cable for video camera

1 x Tupperware medium size, containing: 4 x ship's logs, books: *Webster's Dictionary* , *The 1993 World Almanac, Reed's 1993 Nautical Companion, The 1992 Guiness Book of World Records, Paddle to the Amazon, Saga of a Wayward Sailor, Maiden Voyage.*

Port, Bottom Aft Compartment

Cans of Nutriment, fruit & entrees

Meals Ready to Eat (MREs)

Several gallons water

2 x 1-gallon wide mouth jugs, (M&Ms)

Emergency SSB resonators

Batteries, vacuum-bagged packages of spares. Total on board:
    48 x D cell, 32 x AA cell, 8 x AAA cell

1 x Gallon, Power Bars (22)

Port, Bottom Forward Compartment

Cans of Nutriment, fruit & entrees

MREs

Several gallons water

1 x 1-gallon wide mouth jug containing power bars

1 x Plastic tackle box Medical Kit containing: Book *First Aid at Sea*, A & D ointment, 1.5 oz. for chafed skin, Advil 50 tablets, for headaches, Arthricreme 3 oz. for arthritis and muscle pains, Antiseptic kit, 1.5 oz. (iodine), Benadryl 24 capsules for allergic reaction, Biaxin 36 tablets for skin and internal infections, Cipro 24 tablets for gastrointestinal and urinary infections, Colace 60 tablets for stool softener needed after diet of MREs, Feldene 60 tablets for arthritis, Hypo tears PF, 30 packets, for dehydrated, wind and salt-burned eyes, Loprox, 4 sample packs for skin infection, Lotrimin .85 oz. antifungal creme, Moleskin for blisters, Quinine tablets for leg cramps, Second Skin kit, for blisters, chafe and burns, soap bar, small, Topicort gel, 2 sample packs for skin infection, Toradol 50 tablets for pain relief, Triple antibiotic ointment, 2 oz., for infection, Tums antacid 96 tablets, for stomach aches, Tylenol 100 tablets, for headaches, Zinc oxide ointment, 3 oz., to prevent sunburn, Ace bandage 4", gauze roll 2", 25 sterile-pads 3" x 3", 10 sterile pads 4" x 4", waterproof tape, 16 Bandaids 1", 16 Butterfly Bandaids (small), 2 Triangle bandages.

(Thanks to the following for their help with the medical kit: Doctors Don Elsman, Richard Kernish, Ray Mummery and Fred Vihlen and Nancy Vihlen R.N.)

Starboard, Top Aft Compartment (Glove Compartment)
Safety Harness line, tied to pad-eye

1 x Tupperware, large. Medicine box (daily type items containing): Dental kit, daily medicines, creams, Q-tips, safety scissors, tweezers.

1 x Tupperware, large containing: 2 pairs reading glasses, sunglasses, calculator (vacuum bagged), spare kitchen timer (vacuum bagged), wind speed meter, 2 dividers for navigation, silicone grease, waterproof marker, Swiss Army knives (2 small, 1 large), Spider Co. Rescue knife, Buck knife, safety pins, nail clippers, writing pens and pencils, wallet with 100 dollars U.S., 2 rolls of Canadian pennies for souvenirs.

1 x Tupperware, small. Travel kit containing: Deodorant, 6 chapsticks, 5 toothpaste, dental floss, floss threader, 2 tooth brushes, 2 lens cloths, 1 pair leather sailing gloves, 1 x Casio watch, (backup), 1 x spoon, 1 x can opener, 1 x 25 mm. flare gun (originally kept loaded and bolted to deck, moved due to gas tanks).

Starboard, Top Forward Compartment
1 x Foul weather jacket (thermometer attached to zipper) & bibb pants

1 x Wool sweater, vacuum bagged

1 x Wool gloves, vacuum bagged

1 x Wool watch cap, vacuum bagged

1 x Pullover stocking mask, vacuum bagged

2 x Pair wool socks, vacuum bagged

2 x Pair cotton socks, vacuum bagged

8 x Underwear, vacuum bagged

8 x T-shirt, vacuum bagged

2 x Handkerchiefs, vacuum bagged

1 x Levi Jeans, vacuum bagged

1 x Long johns, top and bottom, vacuum bagged

1 x Long johns top (extra)

1 x Sweat suit

1 x Light-weight shirt

3 x Wash cloths
2 x Hand towels
1 x Pratique Quarantine flag

Starboard, Bottom Aft Compartment
Cans of Nutriment, fruit & entrees
MREs
Several gallons water
Book, *Return with Honor*, by Colonel George "Bud" Day
Aircraft VHF antenna, bolted into place
Winch handle, lightweight
Plastic model of *April Fool* (Signed and presented to the Commodore of the Royal Cornwall Yacht Club)

Starboard, Bottom Forward Compartment
Cans of Nutriment, fruit & entrees
MREs
Several gallons water
6 x Rolls toilet paper, inside zip lock bags then vacuum bagged separately (15 sheets/day)
EPIRB Litton #952 Class II Sat-Find 406

Radio Rack
1 x ICOM M600 single side band (SSB)
1 x Auto-Tuner 120 (for SSB)
1 x SSB microphone
1 x ICOM M120 Marine VHF
1 x Marine VHF microphone
1 x Emergency Marine VHF antenna
1 x Handheld ICOM M7 marine VHF radio, in waterproof case
1 x King KY97A aircraft VHF radio
1 x Aircraft VHF microphone, with hex wrench for radio rack
2 x Aircraft VHF headsets
1 x Ship's log
Spare radio fuses, in pill bottle
Pilot Chart - North Atlantic
Owner's manual for *Father's Day*
Manuals for GPSs, video camera, 35mm. camera, and water maker
Condensed map, showing which chart to use

Passport
4 x sponges

Cockpit Area, Attached
1 x Emergency SSB 4 foot mast antenna, with hex wrench
1 x Emergency SSB resonator
2 x Mini-Mag holders with Mini-Mag flashlights
1 x Flexible tip pen light
1 x Cup holder
1 x Drinking cup, plastic 10 oz. (kept in cup holder)
1 x Digital kitchen timer/clock/alarm
1 x Bilge pump handle
1 x World wide band receiver
1 x Garmin GPS-50
1 x Compass (25 degree deviation due to proximity to radio)
1 x Amp hour gauge
1 x Temperature gauge
1 x Whistle, USCG required
1 x Seat belt
1 x Picture of Johnnie

Cockpit Area, loose or worn
1 x Life preserver, USCG required (Offshore type)
1 x Throw cushion, USCG required
1 x Sleeping bag, homemade (no zippers)
1 x Stuff bag for sleeping bag
1 x Dry bag for sleeping bag
1 x Pillow, homemade, small
1 x Binoculars 7 x 50
1 x Sony video camera inside of underwater housing
1 x 35 mm. Nikon camera in padded bag, with extra film, lens
    cleaning cloths, zoom lenses 28 - 70 mm. and 70 - 210 mm., fil-
    ter, flash attachment, 13 rolls of film and spare battery
1 x Drinking cup, stainless steel
1 x Clip board used for navigation
2 x Emergency "SAM" splints for broken limbs
1 x Floppy canvas hat
1 x Long-sleeve shirt
1 x Pair Levi jeans
1 x Belt

1 x Polartec jacket
1 x Pair deck shoes
1 x Rolex watch used on *April Fool*

Outside area, Attached
1 x Anchor, Danforth with 200 feet braided line and 10 feet stainless steel cable
1 x Sea anchor, (18 inch wide mouth) with 100 feet braided line
1 x Winch for retrieval of anchor (Not needed for sea anchor)
1 x SSB Outbacker antenna
2 x 6-gallon gas tanks
1 x 4 hp. Evinrude outboard, with snorkel and cloth cover
1 x Compass
1 x Boat hook, extendable, with camera mount
2 x Solar panels
1 x Plastic foothold on stern
1 x U.S. flag, radar reflective

And one lucky charm!

GLOSSARY

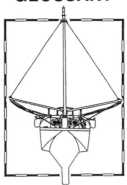

Airex. A semi-hard foam used as the core material encased by fiberglass in boat construction.

Ballast. A heavy substance used to improve the stability and control the draft of a boat.

Batten. To close or secure.

Barometer. An aneroid instrument that reads the atmospheric pressure at a specific place.

BBC. The British Broadcasting Corporation, a world-wide radio service from Britain.

Becalmed. Staying in one spot due to lack of wind.

Bilge. The lower interior area of the hull, where water collects if allowed onboard.

Birdhouse. A water-resistant air vent used on boats, also known as a dorade. The one on *Father's Day* looked a lot like a birdhouse and was called such.

Boom. A long spar used to extend the foot of the sail, and which swings about the lower portion of the mast to regulate the amount of wind on the sail.

Boom gallows. A metal frame used to prevent injury from a boom by restricting its arc across the deck. Also allows the booms to be fastened to it when the sails are not supporting the weight of the booms.

Bow. The very front of a boat (the pointy end).

Bulkhead. Vertical partitions in a hull, corresponding to the walls in a house.

Buoyant. Floats on the water.

Cabin. The inside living quarters of the boat.

Compartment. Interior areas divided off by bulkheads for storage.

Compass. A device for determining directions by means of a magnetic needle pointing to magnetic north.

Variation. Angular difference between true north and the direction of magnetic north at a given point on earth.

Magnetic course. Angular difference between magnetic north and the ship's heading.

Deviation. Error in a magnetic compass caused by local magnetic influences on the boat.

Compass course. Angular difference between compass north and the ship's heading.

True course. Angular difference between non-magnetic North Pole and the ship's heading.

Deck. A hard structure that covers the top of the boat.

Dog house. An enclosed area that the hatch can slide into.

EPIRB. Emergency Position Indicating Radio Beacon, which sends coded radio signals to a satellite indicating position and owner's name. Used only in an emergency. Also allows aircraft to home in on it by a separate radio frequency as well as a strobe light.

Fiberglass. A short name for "fiber reinforced plastic," a material made of glass fibers embedded in a thermosetting plastic.

Gale. Common term for small, local bad weather with high winds (gale force is 35 to 40 knots of wind.)

GPS. Global Positioning System. An electronic means using satellites to find your position within about 49 feet (15 meters) in day, night or bad weather.

Hatch. An opening in the deck to provide access below.

Heel. To lean the entire boat to the side, usually due to wind against the sails.

Hull. The body of the boat excluding the deck.

HF. High frequency radio propagation, used in long-range communication.

Jibe. Occurs when turning the boat around without turning through the wind's direction. This causes the back of the sail to swing violently from one side of the boat to the other when passing through the wind. Can be hazardous if not controlled.

Keel. The major vertical appendage beneath the hull. Keeps the boat on course and contains ballast.

Knot. One nautical mile per hour. A nautical mile equals 6,076 feet.

Leeward. The direction toward which the wind is blowing.

Lee shore. The shoreline which the wind blows onto, a possible danger to a sailor.

Mast. A heavy-duty pole sticking vertically out of the deck to which the sail attaches.

MRE. Meal Ready to Eat, a US military food ration containing about 2,500 calories.

Nautical mile. 6,076 feet, based on a length of one degree latitude. Used in sea navigation. A nautical mile is longer than a statute (land) mile, which is equal to 5,280 feet.

Pilot chart. An oceanic chart for a given month showing average currents, winds, wave heights, ice limits, climate, storms, etc. Used for route planning.

R & R. Military term referring to rest and recuperation.

Reef. To reduce the sail area exposed to high winds. This prevents sail failure and also unsafe speeds.

Rudder. Large, moveable underwater appendage located at the stern. Steers the boat.

Sea anchor. Device deployed underwater to increase drag to reduce lost distance due to adverse winds.

Sextant. Hand-held device for measuring the angle from the horizon to a celestial body. Used in conjunction with time and almanacs for finding a specific location.

SSB. Single sideband radio used for long-range communication.

Stern. The back of the boat.

Tiller. Pole-like device that attaches to the rudder to steer the boat.

Transom. Actual structure of the hull at the boat's stern tying the sides of the boat together.

VHF. Very High Frequency radio used for short range (line of sight) radio communications.

Winch. A mechanical device, hand cranked to exert increased power on a line such as an anchor line.

Wind (direction). As in the direction of the wind ("East Wind" blows from the east).

Windward. Toward the direction from which the wind is blowing.

INDEX

Photo by Ed Navarro

Hugo Vihlen and writer Joanne Kimberlin pore over details of the *Father's Day* voyage. Since claiming his second world record, Hugo spends most of his days at his home in South Florida, planning a third voyage in an even smaller boat. Joanne works as a news editor at *The Key West* (Florida) *Citizen*.